Physics of Blackness

Physics of Blackness

Beyond the Middle Passage Epistemology

Michelle M. Wright

University of Minnesota Press
Minneapolis
London

Published by the University of Minnesota Press
111 Third Avenue South, Suite 290
Minneapolis, MN 55401-2520
http://www.upress.umn.edu

Library of Congress Cataloging-in-Publication Data

Wright, Michelle M.
    Physics of Blackness: Beyond the Middle Passage Epistemology / Michelle M. Wright.
    Includes bibliographical references and index.
    ISBN 978-0-8166-8726-8 (hc: acid-free paper)—ISBN 978-0-8166-8730-5
(pb: acid-free paper)
    1. Blacks—Race identity. 2. Identity (Psychology). 3. African diaspora. I. Title.
HT1581.W693 2015
305.896—dc23   2014005529

Printed on acid-free paper

The University of Minnesota is an equal-opportunity educator and employer.

Contents

Many Thousands Still Coming

Theorizing Blackness in the Postwar Moment

For a few centuries now, Blackness has been big business, attracting attention and reaping raw profit not only in the West but increasingly in the world at large. In one of its earliest and most famous manifestations, Blackness was sold as a balm to white self-regard and resulted in a fantastic boon in profits when African slaves were marketed as "Negroes"—a distinctly subhuman species who possess, Thomas Jefferson remarked, "that immovable veil of black,"[1] thus excusing from further consideration the accusations of inhuman practice lobbed by abolitionists. Today, the myriad ways in which Blackness is sold is dizzying: its social, cultural, and political currency helps sell jazz, pop, hip-hop, a variety of professional sports, Barack Obama, punitive criminal laws in "First World" Western nations, Bishop Tutu, "race" medicines, and degrees in African American, African Diaspora, and African studies—to mention some of the most obvious examples. Yet for all its successful (and less successful, forgotten) deployments, Blackness remains undefined and suffering under the weight of many definitions, not one of which covers every type of Blackness or coheres with all the other denotations and connotations. So what do we mean when we discuss "Black music" or "Black culture" or, for that matter, given the claims of geneticists, "Blackness" as a distinct genetic marking?

At first glance, it appears that it is the Black body that is denoted by Blackness: indeed, to hear some sportscasters and race geneticists express their assumptions, the Black body is often imagined and deployed as if it were a uniform "thing" that automatically grants its owner great athletic ability and rhythm. This mystique, which lifts the body up in the white imagination as an objet d'art, also denigrates it to the animal status of pure instinct. It seems every few years we are reminded of this with a sportscaster's politically incorrect comment or complaint about how Black athletes enjoy "natural" corporeal advantages over their differently raced competitors.

Contrary to the assertion that Blackness comprises a set of genetic qualities, decades of research have borne no fruit confirming this often-repeated claim. Indeed, the concept of Blackness as located in the body cannot be sustained by any serious further investigation because simple observation reveals a broad variety of Black bodies. Many of those bodies can "pass for white" or another ethnicity; many of those bodies do not identify as Black, although they "look" Black to us; and those bodies may in turn encounter other bodies—for example, African Americans touring their ancestral homeland in Ghana—and reject the notion that African Americans are Black, ironically based (at least partially) on perceived physical differences.

While we cannot dismiss social, political, and cultural discourses and practices that clearly link Black communities across the West to their African origins, locating Blackness as a determinable "thing," as a "what" or "who," gives us a conceptualization that exhibits the unnerving qualities of a mirage: from a distance, it appears clearly cogent, but up close, Blackness evanesces, revealing no one shared quality that justifies such frequent and assured use of this signifier.

For those of us who work in Black studies on identity, we are almost wearily familiar with this problem of trying to find a one-size-fits-all definition of Blackness. The absence of any sort of biological evidence that links all Black peoples together hardly surprises us (we are well aware that Blackness was not a scientific discovery but an economic and political argument first used to justify the Atlantic slave trade). Yet even knowing that there is no one gene, history, nationality, language, politics, society, culture, or any other factor that can serve as the basis for the identity category of Black, we nonetheless continue to deploy it as a category and are thus still bedeviled by the question of exactly what constitutes Blackness.

In his introduction to *Once You Go Black: Choice, Desire, and the Black American Intellectual*, Robert Reid-Pharr asks us this very same question through Thomas Holt: "The problem becomes particularly difficult for those of us involved in the study of Black American history and culture because we risk either conceding to outmoded and regressive ways of thinking about human identity and diversity or devaluing as 'unreal' or 'immaterial' a history and culture that many of us take to be precious."[2] There is, of course, a political undercurrent to this dilemma: some scholars (such as Walter Benn Michaels) have seized on the argument that Blackness is socially constructed to then argue that it is unworthy of research.[3]

Some even argue that to identify Blackness as an identity is racist. For scholars like me, these arguments only exacerbate racist perceptions and behaviors, and we reject the illogic that the study of racism is intrinsically racist. Yet to understand Blackness as a construct without explaining what it is—only what it is not—generates old and new paradoxes in our arguments. The largest problem is that of unequal representation of Black collectives in discourses of Blackness generally: despite our best efforts, some groups enjoy being understood as Black, whereas others have to struggle and clamor for recognition. This "problem" is hardly limited to or most heavily burdensome to scholars who work in Black American history and culture—it is, I would argue, endemic to any and all discourses on Blackness that reject a biological origin for race and yet offer little else in its place.[4]

When we ask, "What is Blackness?" we already have a set of answers: it is a collective identity that intersects with many other collective identities that in turn intersect with one another, such as gender, sexuality, or socioeconomic class; spiritual and other performative subcultures, professions, trades, ethnicities, or religious denominations; lifestyles or dietary choices—the list is endless. What we really want when we seek to define Blackness is a common denominator that links the Black presence in all these categories. At the same time, Blackness is simply too many things to be anything but everything. One would be hard pressed to find some way in which Blackness did *not* intersect with all other collective identities (especially given the current understanding that all human life originated in the continent of Africa). While this conclusion is pleasingly inclusive (if annoyingly opaque in its simplicity), it does not answer why, if Blackness is and can be everything, it is so often set off as some "thing" that is distinct.

Pursuing this question requires focusing on the phenomenology of Blackness—that is, *when* and *where* it is being imagined, defined, and performed and in what locations, both figurative and literal. Blackness cannot be located on the body because of the diversity of bodies that claim Blackness as an identity. Blackness, then, is largely a matter of perception or—as performance studies theorist E. Patrick Johnson observes—made up of moments of performance in which performers understand their bodies as Black. Furthermore, because it is not necessary for the audience to understand such performances as Black (except in the matter of ticket sales and perhaps favorable reviews), this further suggests that Blackness is in the mind of the performers.

Physics of Blackness: Beyond the Middle Passage Epistemology argues that Blackness operates as a construct (implicitly or explicitly defined as a shared set of physical and behavioral characteristics) and as phenomenological (imagined through individual perceptions in various ways depending on the context). As such, we can best locate and define Blackness across the African Diaspora by incorporating both of these aspects into our analyses within and without the academy.

Bringing together Blackness as constructed and Blackness as phenomenological is not as difficult as it might at first appear, because both modes comprise notions of space and time, or "spacetime." Our *constructs* of Blackness are largely historical and more specifically based on a notion of spacetime that is commonly fitted into a linear progress narrative, while our *phenomenological* manifestations of Blackness happen in what I term *Epiphenomenal time*, or the "now," through which the past, present, and future are always interpreted. I capitalize my use of the term from its formal philosophical definition, in which the epiphenomenal is not in itself causal but nonetheless correlates with causal phenomena. In *Physics of Blackness*, "Epiphenomenal" time denotes the current moment, a moment that is *not* directly borne out of another (i.e., causally created). As I show in chapter 3, however, Epiphenomenal time does not preclude any and all causality: only a *direct*, or *linear*, causality. In other words, the current moment, or "now," can certainly correlate with other moments, but one cannot argue that it is always already the effect of a specific, previous moment. Read together, they underscore the depth and breadth with which these notions of spacetime pervade Western expressions of collective identity, most especially Blackness. Even further, they underscore that while the linear progress narrative is an invaluable tool for locating Blackness, when used alone its very spatiotemporal properties preclude a wholly *inclusive* definition of Blackness, yielding one that is necessarily inaccurate. By contrast, Epiphenomenal time enables a wholly inclusive definition (appropriate to any moment at which one is defining Blackness).

The use of *physics* in this book's title reflects my use of lay discourses on spacetime in particle or quantum physics, which I bring into conversation with discourses on Blackness—scholarly, creative, and in some cases media based—to uncover how and why these distinct spacetimes operate and to trace their attendant effects on concepts of Black agency and the meaning of Blackness in our *contemporary* "postwar" moment.[5] Thus while this book grounds itself squarely in the humanities, it nonetheless seeks to show how using space and time as analytical categories informs an interdisciplinary analysis that is at once broader and deeper than analyses grounded wholly in the conceptual resources of the humanities.

This introduction reflects the organization of the four chapters that follow: the first half of the book examines the dominant constructs of Blackness that use a linear progress narrative, and the second half focuses on the use of Epiphenomenal time—that is, how Blackness is read in our postwar moment. It is perhaps unavoidable that any analysis of Blackness and its role in the Diaspora will identify certain discourses—collections of linguistic and cognitive practices focused on core sets of concepts—as "dominant." A dominant discourse expresses the will of a center of political, social, or economic power within a given social structure, in effect constructing within that structure the identities of social classes based on presumed degrees of freedom to exercise agency. Thus under both of the central paradigms that organize the conceptual resources I bring to bear in this book—the Middle Passage epistemology and the postwar epistemology—there are dominant and subordinate discourses that shape the terms in which competing interests are debated and pursued.

The goal of this book is to provide a model for defining Blackness across the Diaspora that easily locates and corrects the common exclusions so often found in our everyday speech, scholarly canon, and public assumptions. The need for definitions of Blackness that do not exclude, isolate, or stigmatize is all the more pressing, I would argue, with the increasing proliferation of diverse Black communities of individuals whose histories and current status as "hyphenated" Black identities across the globe call for representation and inclusion. In this manner, *Physics of Blackness* specifically cautions against overreliance on the exclusive use of linear progress narratives to define Blackness and urges equal consideration of the moment of interpretation, or Epiphenomenal spacetime.

Importantly, even as incorporating a phenomenological definition of Blackness into our current understanding sheds light on issues of exclusion and lack of agency, it also raises troubling questions: most pressingly the conundrum of whether Blackness is ultimately in the eye of the beholder or of the performer. For those who seek to ignore or deny the material reality of oppressed Black peoples across the globe, myopically arguing that the *immateriality* of Blackness moots any and all questions about it is a strategic if entirely mendacious way to sanction anti-Black racist practices. Furthermore, this misuse is of deep concern to scholars who see a similar threat in poststructuralist theories of Blackness that appear to detach it from its African origins (most "infamously" in Paul Gilroy's *The Black Atlantic*, still a "must-read" for all scholars of Black collective identity in the African Diaspora).

In their anthology *Race and the Foundations of Knowledge*, African Diaspora scholars Joseph Young and Jana Evans Braziel attempt to strike a balance between the outright rejection of Blackness as perception/performance and Blackness as a historically demonstrable fact. Explicitly rejecting what they define as "poststructuralist dismissals of race," they offer a counterdefinition:

> We do not define race, though we recognize that historically it has been defined in such ways, as any of the following: an ontological category, a biological or psychological essence, a fixed or unchanging category of uncomplicated belonging, a genetically determined classification with presumed intrinsic epistemological interpretations. Like the scholars who insist that race does not (or should not) exist (Anthony Kwame Appiah, Houston Baker Jr., Henry Louis Gates, Jr., Paul Gilroy, and others), we too recognize race as a historical category defined through biological reductivism, a political classification intended to define individuals through difference in oppressive ways, a social and cultural construct, a discursive formation. It is not, however, an "empty" category or a "free-floating signifier," as some would have it.[6]

By characterizing misrepresentations of Blackness as "empty" or "free floating," Young and Braziel reveal a central worry associated with the notion of Blackness that isn't "grounded," or given weight, specifically, through its "historical category." At the same time, by choosing to foreground race as a historical category, Young and Braziel almost dovetail with an article they cite just a page or so before—namely, Caribbean scholar and cultural studies founder Stuart Hall's famous essay "Cultural Identity and Diaspora," in which he argues that there are two types of cultural identity for collectives, cultural and historical, which in fact are conflated:

> There at least two different ways of thinking about "cultural identity." The first position defines "cultural identity" in terms of one, shared culture, a sort of collective "one true self" hiding inside

the many other, more superficial or artificially imposed "selves," which peoples with a shared history and ancestry hold in common. Within the terms of this definition, our cultural identities reflect the common historical experiences and shared cultural codes which provide us, as "one people" with stable, unchanging, and continuous frames of reference and meaning, beneath the shift ing divisions and vicissitudes of our actual history. This "oneness," underlying all the other, more superficial differences, is the truth, the essence, of "Caribbeanness," of the Black experience.[7]

Hall's analysis gets at the heart of the problem of seeking to define Blackness in a way that reflects its diversity yet does not deprive it of its historical materiality. Hall understands the construction of collective identity as agglomerations of individual selves who nonetheless also share a common "history and ancestry." Hall's language echoes his understanding of Young and Braziel's worry over "empty" definitions of Blackness by noting that the "one people" defined by this shared history and ancestry are grounded in a "stable, unchanging, continuous [frame] of reference and meaning"—a counterweight to the threat of "shifting divisions and vicissitudes" that provides a pleasingly solid foundation while more "superficial differences" float at the top. In other words, Hall's argument, like Young and Braziel's, views collective history as something that provides Blackness its "weight"—a grounding in lived experiences rather than the misperceptions of outside groups or erratic individuals.

Hall also offers us a warning here, because those "shifting divisions and vicissitudes" come from "our *actual* history" (emphasis added) rather than anything imagined. A closer look at "Cultural Identity and Diaspora" reveals that history achieves two aims—on the one hand it provides stability, while on the other it constantly threatens change and, with that change, divisions. If collective Black identities are historical, how do we unravel the warp and woof of this history?

Most discourses on Blackness in the United States and the Caribbean locate themselves in the history of the Middle Passage, linking our cultural practices and expressions, our politics and social sensibilities, to the historical experience of slavery in the Americas and the struggle to achieve full human suffrage in the West. These histories are both constructed and phenomenological: they are a chosen arrangement of historical events (spaces and times) perceived to be the defining moments of collective

Blackness. At the same time, for the purposes of this theoretical analysis of Blackness, it is important to underscore that these are not so much histories as epistemologies: narratives of knowledge that are taught, learned, relayed, exchanged, and debated in discussions on the "facts" of Blackness.

These historical-cum-epistemological events are usually linked by or narrated under the theme of overcoming obstacles through struggle (or "uplift"), with the defining aspect of contemporary Black collective histories focusing primarily on slavery (Middle Passage histories), European colonization (postcolonial histories), or the dominance of ancient African civilizations (Afrocentric histories). These themes create either a linear progress narrative or, when reversed (as in Afropessimism), a reverse linear narrative indicating that no *Black* progress has been made because of the continual oppression by white Western hegemonies that began with slavery, moved through colonialism, and now deploy an array of cultural, political, economic, and military power through social and governmental technologies to keep Blacks not only as subalterns—those who are subordinated by power—but also as the (white) Western Other.

The question of defining Blackness has become more urgent as the collectives that perceive themselves through these multiple histories find themselves encountering each other more frequently. As recent anthologies such as *The Other African Americans* show, many Western nations are now (and in many cases have been since the postwar era) receiving Black African immigrants whose histories, while certainly tied to Atlantic slavery, more often narrate themselves through colonialism or postwar socioeconomic changes than through the Middle Passage. These two collectives of historical and ancestral Blackness, while most certainly intertwined (and at times also often facing the same kinds of racist violence) nonetheless understand themselves differently. Denoted simply as "Black" almost anywhere outside of Africa, their encounters must negotiate their differences even as Blackness enjoins them to work together toward the common goal of racial uplift. In short, they have experienced differences that these linear progress narratives of Blackness strongly encourage them not to discuss, perhaps not even to *see*, much less acknowledge. However, in many of these moments, experienced or expressed, the phenomenological aspects of Blackness subvert even the most eloquent construct of collective unity. In other words, perceived differences *will* be expressed, but because most dominant constructs of Blackness cannot understand differences within, difference is often expressed as a dichotomy between "Black" and "not Black."

In "Colorblind," her 2007 opinion piece from Salon.com, conservative Black columnist Debra Dickerson produces a cartoonishly distorted imagining of those differences that nonetheless reflect some of the greatest reservations some Black collectives harbor about others.

> Obama isn't Black. "Black," in our political and social reality, means those descended from West African slaves. Voluntary immigrants of African descent (even those descended from West Indian slaves) are just that, voluntary immigrants of African descent with markedly different outlooks on the role of race in their lives and politics. At a minimum, it can't be assumed that a Nigerian cab driver and a third-generation Harlemite have more in common than the fact a cop won't bother to make the distinction. They're both "Black" as a matter of skin color and DNA, but only the Harlemite, for better or worse, is politically and culturally Black, as we use the term.[8]

Like most arguments seeking to separate some Blacks from Blackness, Dickerson's plays fast and loose with history and in doing so also reveals (unwittingly) temporal and spatial gaps that belie the notion of the linear progress narrative. While most scholars of contemporary African immigration would take issue with her qualifier of "voluntary"[9] (when one's family is faced with death by starvation, violence, etc., is emigration truly born of free will?), it is her focus on the differing "outlooks" of the Harlemite and Obama/Nigerian cabdriver that bear the greatest scrutiny. Under this logic, histories not only uniformly shape collectives in the "now"; they are also unbroken, passed perfectly from one generation to the next.[10]

Chapter 1 analyzes Dickerson's article more thoroughly, but for the purposes of this introduction, I will simply note that Dickerson assumes, and Hall explicitly locates, a concept of history as the producer of a common memory passed down through generations. Because, of course, human beings are mortal, the only way to establish a "stable, unchanging" history of the collective is to locate something that is immortal—or, at least, capable of living beyond mortal memory. In Dickerson, one cannot simply receive this memory. The third-generation Harlemite (loaded, it is implied, with three generations' worth of experiential knowledge about the social and political reality of being Black in the United States) cannot imbue Obama's Black consciousness with this same empirical knowledge and thus render him "Black" under Dickerson's terms. We can further infer that imparting this information would not change his outlook because the status of his Black ancestry is not enslaved, not rooted in an involuntary migration (putting it rather mildly).

The wholehearted embrace of Obama by most U.S. (and global) Black communities belies Dickerson's later assertion that Obama cannot win the presidency due to this difference in outlook, but there is another equally important flaw in her logic of defining collectives through a shared history or outlook: the spatiotemporal gap inherent in all linear progress narratives that she is trying to erase. While oral histories and traditions passed down through generations are facts, not simply false claims, the historical documents and our interpretations of them are always changing, most especially with a collective such as Blackness because its history is so deeply intertwined with most other global histories. Case in point—a July 30, 2012, article by Sheryl Gay Stolberg for the *New York Times* reported that Obama's mother, Ann Dunham, may be descended from a branch of the Punch family whose earliest U.S. ancestors were West African slaves.[11] In other words, Obama may in fact possess that Middle Passage Blackness Dickerson denies, pointing to a production of Blackness that emerges only through two separate histories and is "interrupted" by whiteness (Obama's mother): a whiteness that also exhibits Black ancestry. With Obama, we do not have a Blackness that is wholly outside Middle Passage Blackness; in fact, another one of his ancestries connects him through a heavily interracial family history that is a far larger part of the Americas than most dominant discourses admit.

Whether or not Ann Dunham is a descendant of the Black John Punch, there remains this daunting obstacle in defining Blackness—in this case Middle Passage Blackness—through an unbroken chain of ancestors whose experiences inform our contemporary outlook. Hall's historical reality has come crashing in as we stand back to take a second look at our ancestral trees, which, even if we squint, can no longer be mistaken for a linear growth of branches stemming from one root; instead, we are presented with the tangled roots that theorists such as Paul Gilroy have defined as "rhizomatic" (more horizontal than vertical in structure and with no one clear direction). We are returned to our blankly banal observation that Blackness is everything, intersecting with all humanity, indistinct.

Consider what happens during Internet searches as a useful analogy to horizontal and vertical interpellations. Search engines stress the "horizontal" capability of their software: the ability to take search terms and provide links to websites ranked according to the quality of their service or content. In other words, the process is meant to be democratic: no matter what you are searching for, you will be provided with a broad array of links from a broad array of sponsors, but the first ones listed presumably return the best information (breadth and depth) or service. Yet consumer groups, other nonprofit organizations, small business owners, and Internet activ ists often dispute this claim by pointing to the *vertical* nature of the results: ranked first are the largest for-profits and most heavily funded nonprofits.

Chapter 4 examines the effect of "verticality" on Black epistemologies in the West, suggesting that many of these effects can be meliorated through a "horizontal" reading. For example, an online search for "Africans in World War II" returns almost one billion hits, the majority of which reflect a colonial definition of "African" as a synecdoche for a landscape that is owned and controlled by white Western nations. The search primarily returns links to African campaigns carried out by the Axis and Allies, African colonies, and the Afrika Corps, and their sheer preponderance almost smothers what few horizontal links there are to narratives in which Africans are subjects, much less agents. Rather than a vertical, hierarchical interpellation of "African" as a colonial possession, the savvier scholar can navigate past these vertical returns by inserting more "horizontal" search terms, such as "African civilians," and even more horizontal temporal parameters (which I reveal at the end of the book).

However, we can (severely) prune this tangled skein of ancestries by imposing Hall's and Dickerson's argument about perception—that we "chop off" all those lives that we do not perceive as having lived the social and political realities of their times of being Black (and, ideally, those persons who did not perceive themselves in this way). Yet perception also produces its own problem: for example, if we want to consider Barack Obama "Black," we must allow for a diversity of perceptions and performances of what it means to be Black. We must reattach all those ancestors whom Dickerson sheds and thereby precludes from concern and who bring their own definitions of Blackness that will likely challenge one another as well as the contemporary definition of Middle Passage Blackness through the sociopolitical outlook to which she alludes. To what degree would Barack Obama Sr.'s ancestors identify as "Black," adhering to the outlook of Ann Dunham's "Middle Passage Black" ancestors? It also stands to reason that those possible Dunham ancestors who passed as white Punches would not share contemporary views of Blackness. In reading President Obama's

Blackness as the product of both constructs and phenomenology, many Blacknesses appear, but they are not easily represented on *any* of the linear timelines that define the Black collective, including the most frequently discussed, published, and assumed epistemology: Middle Passage Blackness. Obama is far from the only Black individual who often finds his identity excluded from the linear progress narrative of Middle Passage Blackness. Indeed, *most* Black bodies are excluded from most discussions on Blackness because the majority of dominant discourses in Black studies, like most white discourses, implicitly or explicitly favor and focus on the heteropatriarchal male body as the Black norm in these histories and theories. It should be stressed that this exclusion is rarely accompanied by sexist or misogynist expressions. Unfortunately, these exclusions, conscious or not, can manifest many of the same effects that a deliberate and explicit bigotry would. When women, LGBTTQ (lesbian/gay/bisexual/transgender/ transsexual/queer and questioning) Blacks, and other students of these narratives struggle to apply the examples and abstract theorizations to themselves and cannot, this implicit exclusion of their voices and experiences from the "main narrative," in spite of the occasional paragraph or perhaps chapter giving voice to their existence, reinforces a sense that they are somehow not "normally" Black.

This problem has hardly gone ignored or neglected: there are generations of scholars who have lastingly contributed to their disciplines by both recovering marginalized narratives and theorizing them back into dominant epistemologies in Black studies. Yet as those works—most recently of Marlon Bailey, Stanlie James, Audre Lorde, Roderick Ferguson, Deborah Gray-White, Robert Reid-Pharr, C. Riley Snorton, Darlene Clark Hine, Sharon Holland, E. Patrick Johnson, Thavolia Glymph, Tera Hunter, Dwight McBride, Paula Giddings, Daylanne English, Nikki Brown, M. Jacqui Alexander, and many other distinguished scholars of African American women's and queer histories—make clear, Black women do not always share the same historical timeline as men. Black women gain the right to vote decades later; African American women are formally removed from leadership positions as the Civil Rights movement achieves its official structure; and LGBTTQ Blacks find themselves consigned to the shadows, often as victims of white brainwashing like their white counterparts until the Stonewall Rebellion, but now encounter a Stonewall almost wholly reappropriated by queer white representations accompanied by statements that implicitly exclude Blackness from queerness (i.e., "Black have their Civil

Rights—now we want ours!"). As a result, these identity narratives, even after famous and influential books that create and theorize them emerge from the aforementioned authors, do not change the focus favoring the heteropatriarchal Black male body in the mainstream scholarship that follows.

At the heart of this problem of accurately representing a Black collective is the fact that "Blackness" does not exist outside of its intersection with other collective identities. If I cannot tell you whether the collective or individual under discussion is male, female, gay, transgender, Brazilian, an adult, or a child—if I can tell you nothing other than that the "person" is Black, I truly have the "empty," weightless identity of which Young and Braziel warn their readers, signifying nothing. Because trying to narrate all these collective identities appears impossible, they are primarily narrated through the lives of perspectives of Black men, under the default assumption that they are the leaders and therefore the agents of the collective. These narratives rarely claim to be speaking for *all* members of the Black collective *all* the time; instead they hope to represent *most* of the collective *most* of the time by considering various historical events, ancestral narratives, cultural practices, sociopolitical movements . . . the list continues. While the problem of holistic representation is understandable, its effects are hard to swallow: as certain bodies crowd the foreground of our representations, we begin to assume and look only for similar bodies, producing an inaccurate history of which peoples, groups, movements, or individuals were part of which events, much less of the (interpretive) effect of those moments on their lives. In other words, we run the risk that our mistakes will only be compounded in future generations: raised on histories that primarily feature men, we grow up to assume that women didn't accomplish anything and same-sex desire and relationships rarely if ever occurred.

This conundrum that accompanies all attempts to inclusively represent Blackness is not merely abstract; it affects which groups become forgotten in history when we historicize Blackness (as historians are always so painfully aware), and it affects the ability of county, state, federal, and private nonprofits to draw attention to, accurately represent, and effectively advocate for Black populations that are either passively or actively disqualified from city, county, state, or federal support; educational grants; and health studies—to mention just a few of the resources that Black communities struggle to access. As the Middle Passage epistemology itself attests, there is something truly soul-destroying in the repeated discursive erasure from or marginalization of vulnerable identities, whether in the media, on the street, in the classroom, or in the legislative chamber.

The only way to produce a definition of Blackness that is wholly inclusive and nonhierarchical is to understand Blackness as the *intersection* of constructs that locate the Black collective in *history* and in the *specific moment* in which Blackness is being imagined—the "now" through which all imaginings of Blackness will be mediated. Constructs of Blackness are produced through history, culture, and ancestry, which are predicated on a notion of time and space that is linear and driven by progress (with setbacks along the way); however, this linear spacetime, while offering the necessary "weight" of a material Blackness, at times excludes those who, in the contemporary moment, perceive and perform themselves as Black but do not share that linear timeline.

As the linear spacetime that dominates the academic canon on Black diasporic identities, the Middle Passage epistemology is a commanding one: it negotiates the complexity of the origins of Blackness in the West by stressing the process of being ripped from one existence and brutally thrust into another; it forces us to question the very heart and intention of white Western democratic discourses by presenting centuries of the moral and ethical corruption of chattel slavery and the equally corrupt logic that attended its constant justification; it belies those anti-Black discourses of African inferiority by presenting an endless fountain of thinkers, warriors, scientists, politicians, activists, artists, and entrepreneurs who achieved far more than the supposedly superior white majority. Intellectually, its counternarrative to Western claims of Enlightenment and modernity do not erase but complicate our understanding of those claims. Morally, it has not only been invoked and successfully used to critique older and contemporary forms of slavery but also been borrowed by Western women's movements and LGBTTQ movements to locate these identities within Western history writ large and assert their progressive nature. In other words, those scholars who have toiled in previous centuries and decades to bring the Black experience to light have inspired and driven not only Black studies but also a host of other disciplines such as sociology, history, literature, psychology, education, and so on.

Western physics and philosophy define in large part the linear spacetime that shapes and informs the Middle Passage Epistemology. Newtonian laws of motion and gravity, a hallmark of the European Scientific revolution, reveal, as Newton himself asserted, that "absolute, true and mathematical time, in and of itself and of its own nature, without reference to anything external, flows uniformly." Nevertheless, as Dan Falk's *In Search of Time* suggests, "Newton's view of time built on—but also departed from—the recent work of Galileo and Descartes. Galileo had envisioned time geometrically as a line marked off at regular intervals. . . . Newton went further by envisioning both time and space as geometrical structures that had a real existence."[12] Indeed, this "real existence" therefore rendered them, as Newton also asserted according to Brian Greene in *The Fabric of the Cosmos*, "absolute and immutable entities that provided the universe with a rigid, unchangeable arena. According to Newton, space and time supplied an invisible scaffolding that gave the universe shape and structure."[13]

While Falk and Greene add "space" to their discussion of Newton's theories of time, not all physicists or Newton scholars agree that Newton did indeed understand his theories as implicitly applying to space. This is where the humanities offers its own distinctive lay discourses on time; borrowing from my own fields of postcolonial studies and poststructuralist theory, which argue that time and space are inextricable from one another because each informs the other in our *discourses* (i.e., not the physical world), this book uses the term *spacetime*.

"Newtonian spacetime" is *not* equivalent to Newton's theories but rather is how philosophy and political science—as well as nearly all Western discourses, really, academic and lay—have (mis)translated Newton's concept of linear time into a linear spacetime or progress narrative. Newton's laws, with the addition of Einstein's argument that time is complemented by rather than wholly separate from space, operate quite well in the observable physical world and related technological applications. The problem arises with the translation of this concept of linear spacetime into the humanities and social sciences. The idea that time, as we experience it, only moves forward became popular among eighteenth- and nineteenth-century European philosophers and political scientists who increasingly came to argue that if we do not already see the evidence borne out by science (we see the young only growing old, not the other way around; an egg hatching, not reassembling), we can see it in the progress of "mankind" from huts, villages, and tribal chiefs to buildings, cities, machines, and "more advanced" forms of government.[14]

Given the immediate cogency it provides in presenting information and knowledge, it is no surprise that the linear progress narrative is what organizes most of our knowledge and knowledge production in the West. Today across the natural sciences, social sciences, and humanities, we organize most of our epistemologies according to this spacetime, teaching and arguing that our current knowledge is the result of or based on previous achievements and that we are more "advanced" than previous generations of scholars and practitioners—that word itself presuming a linear movement forward. Sometimes we use *post* to further indicate how far we have come—as in postmodernism, poststructuralism, postcolonialism, postlapsarian, the postwar era, postfeminist, even "post-Black"—even though scholars who work with all these ideologies point to the illogic of claiming to be "past" that which one still needs to define oneself (post-Blackness defines itself *through* Blackness, not outside of it, and so forth).

In physics, Newton's assertions that linear time provides the "scaffolding" of the universe no longer monopolize all theories of spacetime. Einstein's equations—later demonstrated to be true—revealed that time does not move uniformly but in fact can speed up or slow down. In particle physics, experiments on subatomic matter, most famously Wheeler's 1980 "which path" experiment, demonstrated that subatomic particles travel haphazardly through space and can even exist in two places at the same time. This means that one cannot attempt to track a particle though linear space or time; one can only use the present moment, more specifically, the *now*, to determine the location of an object. In philosophy, the "now" moment is understood roughly as epiphenomenal time. As noted before, because my own deployment of Epiphenomenal time is not tripartite but consists of one moment, it is not based in a linear relation between cause and effect; that is, as in the history of collectives, causalities abound in physics, but it is always impossible to assert convincingly that there is one single reason for any effect. No moment one experiences depends directly on a previous moment in order to come into being. We do not come from the past but exist only in the now, and we are repeatedly mediating that now with recollections, readings of, discussions on, and experiments about the past.

This idea that time does not flow forward in a linear fashion—that is, as a progress narrative—has also achieved some popularity in lay and academic discourses outside of the natural sciences. Performance studies and poststructuralist arguments (in gender and sexuality studies especially) have introduced arguments that social identities are performed and, as such, are at least partially phenomenological. Religious studies scholars are very familiar with epiphenomenal time as an enduring conceptual touchstone that has been adopted by theologians in various centuries to explicate some of the more preternatural aspects of religious dogma concerning embodiment. Unsurprisingly, theories of embodiment also explore the "now" of performance.

Exploring identities through intersecting spacetimes can produce a diverse but coherent narrative. When applied to an exploration of Blackness in the African Diaspora, we can not only produce Blackness as a "when" (rather than as a "what" or "thing") that is richly incorporative of a diversity of identities but also bring to light Black identities that had been erased, marginalized, or forgotten until our postwar moment of interpretation. At the same time, as all these readings of postwar Blackness show, we cannot find these moments until we first locate them on a linear timeline. That timeline is most often the Middle Passage Epistemology in academic discourses in Black studies, but it can also be a postcolonial or Afrocentric spacetime, both of which locate Africa as an origin but differ at times regarding the events, personalities, and ideas that mark the advance or block the progress of the collective.

Blackness is well suited to a progress narrative. Its linear structure offers immediate clarity and representation; its dynamic of cause and effect appear rather self-evident in our lived experiences scientifically, physically, and psychologically; and the progress narrative's philosophical tenet that knowledge can be accumulated and we can progress to a greater state of understanding offers an almost altruistic and thus worthy goal: to improve the lived experiences of the Black collective but also humanity at large. One can understand why so many scholars try so hard to cram the dizzying diversity of Blackness into this particular notion of spacetime.

Just as the microcosmos, which resists Newtonian behavior, has created a Holy Grail in physics, the Grand Unified Theory (GUT),[15] so do our most traditional theorists struggle to reconcile Blackness, in all its diversity, with our most dominant notion of a linear Black "spacetime." In their authoritative anthology *Black Imagination and the Middle Passage*, leading scholars Henry Louis Gates Jr., Maria Diedrich, and Carl Pedersen wrestle with these limitations of Newtonian spacetime. Seeking to encompass the global diversity of the African Diaspora produced through the Atlantic slave trade (a.k.a. the Middle Passage), they argue that the linear can in fact encompass all forms of Middle Passage Blackness:

In arguing for a spatial and temporal continuum of a Middle Passage sensibility, the editors and contributors of this volume define a topography that extends from the interior of Africa across the Atlantic and into the interior of the Americas. . . . Several intermeshing elements constitute this new conceptualization. Instead of looking at the Middle Passage as a phenomenon of constricted space and limited time, the essays collected here extend its meaning in time and space from the particularities of internal African migration to current meditations on the relationship of African Americans to their past, from the hierarchical spatial relationships of above/below (the deck of the slave ship and its hold) and center/periphery (e.g., the Great House and its slave quarters . . .) to the syncretic notion of a space in-between that links geographical and cultural regions.[16]

The "spatial and temporal continuum of a Middle Passage sensibility," as the authors put it (or the linear progress narrative that comprises the Middle Passage epistemology) addresses that key element that is so desired by discourses defining collective identities: a "continuum" or historical continuity for any given group. Yet that continuum, that unbroken continuous line, no matter how far one stretches it, cannot encompass all the Black Africans directly impacted by the slave trade, nor all the African-descended Black communities in the Americas (or South Asia or, in a few cases, Europe) over the centuries.

The editors acknowledge the reality of spatiotemporal "gaps" by filling them with a "syncretic notion of space in between that links." Yet they leave the "notion" as a placeholder and do not define its nature or full function. In order to enjoy continuity (and this is true of all collective identities), one must sacrifice diversity—after all, human beings are like cats (perhaps a bit more diverse) and have the "bad habit" of wandering off from the group, weaving in and out, or disappearing entirely from the linear progress narrative of history.

To date, discourses on Middle Passage Blackness that account for its formation through this spacetime are stuck in this baffling state of affairs: how can one retain the historical continuity (and thus be able to point to the existence and pedigree of Black culture, Black politics, Black music, Black literature, etc.) of Middle Passage Blackness *and* accurately represent all its many manifestations? It is the continuity that is the problem, the linking of events through a logic bound by cause and effect that ties the past to the present and provides direction for the future—in short, it is the very basis of this timeline's continuity that is preventing all Black peoples from being represented within the "when" of Middle Passage Blackness.

In *Warped Passages: Unraveling the Mysteries of the Universe's Hidden Dimensions*, Harvard physicist Lisa Randall discusses resolving this contradiction: "In theoretical particle physics . . . an object of study increasingly appears to possess a phenomenon that cannot be synchronized with the dominant phenomena observed. . . . Selecting relevant information and suppressing details is the sort of pragmatic fudging everyone does every day. It's a way of coping with too much information. . . . When appropriate, you ignore some details so that you can focus on the issue of interest, and not obscure it with inessential details."[17] Understanding Randall's "dominant" phenomena observed as Middle Passage Blackness, we can equate this "pragmatic fudging" to our current treatment of Black identities that do not adhere to the linear timeline of the collective (whether it be postcolonial, Afrocentric, or Middle Passage in its history). Rather than highlight this contradiction, our discourses "ignore some details" so we can "focus on the issue of interest"—that is, select those Black collective identities that adhere to the Middle Passage collective identity we are interested in exploring. There is a cost to this, as Randall explains, because those "inessential" details that stubbornly refuse to adhere to the timeline do not go away—or else they disappear and others arrive. In discourses seeking to accurately represent Blackness through not just the Middle Passage but the entire African Diaspora (such as postcolonial theory writ large), "pragmatic fudging" only puts off or delays the problem.

Randall explains that "multiverse" theorists such as herself (i.e., those who believe that we exist in one of many universes, most of which we cannot perceive or experience with the naked eye) understand these diverse phenomena as distinct "dimensions": distinct spacetimes that exist all around us and produce the phenomena that we observe and struggle to integrate into the laws of our "Newtonian" spacetime. Without committing to the multiverse theory, I find Randall's explanation of dimensions for her lay reader especially informative because she likens them to social identities. Her comparison helps this project to make a more cogent argument in discussing the difficulty involved in integrating more Black identities into our discussion, lectures, interpretations, and scholarly studies.

The Middle Passage epistemology operates as a formidably successful structure in analyses in the social sciences or humanities of Black identity because it provides us with the basic dimensions of Blackness—(three-dimensional) space with the added dimension of time to form a linear progress narrative. Nonetheless, *Physics of Blackness* shows how Black discourses can endlessly expand the dimensions of our analyses and intersect with a wider range of identities by deploying an Epiphenomenal concept of spacetime that takes into account all the multifarious dimensions of Blackness that exist in any one moment, or "now"—not "just" class, gender, and sexuality, but all collective combinations imagined in that moment.

If the spacetime of the Middle Passage Epistemology can be represented by a line (or an arrow), then the postwar epistemology (a more convenient form of the more properly named World War II/postwar epistemology) should be represented as a circle with many arrows pointing outward in all directions. This nicely sums up the argument of *Physics of Blackness*: *in any moment in which we are reading/analyzing Blackness, we should assume that its valences will likely vary from those of a previous moment.*

The circle denotes the "now" of the present moment, and the arrows represent all the spacetimes that intersect with that "now." Reading Blackness from the "now" does not mean erasing or marginalizing the past: on the contrary, many historians take care to remind the reader that all engagements with the past are mediated by the present so that we do not radically distort the past with "presentist"—that is, unmediated—questions, concepts, categories, or even conclusions. A badly rendered history, we are often told, is one in which the narrator refuses to honor the present moment and instead insists that the totality of a past moment can be wholly captured (not unlike an anthropologist insisting that the totality of a culture can be captured and represented by the interpretive dominance of the moment in which he, she, or they[18] are present).

The World War II/postwar epistemology is in fact very much caught up in the past and relies on the Middle Passage Epistemology to orient and situate any reading of the "now" that draws on the past, the present, or the future. Indeed, one could argue that, in its insistence on honoring the past as an object of study that is far more complicated than anything our "now" could ever possibly capture, the Middle Passage epistemology offers nuances and ambiguities worthy of our respect while never foreclosing on the possibility that there are more to be discovered.[19]

In the social sciences and in some areas of the humanities, many of the tenets that guide postwar spacetime will be familiar. After World War II, the demand for more "public histories" in the field was accompanied by a change in methodologies of representation. The viewpoints of the ruling classes were challenged more frequently by the viewpoints and recorded lives of those they ruled, shifting scholarship from a more hierarchical, or vertical, system of denotation to one that examined a variety of peer, or horizontal, relationships. Today, for example, a history of U.S. slavery that relied entirely on the viewpoint of slave owners and white politicians would quickly be dismissed by historians, public intellectuals, and others who hold the view that the ruling classes cannot speak for those that they ruled. This hypothetical problematic history would have to be corrected by either honestly recasting itself as a study that considered only how the ruling classes represented their lives or expanding it to truly become a "history of U.S. slavery" that incorporates slave diaries, Amerindian histories, white working-class accounts, freed slave narratives, and so forth. The vertical or hierarchical nature of this "expanded" history would remain in place—if for nothing else than to inform an exploration of the disparity of perceptions involved! At the same time, its reading of collective experiences would incorporate data and narratives based on peer relationships—how the slaves understood their identity not only through those who ruled them but through their daily (nay, hourly) exposure to and relationships with other slaves.

In sociology, the vast majority of studies on African Americans conducted today focus considerable attention on both vertical and horizontal relationships. Vertical representation is pursued through studying how participants might perceive the effects of the state and its formal and informal representatives on their lives—including those running the study. Horizontality would come from studying how participants interact with one another and considering, among other things, how they narrate those interactions. In African Diaspora studies, theories of Blackness almost always predicate themselves on seeking total or near-total inclusivity, but as many, including myself, have complained, we lack a model that could accurately represent the majority of the Black Diaspora at *any* historical moment.

Advocates of twentieth-century sociopolitical theorist Mikhail Bakhtin (or of Voloshinov, who may be either a pen name or a separate person)[20] will find resonance in Bakhtin's theories of the novel and the epic, in which the spacetime or "chronotope" of the latter is rigidly monologic, reflecting only the spacetime of the hero even when it produces contradictions (such as minor characters whose imminent peril is forgotten in the course of the story or who fail to age or change in the absence of the hero even though the hero does so, or vice versa). The novel, by contrast, is understood by Bakhtin to be dialogic, comprising the competing spacetimes of both major and minor characters (although Bakhtin never explicitly works out how all these spacetimes actually cohere through one narrative).

In Black studies, Mae G. Henderson, in her foundational "Speaking in Tongues: Dialogics, Dialectics, and the Black Woman Writer's Literary Tradition," builds on Bakhtin's dialogic and philosopher Hans Georg Gadamer's concept of intersubjectivity to argue that individuals such as Black women, who often intersect with other minority collective identities, speak to all identities and are thus "dialogic" rather than "monologic" in their expressions. Yet like Bakhtin, Henderson also does not explain what this kind of dialogic spacetime or chronotope looks like.

Physics of Blackness distinguishes itself from these arguments by asserting that all collective identities are, in fact, dialogic in varying ways when read at distinct moments through intersecting linear and Epiphenomenal spacetimes. To be mercifully less abstract, the academic discourses surrounding the historical figure of Olaudah Equiano also serve as a useful example. Equiano, a.k.a. Gustavus Vassa, is famous in both African American and African Diaspora history as the author of the canonical *The Interesting Narrative of the Life of Olaudah Equiano*, an autobiography that contains a narration that takes the protagonist from initial enslavement (at the age of eleven) through the journey of the Middle Passage into the equally unfortunate and brutal fortunes of Atlantic slavery until he secures his freedom and eventually enters posterity as an ardent transatlantic abolitionist.

Equiano's text is a rich and valuable link in history, literature, cultural studies, and political science courses (among others) that use a Middle Passage Epistemology to explore Blackness. It quite literally links, through personal narrative, the nearly incomprehensible journey from Igbo (and nobility at that) to Atlantic Negro slave to, astonishingly, self-emancipated Black Briton/Igbo abolitionist activist and scholar. Equiano's career, both within and without his *Narrative*, is one of the rare embodiments of the highest ideals that drive this progressive spacetime—the incorruptible drive for freedom for the Black collective and the achievement of concrete goals for the Black/African collective. Equiano's life thus not only represents the Middle Passage Epistemology; it also reconnects African and Black Diasporans because his abolitionist career took him back to Africa, where he worked in Sierra Leone while raising money in the British Isles and helping the Black Londoner community of which he was also a part. Teaching, discussing, and analyzing Equiano and his narrative, therefore, is an effective and compelling way to represent the extraordinary individuals who are part of Middle Passage Blackness and its understanding of that collective as always driven toward higher or more complete states of freedom and knowledge.

Yet several years ago, a prominent Equiano scholar, Vincent Carretta, came across new and unwelcome evidence that suggests that Equiano might have been born in South Carolina, not an Igbo village as he claims in his *Narrative*.[21] For scholars seeking to discuss Equiano through a Middle Passage Epistemology, this makes for a difficult situation: even if the rest of Equiano's narrative (following transport) is more or less accurate, how does one celebrate an African American who pretended to be African royalty? One could understand affecting such a ruse, as Carretta surmises, to escape one's captors (and the *Narrative* tells of more than one instance of slave owners reneging on their promise of emancipation); yet why then keep up the ruse, deceiving that very collective that he claims to represent so proudly?

This ambiguity about Equiano makes it difficult to locate him in the linear spacetime of the Middle Passage epistemology, because we can no longer be sure about the truth of his *Narrative*. If we cannot know where Equiano was born or exactly where he traveled before arriving in England, we cannot be sure that his life reflects a heroic drive for freedom rather than a compromised and self-interested career in pseudoheroics (perhaps hiding yet more deception)—or something in between. The meaning of his *Narrative* now escapes us. He cannot be pinned down because his extensive travels across the Atlantic and his status in most of those geographies as something he was not (the equivalent of an object rather than the resourceful human being he was) make him unlocatable without his *Narrative* to provide the coordinates—which are now in dispute with other coordinates left behind in state, county, and maritime archives. We cannot ask, "*What* was Equiano's Blackness?" and receive a satisfying answer with the archives in such direct dispute.

We can ask, however, "*When/where* was Equiano's Blackness?" and receive not one but a revealing multitude of answers produced by the multidimensionality of Blackness in the African Diaspora at that moment as we read it in the now, with all its possibilities. Unlike a progress narrative, which must move ever forward, reading oneself in the now allows for a broad variety of possibilities, some or all of which might be true in another spacetime, but at present exist as possibilities presented in all the conflicted discourses that make up the "evidence."

This argument that any one given moment of the "now" contains several viable possibilities is not wishful thinking—in particle physics, it is called the "principle of superposition," which, according to Adam Frank, a physicist at the University of Rochester, "holds that things at the subatomic level can be literally two places at once. Worse, it means they can be two things at once."[22] In applying the concept of superposition to our "now," when we do not know exactly where/when Equiano was at certain moments of his narrative, we need not cancel out any possibility that has not been proved false. As such, Equiano exists in several "places at once," because it is possible that Equiano existed in any and all those places. After all, we are not looking for Equiano in spacetimes that are clearly impossible—that is, Nigeria in 300 BCE or eighteenth-century Antarctica. Should we ever discover the exact place and time of Equiano's birth, all the falsely hypothesized birthplaces and times will disappear. Yet, in this moment, this "now," we do not know where and when Equiano was born—we only have several educated guesses. This ambiguity serves us, because it means that we can investigate not only his possible birth places and times but also other possible spacetimes that intersect with his life through Black collective identity or identities that exist in other possible spacetimes. Most of these identities are "horizontal"—that is, they involve Equiano's membership in peer groups among Black slaves and freemen of South Carolina (or possibly beyond) or citizens of his home village in what is now called Nigeria (and again, perhaps beyond). In other words, allowing for these possibilities does not further compound the ambiguity but instead produces many specific dimensions of Blackness that intersect through Equiano in all these possible manifestations.

Equiano exists in South Carolina, in the birth record of a slave child; Equiano also exists in the little Igbo village in, some scholars insist, a traditional oral narrative of his birth and childhood; in the possibly true *Narrative*, Equiano exists on the sea, as both captive and seaman, as a successful deceiver and courageously intelligent former slave now more than ever devoted to seeking abolition. Because we have so many more spacetimes opened up (and this list is not exhaustive) in which Blackness operates, we can then ask whether and which other horizontal (peer-collective) identities for Equiano may come forth in West African oral narratives, contradictory slave archives, naval archives, the records that may exist of those poor Black Londoners and Blacks who worked for total suffrage in Sierra Leone, and other scholarly enigmas of the African Diaspora. In other words, in how many other unanticipated ways might we find Black collective identities intersecting with the discourses of that era, whether oral or written, self-notated or set down by authority? We cannot read Equiano accurately through the standards set by the Middle Passage Epistemology itself, because his seemingly limitless intersections with so many geographies, traditions, archives, and so forth point to his multidimensionality in this moment—the endless possibilities of this "now."

The Middle Passage Epistemology produced and was in part produced by Equiano's text, and that does not change. When our attempts to read him within that epistemology achieve a difficult moment, the fixed orientation of that linear spacetime allows us to then "spin 'round," as it were, in the now and look for all the possible "Equianos" that occur when we read, listen to, or debate the historical and academic record. If we read Equiano as a "what," it is difficult to do this, because a "what" cannot occupy several spacetimes at once. If we ask "when and where" Equiano was and frame this question in the now, using space and time as our categories for analysis creates the greatest number of Blacknesses that are possible and viable.

Both the Middle Passage and postwar epistemologies seek to understand Black collectives within vertical *and* horizontal frames. Both are concerned with questions of equality, nuance, and accuracy in representing Black collectives. There are moments, however, at which the former is limited in its ability to achieve its goals by the spacetime it uses. Because it tracks the collective as a whole—those moments in which some Black identities do not fit on the timeline (e.g., LGBTTQ Blacks during decolonization and Black Power movements in Africa and the West)—it implicitly reformulates that collective into an ever narrower and more homogeneous membership. The qualitative value of Blackness is much lower in this moment, failing to accurately reflect important nuance and diversity, or a "qualitative collapse" in the moment of interpellation (as chapter 4 explains). Furthermore, the tendency to misread this Blackness as a "what" imposes even more fixity so that Blackness, as a vaguely biological "what," takes on an eerie resemblance to those anti-Black discourses that first claimed Blacks were indeed a "what"—a distinct subhuman species "marked by Nature," as Jefferson opined.[23]

Because our Western notions of linear time borrow heavily from classical or Newtonian physics, and analyses of Epiphenomenal time are currently most extensive in particle or quantum physics, these lay discourses written by science journalists and noted physicists inform my argument but also make clear the disciplinary distinctions. Methodologically and theoretically, this book locates itself at the intersections of poststructuralist and postcolonial theories of identity that use discourse analysis. As a result, lay discourses on spacetime from physics operate as vigorous and rigorous interlocutors for my theorizations of Black spacetimes; there is no place for judging whether they are subordinate or superior to the latter.

Chapter 1, "The Middle Passage Epistemology," argues that, like most collective identities in Western discourses, discourses on Blackness in the African Diaspora explicitly or implicitly interpellate it through a linear progress narrative. While this narrative is crucial for all collectives that are part of Western discourses on identity, when used alone it fails to do the job with which it was charged: to provide an accurate representation of that collective.

While Sir Isaac Newton is not the author of the progress narrative, I show how his famous laws of motion and gravity in classical physics usefully correlate with the linear progress narratives that developed during the Enlightenment and that we use in the West today (across *all* disciplines, including the way in which all sciences organize their epistemologies). The chapter begins with an analysis of how mistranslations of Newton's three laws into discourses that use linear progress narratives specifically create three logical problems for any collective identity seeking to interpellate itself through this linear arrangement of spacetime. First, the assumption of fixed origins forecloses the inclusion of members who do not share in this origin but appear elsewhere in the narrative. Second, Newton's laws establish cause and effect, a dynamic that translates badly into theories of identity for two reasons: (1) the assumption of cause and effect in a collective's linear timeline simplifies collective memory by asserting it as perfectly preserved knowledge enjoyed by every member of the collective such that each succeeding generation accumulates yet more knowledge (but does not lose or change any) and (2) the cause-and-effect framework, when translated into theories of collective identity, deeply inhibits agency by asserting that all members of the collective are the product of and reactors to history rather than agents with choice. Third, the linear nature of the progress narrative forces the collective to be represented through one traditional body (usually that of a heterosexual man), which can distort and marginalize the specific experiences of unrepresented members (most often women, queers, and those with the least economic power).

Using the earliest and only other use of the Middle Passage epistemology I have found, educational scholar Annette Henry's "There's Saltwater in Our Blood," chapter 1 reveals how Henry's reservations about this epistemology, which she otherwise strongly advocates, can be best understood through the aforementioned laws and their problematic mistranslations. More specifically, Henry opines that, while the "Middle Passage Epistemology"[24] provides a necessary service in raising her two informants, Mavis's and Samaya's respective daughters, it lacks the ability to interpellate experiences specific to Black women or girls. Also, she notes, it never fully explains how it understands its relationship to dominant white racist epistemologies: designed in part to resist them, it is therefore part of them and yet at the same time implies or states that it is wholly separate.

In order to retain as much clarity as possible, and to demonstrate that the Middle Passage epistemology, as I understand it, does in fact cohere with Henry's designation, chapter 1 reads Mavis, Samaya, and their daughters through the scholarly versions of the "Middle Passage Epistemology" that Henry cites. When interpellated through the cited Middle Passage epistemologies of W. E. B. Du Bois's *The Souls of Black Folk*, Henry Louis Gates Jr.'s *The Signifying Monkey*, and Paul Gilroy's *The Black Atlantic*, Mavis, Samaya, and their daughters do enjoy a rich history that logically justifies their presence in the West even as it condemns the white racist timelines that attempt to read all Blacks as located outside of Western civilization's spacetime as inferiors.

Yet while the Middle Passage epistemologies created by Du Bois, Gates, and Gilroy seek to interpellate entire Black collectives (or most of the people most of the time), those identities that ultimately do not fit a heteronormative masculine definition of Black progress are erased or marginalized in these texts. These exclusions can become yet broader when the Middle Passage epistemology is deployed to exclude U.S. Black Africans and their offspring, as well as U.S. Middle Passage Blacks of recent white or Caribbean ancestry. Using commentaries on Barack Obama's Blackness by the aforementioned Debra Dickerson and political scientist Ron Walters, as well as a *New York Times* interview with Gates and Lani Guinier on "Middle Passage Blackness" and college admissions, I show that intentional, explicit exclusions (as opposed to the implicit and likely unintended ones found in Du Bois, Gates, and Gilroy) produce even larger and more obvious problems in the interpellation of Blackness when the Middle Passage epistemology is used alone.

Chapter 2, "The Problem of Return in the African Diaspora," concludes the two-chapter analysis of the Middle Passage epistemology by focusing on its use as a spatiotemporally *diasporic* identity for Blacks outside of Africa; that is, in addition to the linear progress narrative, there is another line, dotted perhaps, that *returns* to West Africa, confusingly reversing the progress narrative's movement "forward." The introduction to chapter 2 also begins with an examination of the "arrow of time" as explained by theoretical physicist Sean Carroll in *From Eternity to Here*. Theoretical physics, Carroll relates, also struggles with the notion of "moving backward" through time. Simply put, the problem appears to be entropy, or the way in which time is defined at the atomic level and above. While everyone is familiar with experiencing entropy in the context of forward movement (growth, expansion, decay), no one has ever witnessed the reverse occurring: a grown woman becoming a baby, shrapnel and debris reassembling into a bomb and its target, or rotting food turning fresh.

There is a correlative to the "arrow of time" in African Diaspora discourses that explore the meaning of return; they also contrast the idea of traveling back in time with the physical journey itself. More specifically, whether understanding return as a matter of survival (Hortense Spillers's "Mama's Baby, Papa's Maybe"), involuntary (Octavia Butler's *Kindred*), an informed choice with ambivalent yet insightful results for Black Atlantic women (Maryse Condé's *Heremakhonon* and Saidiya Hartman's *Lose Your Mother*), or an opportunity to explore the U.S. Black male psyche (Mat Johnson's *Pym*), all these works, as I will show, ask us to rethink any assumptions we may harbor about return. All five works demonstrate that embarking on return is insightful but also paradoxical—difficult and, ultimately, impossible. Indeed, return always seems to end in failure, most especially when the subject thinks the journey has been wholly successful—that is, that a utopian past has been accessed.

Hortense Spillers's landmark essay "Mama's Baby, Papa's Maybe: An American Grammar Book" provides the entrance to the theme of return for chapter 2 because of its compelling interpretation of return as central to the intellectual, physical, and spiritual well-being of U.S. Blacks. Spillers famously determines that U.S. whites' pursuit of progress on their own timeline relies fundamentally on the vicious and unending interpellation of U.S. Blackness as Other. While Spillers begins the essay by calling for the reader to take her own body as representative of the Black female experience, her definition of return as the need to embrace pre–Middle Passage West African heteropatriarchal mores excludes those men and women who cannot or do not want (often because of queer loved ones) to belong to a collective that espouses such questionable values. Yet in an interview conducted several years later, Spillers explains that she herself struggled to see any other solution at the time of writing "Mama's Baby" and calls on today's generation to find a way to understand Blackness that is broader and more inclusive.

The rest of the chapter takes up this challenge through *Kindred*, *Heremakhonon*, *Lose Your Mother*, and especially *Pym*, a novel of speculative fiction, a pessimistic postmodern narrative of return, a travel narrative, and a surreal satirical novel, respectively, all of which offer possible solutions to this problem of return. Unlike Dana's literal return to the antebellum South in *Kindred*, which reaps equally literal damage through the loss of an arm, Veronica Mercier, the savvy yet selfish bourgeois Guadeloupian and Parisian protagonist of Maryse Condé's *Heremakhonon*, embarks on a more figurative return and pays a cost in the same register through psychic damage. Like the character Dana, Condé the writer also attempts a vertical interpellation to explain her "return," here a historical one to an unnamed twentieth-century postcolonial West African nation. Butler's Dana returns from her adventure with part of her body left behind (supposedly ensuring her own continuing existence on the linear timeline), but this appears to have been the price she was required to pay to ensure her return to her "normal" spot in the present on the Middle Passage timeline. By contrast, Veronica returns "punished," it seems, for her failure to recognize the reality of postcolonial West Africa, where she is violently disabused of any notion that Africa could be her "home." For Veronica does not seek to engage or bond with working men and women, much less the impoverished citizenry, instead seeking out sexual relationships and friendships among society's socioeconomic elite—those who, like her, directly benefit from an oppressive military-industrial complex and its neoliberal justifications.

Saidiya Hartman's tale of "return" highlights horizontal rather than vertical relations between herself and those she encounters. In those rarer moments in which Hartman interpellates herself as somehow subaltern in her relation to West African collective identities, the text also switches to vertical viewpoints and logics, away from those she encounters in the now and away from the knowledge and questions and the connections they bring, however friendly or hostile. Mat Johnson's *Pym*, the focus of the last half of the chapter, is an intertextual satire that takes Edgar Allan Poe's *The Narrative of Arthur Gordon Pym of Nantucket* as its point of departure and goes furthest in its rejection of linear logic when its characters embark on a return to an unfinished American interracial literary past: *Nantucket*'s fantastic lands of Black Tslal and white Tekelia.

Chapter 3, "Quantum Baldwin and the Multidimensionality of Blackness," turns the discussion to postwar epistemology, exploring Epiphenomenal time and its ability to interpellate Blackness "multidimensionally" by locating an individual at the intersection of multiple collective identities, or epistemologies. The chapter begins with theoretical particle physicist Lisa Randall's "multiverse" theory to introduce its own concept of identities as "dimensions" when interpellating Blackness. While Randall seeks a single unifying spacetime for all possible dimensions, chapter 3 more generally emphasizes how Epiphenomenal time interpellates a single individual as the point at which many collective identities intersect—but that individual does not become the unifying umbrella for those identities. In other words, the individual being interpellated is an intersecting site for a broad variety of other collective epistemologies; in Epiphenomenal spacetime, unlike in linear spacetime, the individual does not then become the dominant representation that subsumes all those collective identities.

James Baldwin's collection of essays *Notes of a Native Son* is a uniquely instructive, if also flawed, example of exploring Blackness through a broad array of intersections with other *peer* collective identities, or the many unlimited dimensions of Blackness in any one moment. Unfortunately, as I also note, Baldwin's essays are woefully devoid of Black female agents. While the essays that make up the first two sections of *Notes* are used to explore Baldwin's ambivalence about the Middle Passage epistemology (he both uses it and advocates expunging it from discourses of Blackness), the chapter concentrates on the four Europe-focused essays that conclude *Notes* and the way in which they interpellate Blackness as global, intersecting, boundless, and unpredictable by understanding encounters with other Black and white identities as equal, peer, or "horizontal" rather than as "vertical" or hierarchical (i.e., the Black African is rendered subaltern in her encounter with the white European; the U.S. Black is rendered less authentically Black, and therefore subaltern, in his encounter with the Black African).

Most specifically, "Encounter on the Seine: Black Meets Brown," which opens the third section, moves us through Paris at eye level as the African American reflects on and encounters fellow U.S. Black expatriates, white Parisians, and finally a French African soldier. Baldwin largely uses these spatially horizontal, eye-level devices, moments of chance meetings (on street corners) and encounters at intersections (the Eiffel Tower), to explore the temporally horizontal: an open and shared moment of postwar Paris in the 1950s.

While "Encounter" creates a space in which Blackness productively intersects with other collective identities and even another interpellation of Blackness, those textual interpellations are many but brief and do not begin to reflect the broad array of Black identities that could intersect in this otherwise very promising spacetime established by "Encounter." Chapter 3 therefore first intersects through this spacetime coordinate (Paris in the 1950s at the Eiffel Tower) with Bernard Dadié's *Un Nègre à Paris*, before linking Dadié's text to other Black creative and biographical discourses from Ghana, Mali, and Brazil that reflect on Blackness in World War II and the postwar eras. Baldwin's encounter at the Eiffel Tower is turned into a diasporic trope for encounter, producing a broad array of positionalities and views on Blackness that also reflect its diverse national, economic, social, and political identities.

The chapter concludes with a closer examination of *Notes*'s use of vertical interpellations, using the chiefly vertical structure of the Eiffel Tower to explain how even the horizontally focused set of interpellations offered by *Notes* cannot be assumed to be free of verticalities. Using Geraldine Murphy's "Subversive Anti-Stalinism," the chapter concludes by looking at how *Notes*'s own deployment of the Middle Passage epistemology ends up condemning Richard Wright through a strangely homophobic and heterosexist linear logic.

Chapter 4, "Axes of Asymmetry," brings together Epiphenomenal time and the World War II and postwar eras (but mostly World War II) to outline the problems and solutions offered by World War II/postwar epistemology. The vertical hierarchies one finds in Baldwin are endemic to most dominant discourses on World War II, showing that the *quantitative* richness the Second World War offers in terms of geographic breadth, archival material, and accessibility on a global scale is threatened by moments of *qualitative* superficiality. For example, although the Second World War was a truly global war that affected all inhabited continents, most dominant histories fail to reflect that diverse territorial and demographic reach.

This leads to "qualitative collapse," a term I use to define discursively the moment at which interpellating a collective identity through World War II discourses will yield almost no search results, as in the case of interpellating Black African women's identities through World War II. The chapter explains the solution—namely, recognizing the vertical logic in one's question (i.e., "What did Black African women do during the Second World War?") and changing the question to one that is horizontal. Using Evan Mwangi's concept of "internal heteroglossia" (or dialogic exchanges between peer groups) advocated in *Africa Writes Back to Self*, the last chapter reveals how even seemingly "neutral" terms such as *African women* and *World War II* rely on hierarchical reasoning, a verticality under which the answers we seek to our questions are not likely to be found. In other words, we cannot presume that the answer we seek is *subordinate* to our question; it is problematic to assume that the answer was created, written down, or recorded somewhere in the archives with the expectation of satisfying our future question. Instead, we must consciously frame ourselves and our question in the "now" *and* understand the answer we seek as having been written in the *now*, the product of "internal heteroglossia" or conversations between peers.

After showing how Black African women's histories during World War II can be found through this spatiotemporal reframing of the question and the anticipated answer, the chapter and the book concludes with a final framing in the now: where did Newton receive the ideas that interpellated the phenomena he observed in experiments into his theory of linear time? The answer, as one might imagine, does not honor the verticality of our question, but it does, I hope, launch us into another productive set of questions that further reveal and underscore Blackness endlessly intersecting across the globe through a multitude of radiantly meaningful identities.

Writ large, *Physics of Blackness* is intervening into two large debates: one on knowing, and the other on being. The first, extending back at least as far as the European Enlightenment, is about the shape and formation of knowledge itself—how we know what we know. By underscoring, as I do in chapters 1 and 2, the logical flaws and paradoxes inherent in the linear progress narrative, I am also jabbing a finger at the central and dominant way in which we imagine knowledge formation in both the West and beyond. Although tens of billions of dollars are invested in the notion that knowledge constituted by the linear causality created by the past and present allows news analysts, investors, matchmakers, economists, seismologists, meteorologists, political and social scientists, technology geeks, politicians, urban planners, business leaders, and so on to predict our future, we all, on some level, know that this is very, very difficult to do if not impossible. We are not shocked when economists fail to predict financial crises, and we even turn to them again the next day to find out what set of concerns should preoccupy us next. At least since Newton, bold statements in physics have claimed that the key to understanding the entire universe is just around the corner—only to find that the next discovery opens up a whole new series of inquiries because that "key," or answer, actually requires a wholly different kind of lock, or set of questions. Even those things that we label "predictable" are not, as we well know, assuredly so: Medical researchers cannot explain how some bodies, infected with a fatal disease, nonetheless recover without remission (meaning that a "fatal" disease is not always fatal), and we do not fall back in shock when a computer, cell phone, car, or some other electronic or mechanical device fails to work—nor do we look agog when on the second, sixth, or twenty-fifth try the device now does work. We might even argue that the way we marvel at accurate predictions is testament enough to our experience that such things are not commonplace.

At the same time, it is difficult to imagine navigating any sort of human day that didn't take certain predictions into account: the sun rising, our place of work still existing and expecting us, our loved ones recognizing us when we see them. We must assume if we are to act, but we must also understand those actions as performance: the spatiotemporality of our identity manifested in the moment rather than a thing we have carried with us since our first breath. If identities are not "things" but moments in space and time, then it makes no sense to mindlessly insist that all women, all Blacks, all trans folks, all Kazakhs, or all airline pilots, surgeons, or soldiers all think, behave, and act exactly alike in all moments—not the least because individuals who read themselves into specific sets of identities in one moment may not do so in the next. In order to imagine itself as progressive, Western civilization rests on this notion that identities are fixed, physical things are possessed by bodies, because progress also requires a notion of fixity (how else can one know how far one has come?). The recently renewed craze for researching one's ancestral and genetic histories reveals not only the degree to which state, nonprofit, and academic institutions believe in this myth of fixed identity and Western progress but also the degree to which so many individuals also seek to "know" who they are by supposedly unspooling their long chains of genes back through a linear past until arriving at a fixed origin.

Yet to claim we have progressed is a hard qualitative argument to make: the corruption, violence, and bigotry that infest contemporary societies are no better or worse than the ills of preceding societies, only sometimes different. The earth's human population has not progressed from a fixed origin, much less seen any bodies, religions, ethnic groups, or nationalities "improve" on their predecessors or contemporaries. Those living today are not in fact more advanced than those now dead; men are not more advanced than women; heterosexuals not advanced over queers, liberals over conservatives, Northerners over Southerners, and so forth. If identities are performances, then we cannot claim to possess superiority or inferiority in our being: we are a series of performances in distinct moments, and thus we are impossible to compare as if we were hypostatic entities. This links us to the second debate into which this book wades, and one that has gripped me for as long as I have been interested in issues of race, gender, sexuality, and class: how does one define, much less establish, equality in the midst of diversity? If we are not all "the same" (not even the same individual from one moment to the next), how can we establish equal relations between us? Sometimes this question has been misunderstood or even posed in the assumption that some people are superior to others. The last two chapters of this book take up this issue of ontology by showing how we are not fixed quantities but ever-shifting qualities. Equality, then, is a matter of qualitative connection rather than quantitative sameness. We achieve an illusion of superiority only when we create a false rubric for it: we ask, for example, which nation carries the highest suicide rate and inevitably find one that takes the top spot so we can ask what is wrong with that nation—what is its cultural, social, economic and or political failing? What we do not ask is whether it matters when other nations top that nation's suicide rate on certain days, or in certain months, and whether it did in the years before and whether it will do so afterward—and this is before we ask what kinds of people make up the statistics. In other words, by ignoring time, the moments in which we create our questions and come to our answers, we create illusory hierarchies that primarily reflect our prejudices, anxieties, and obsessions.

Many years ago when I began my graduate studies, my focus was on poststructuralist theories, but the inability of these discourses to theorize racial difference—that is, the degree to which their premises held only if one assumed a white masculine norm—intrigued me, to say the least. While I had never assumed that these vaunted theorists had solved "everything," I was surprised at how heavily they relied on a narrow set of parameters in order to theorize supposedly global phenomena. As I became more deeply engaged with African American, African Diaspora, Black European, and Black Atlantic studies, the lack of a detailed, explicit definition of Blackness became a dynamic touchstone for me, mostly because Blackness intersects with so many identities so frequently. In "uncovering" what ultimately drives and defines our concepts of Blackness—space and time—*Physics of Blackness* argues that becoming aware of how spacetime operates in our everyday and more formal discourses on identity can help us retrieve those identities that have been consigned to the margins as "rare" and "unique" and bring them into their true place as a site for enriching intersections with other bodies, other times, and other histories. This mechanics, or "physics," of Blackness ticks in every one of us, because in any given moment we are in the hearts of all sorts of human diasporas.

1

The Middle Passage Epistemology

This chapter focuses on how the Middle Passage epistemology both operates and "stalls," revealing how it sometimes fails in its attempt to represent an integrative and diverse representation of Blackness in its construction of collective Black identities in the West. It also shows how these limitations are caused by logical paradoxes that result from understanding time as linear and progressive. I begin with a brief exploration of the linear progress narrative as it is defined in lay discourses on theoretical particle physics and then discuss the specific behavior of this spacetime when it is used to define Black collective identities. As noted in the introduction, this mistranslation of Newton's laws of motion and gravity into the linear progress narrative was not committed by the humanities alone but in fact dominates how all disciplines and laypersons organize knowledge as *progressive*, from discoveries in physics to the history of pop music to autobiographies to self-help books. Most significantly, as the book's final chapter will show, many religious doctrines also espouse a linear development toward a higher or more divine consciousness.

Interpellating a collective through a progress narrative assigns the collective itself to a cause-and-effect framework, but the "cause" is not the collective but what (supposedly) drives its members forward: the desire for equality and inclusion into a nation, nationhood, the dominance of its nation-state or group, and so forth. Yet because individuals belong to many distinguishable collectives, not just one, attempting to interpellate a given collective through a certain effect, such as the passing of the Fifteenth Amendment, which supposedly guaranteed the right to vote to African American men, creates ambivalent interpellations of Black women in our "now." For example, regarding activists who helped to "cause" the amendment to be passed, some readers would criticize Black women for fighting for the enfranchisement of men but not of themselves because Black women are not relevant to the "effect" (their status remained unchanged; they had not progressed). Yet even when the Black collective can be securely interpellated as a cause, they are not true agents; they always react to or act against white racism. In the strict logic of cause and effect, white racism is the agent that sets the historical agenda for the Black progress narrative because it initiates the *Atlantic* slave trade (as opposed to slavery within Africa), Atlantic slavery, segregationist laws, racist violence, terrorist acts against Black communities, and exploitation by the state, medical professionals, science, industry—the list goes on, and in each moment, whiteness is the actor and Blackness the reactor.

While the crude fact of racism and its effects cannot be denied, the mistranslation of Newton's laws into the linear progress narrative and its cause-and-effect framework reduces Blackness to something far simpler than what it actually is. The history of Blacks in the West, like the history of all peoples, is a history of negotiations. Even when enjoying superior numbers and superior weapons for murder and terror, oppressors must constantly threaten and terrorize or torture and kill members of the oppressed collective in order to maintain their compliance. Even so, not all members will comply; some will resist until they are dead, some will escape, and a rare few will become quite famous, even historically success-ful, subversives and revolutionaries. These horizontal negotiations deeply inform everything from how lives are actually lived (versus the historical records left by the oppressors) to how laws are inaugurated and how some historical events occur and conclude, but they are often lost in linear prog-ress narratives unless they fit neatly on the timeline.

Newton's concept of linear time was adapted to the idea of linear prog-ress with space as well—hence the appellation "spacetime." One already denotes spacetime when speaking, for example, of the "pre-Columbian" era in the United States, or its "colonial" era—that is, we rename geogra-phies depending on which temporal era we mean to denote. These markers are also often marked explicitly or implicitly by notions of progress. We use "prehistoric" to denote an era that precedes human dominance and therefore in which no "history" took place; time passed and organic mat-ter changed, but that is all.

In *Black Bodies and Quantum Cats: Tales from the Annals of Physics*, science journalist Jennifer Ouellette offers a useful set of definitions for understanding the Newtonian laws on the basis of which the linear prog-ress narrative was established across academic disciplines. Indeed, it is hard to dispute the apparent logic of what are among the most famous dicta of Western civilization:

1. A body at rest will remain at rest and a body in motion will remain in motion, unless an outside force—such as the friction of a collision with another solid object—intervenes.
2. The greater the force applied to an object, the greater the rate of acceleration.
3. For every action there is an equal and opposite reaction.[1]

These three laws have become so deeply embedded in the consciousness of so many individuals that they might first strike us as disappointingly obvious, but their implications are vast and astonishing. These three laws are meant to tell us how everything, from kings to crocodiles to diamonds, comes into being and behaves while it exists.

Equally important, these laws assert that their application not only can reveal an object's *past*, how it came to be, but can also predict its *future*. Reflecting on this, we assume as much—the king was once a baby and will go on to become an old man; the log was once part of a sapling and will eventually fossilize (if it remains undisturbed); we know that diamonds were once mere coal but over a billion years or so of heat and pressure became precious gemstones, which they will remain for an even longer time (if no longer rare). As science writer Dan Falk relates in *In Search of Time*, Newton summed up time thus: "Absolute, true, and mathematical time, in and of itself and of its own nature, without reference to anything external, flows uniformly."[2]

The concept of time as flowing in one uniform direction (forward) was not unheard of before Newton. As Dan Falk narrates, long before Newtonian physicists, mathematicians and other scientists and philosophers had explored notions of time as possessing movement or direction:

Newton's view of time built on—but also departed from—the recent work of Galileo and Descartes. Galileo had envisioned time geometrically, as a line marked off at regular intervals; Newton's predecessor, Barrow, shared that vision. René Descartes (1596–1650) saw time as a measure of motion but considered the idea of duration as something subjective, "a mode of thinking". . . . Newton went further by envisioning both time and space as geometrical structures that had a real existence. Newton's universal clock ticked away at a rate independent of stars and planets, independent of our perceptions. It was simply *there*. . . . It was fundamental.[3]

The central concept emphasized here is that space and time form a neat line; space moves "forward"—that is, *chronologically*—pushed by time's natural progression. This is, in a nutshell, linear spacetime—and even today, despite the contrary findings since,[4] it dominates the Western imagination to such a degree that it is difficult to think of space and time functioning in any other fashion. Newton, by building on and confirming established concepts of time with his laws of motion, gave the linear progress narrative of time its appeal as the "divine mechanism that drove God's great creation of the Earth."[5] By imagining time as a *natural* force that moves development *forward*, Newton provided Enlightenment philosophers with a stunningly simple yet compelling understanding of time through which they could interpellate Europe as the vanguard of civilization.

Their resulting argument, that Western civilization is more progressive than other civilizations, remains a central tenet of conservative intellectual thought in the West. Indeed, this shared view of spacetime as linear and more progressive in Europe may be the one shared viewpoint of the Enlightenment's alpha and omega of phenomenology: Emmanuel Kant and G. W. F. Hegel. Moving against claims that Hegel opposes Newton, philosopher Terry Prickard argues, "Thus like Kant, Hegel takes Newton's use of the concepts of absolute space and time as paradigmatic for how proper science is to proceed since these concepts function in just that kind of a priori way for Newton, although they were hardly there before Newton introduced them. Unlike Kant, of course, Hegel ascribes objective reality (not transcendental ideality) to both space and time."[6] In other words, what is most compelling about this linear progress narrative is its transcendence, according to which it assumes a divine status because it is not controlled by earthly endeavors but operates the other way around: time predicates motion. Even though it still holds fearsome sway today (one is hard-pressed to find a book, article, or documentary on Western civilization that does not define linearity as exemplary of progress), on closer inspection the white Western linear progress narrative is linear only through strenuous manipulation of the facts. It is hard, for example, to claim that the European genocides and mass murders committed against Africans and Asians[7] and in the death camps of Europe are more progressive than the barbarity sanctioned by the emperors of ancient Rome or the Spanish Inquisition.[8] Making the line progressive requires defining European colonialism as altruistic and Nazism as a pure aberration, the exception that proves the rule of progressive (white) Western history.

Western civilization does not use linear spacetime only, however; it also uses "Epiphenomenal" spacetime, albeit often implicitly. A variation of this model (which is tripartite and partially causal) of spacetime is found not only in discourses from theoretical physics but also in medieval Christian discourses. Whereas linear time and standard models of Epiphenomenal time are at least partially, if not wholly, tripartite, moving from past to present to future, my version of Epiphenomenal time comprises only the "now"—but a "now" that encompasses what is typically labeled the past and the future.

In physics, Epiphenomenal time correlates with a definition of entropy, or the movement of molecules from "low" entropy (order) to "high" entropy (disorder), which means that the "now" is always in process—that is, the present and future are not discrete moments but rather are conflated into the one moment that is the now. This supposition is currently further borne out by Wheeler's 1980 "which path" experiment, in which it was discovered that when subatomic particles traveling at the speed of light encounter changes in their paths, the particles can somehow anticipate the changes and adapt to them *before* having encountered them. Rather than interpret this as the ability to "change the past" by "seeing into the future," physicists theorized that it indicates the primacy of the present moment, which is *neither an effect of the past nor a cause of the future.* The "now," or this book's definition of Epiphenomenal time, corresponds to the "indeterminate, fuzzy, hybrid reality consisting of many strands" that physicist Brian Greene describes in *The Fabric of the Cosmos.*[9] The present, Greene argues, can even influence the "far away" past because "an observation today can therefore help complete the story we tell of a process that began . . . a billion years earlier. An observation today can delineate the kinds of details we can and must include in today's recounting of the past."[10] As he also admits, "In the psychological arena, rewriting or reinterpreting the past is commonplace; our story of the past is often informed by our experiences in the present. But in the arena of physics—an arena we consider objective and set in stone—a future contingency of history is head-spinning."[11]

Yet the primacy of the moment that is Epiphenomenal time reaches us not only through theorizing the results of subatomic experiments but also as phenomenology—we experience time as sometimes overlapping, sometimes disconnected, moments. If we study a subject at school or learn a trade, we do not experience a reassuringly steady progression in our abilities in hour-by-hour, day-by-day, or even week-by-week or month-by-month fashion. What we forget in one moment we remember in another, and despite the ubiquitous encouragement to live our lives as progress narratives, we often look back at earlier moments as perhaps unsettling evidence that we have already "peaked," whether in high school or in achieving our last noted accomplishment.

Creative works have of course played with Epiphenomenal time—reading one moment through the experiences of many, or perhaps a series of moments through the experiences of one. Social histories often take a single murder case or political scandal and explore all the lives that intersected with it. In this way, Epiphenomenal time can also be understood to empower the exploration of a spacetime *horizontally* rather than *vertically*. The movement can be horizontal because instead of simply interpellating the plot of the situation comedy or novel through the eyes of one character alone, the views and experiences of many others are presented as all equally valid, exactly like dialogism. This, in turn, renders the moment under interpretation as multivalent with no one truth that dominates and thus orders the importance of the various participants in that spacetime. As Brian Greene explains in *Cosmos*, "The alternate paths an electron can follow from [one point to another] are not separate, isolated histories. The possible histories commingle to produce the observed outcome."[12]

Yet Greene also notes, "Some paths reinforce each other, while others cancel each other out"—and linear spacetime does the latter through its vertical relationships. In many moments of reading about or listening to dominant discourses on Western civilization, many peoples who understand themselves as part of it are either ignored or marginalized in progress narratives that detail the birth and growth of a collective or a nation state. Women, queers, and socioeconomic and political minorities often make fleeting appearances, exceptions that prove the rule of male dominance; until the past few decades, the working classes were wholly ignored, and ethnic and racial minorities alternately symbolized an empire's greatness or else elicited pity for their primitive sufferings. As Heather Love has argued in *Feeling Backward*, (white) queer historical narratives are routinely ignored, and no amount of evidence will convince textbooks or other dominant discourses to amend their inaccuracies. Western civilization is often, when boiled down, a pageant of white heterosexual masculinity firmly in tune with progress. Other bodies are affected, but they are rarely agents.

It makes sense, then, that those Western collectives that are routinely excluded by dominant discourses would revise these narratives to insert their own rightful places within the terms of "progress." Most often, when revising these narratives, the question of progress is redefined—dominant groups and nation-states are found wanting in their treatment of the oppressed, and the oppressed are represented as progressive in their scientific, economic, political, and cultural contributions to Western civilization—above all else in their fight for equal rights.

The Middle Passage epistemology is a compelling narrative used by millions to tell themselves how they "know" they are Black because they can locate their ancestry within this history. It is also, it should be stressed, at least a little bit different every time it is enunciated (like all dominant narratives) but *always* operates on the assumption that the "natural" flow of time is supposed to be progressive. Unlike dominant collective epistemologies that, for example, narrate the history of a nation, the Middle Passage epistemology is often more deeply grounded in historical fact than in wishful myth (such as the myth of freedom-loving Founding Fathers seeking a class-free, gender-neutral, and raceless society), rendering it one of the most compelling narratives in the West, told and retold in literature, film, documentaries, and high school and college courses, as well as popular music. Its central historical events, arranged on a linear timeline, move from slavery to rebellions to civil disobedience and some form of social, political, or even economic gains in the present moment, in which reactive, racist state, corporate, or even military interests seek to deprive Blacks in the West of what few sociopolitical and economic gains they have secured.

Constructing Black collective identity through a linear progress narrative and thus underscoring Black achievement and drive makes good sense, especially when one considers the oppressively racist conditions under which "Blackness" was first invented by Western thinkers, politicians, scientists, and fervent advocates of a racialized slave trade.[13] It is no wonder that we find this narrative at work in much of the early Western Black studies canon, advocating universal racial suffrage for those directly connected to and impacted by the Middle Passage. Such Black texts include those written by Mary Prince, Ignatius Sancho, Alexander Crummel, Martin Delany, Ida B. Wells, Frances W. Harper, W. E. B. Du Bois, and Sutton E. Griggs. The Middle Passage epistemology allows us to cogently and compellingly graph the antiprogressive thrust of white Western politics and practices, all the while documenting a history of defiance and collective uplift, and one in which reason and justice triumph over the nonsensical and uncivilized cruelties of racism. In the late decades of the nineteenth century and the early decades of the twentieth, progress and uplift were the official watchwords of African American leadership; during the 1960s and 1970s, throughout the Atlantic, their revolutionary histories continued to coalesce with African collectives, as Middle Passage, Pan-African, postcolonial, and Afrocentric linear progress narratives converged, while unfortunately also consolidating a false notion of normative Blackness within the heterosexual male.

The Middle Passage epistemology is just as important today as it has been since its codification in antiracist discourses in the West at the beginning of the twentieth century, because new racist arguments are constantly being invented based on old and long-disproven beliefs. Its distorting representation, one in which the majority of Black collectives (women, children, LGBTTQ Blacks, and Blacks outside the United States or the Caribbean) are not represented the majority of the time, has been tended to and amended, leading to partial inclusion. Absolutely crucial and critically acclaimed work has been accomplished by a broad variety of scholars of Black and African Diaspora queer, feminist, Lusophone, Hispanophone, European, and Asian studies. Yet despite the value of these contributions, they rarely find their way into most mainstream narratives that are based on the Middle Passage epistemology. From high school history textbooks and college courses, television programs and hip-hop lyrics, to websites for students and advanced scholars, histories of the Middle Passage tend to include only a fraction of the contributions, viewpoints, and struggles faced by Black women, Black queers, and Blacks from outside the United States (and only sometimes from the Anglophone Caribbean). Because these millions in fact make up the overwhelming majority of Black identities who understand themselves as possessing Middle Passage origins, this distortion should give us pause.

However, given the vast proliferation of Black identities in the United States alone (differing by gender and sexual identification, national origin, religious affiliation, etc.), one cannot hope to encompass all of them within a linear timeline. As noted before, some bodies find their marginalizations erased or even justified, while others trace an immediate or even slightly more removed ancestry through other geographical pathways—from Africa to Europe or Asia or the Middle East, or from Africa to the Caribbean, or from Africa to South and Central America—before arriving in the United States. To represent them all, we must separate all these linear progress narratives from one another, perhaps allowing them to intersect when and where all groups can agree that the experience of progress or setback is equally shared. Indeed, this is what a comprehensive graphing of all these progress narratives might look like. Visually, it is enticing, but when fleshed out into narratives, it is a nightmare—more than a triptych, an all-encompassing narrative of our "master graph" would interrupt any linear flow, challenged by the attempt to unite the multiplicity of narratives through common themes.

As an instructive case in point, I recall the late eighteenth- to mid-nineteenth-century Jamaican Creole entrepreneur and Crimean War "doctress" Mary Seacole, who at least in our present understanding stands alone in her narrative, yet in her celebrity and uniqueness always begs further study and engagement. As told in her autobiography, *Wonderful Adventures of Mrs. Seacole in Many Lands*, Seacole was born to a Scottish father and "Creole" mother. She inherited their inn and later married a white English sea captain. Once widowed, Seacole took her (self-proclaimed) formidable talents in both enterprise and medicine to first run boarding houses in Central America and then tend to wounded British soldiers on the battlefields of the Crimea.

Seacole barely intersects with slavery except as an outraged observer. Rather than devote her life to the cause of abolition as a Middle Passage Black (as so laudably undertaken in Olaudah Equiano's, Mary Prince's, and Frederick Douglass's narratives, to name just a few), she revels in her devoted service to her "sons" of the British army—although the primary reason for writing *Wonderful Adventures* was to exact donations from a patriotic British public to escape penury. The titles of these autobiographies themselves indicate the dominant spacetimes each author uses: Equiano and Douglass with "narrative," Prince with "history," and Seacole with "adventures"—the latter suggesting that the textual structure will foreground a series of moments rather than a chronology along which events are causes or effects of one another.

The immediate clarity of the linear progress narrative allows individuals to grasp a series of events in a cohesive fashion, something that Epiphenomenal narratives do not facilitate. In an Epiphenomenal narrative, they must be taken together, but in order to take them together, it is crucial to identify the three properties of linear progress narratives that limit or "stall" more inclusive interpellations of the collective and of events involved.

The first limit on linear progress narratives is that of origins, which, under scrutiny, can never be absolute, because the causal antecedents of an event or an era can always be traced just a bit further back—indeed, it is often the goal of the ambitious historian or archaeologist to subvert established origins—to find an even earlier example of Black European writing, evidence of even earlier Mayan settlements, and so forth. On a linear timeline, origins also hold pride of place, which becomes problematic because they define the entire timeline—meaning that each event on the timeline must reflect the thematic of the origin. A (progress) history of medicine does not continually note that we have failed to cure the common cold and at times have misdiagnosed both the cause and the cure of various illnesses. While this provides what is likely a necessary clarity, it also helps inhibit radical revisions: those realizations and breakthroughs that cannot be incorporated because they threaten the entire premise of the timeline—its origin.

The second limit, also noted before, is that linear narratives must use hierarchical or vertical means of representation. Histories of collectives can therefore track the progress of only the "leaders" of the collective—and in the majority of Western collective histories, these are men. While women and queers might achieve marginal mention, their achievements and contributions are erased, thus perpetuating the false belief that men did indeed dominate the intellectual, cultural, political, and economic contributions of that collective's timeline. Detailed histories of scientific discoveries, for example, often point out that the person credited with the invention in popular or dominant historical narratives was not the only one—or perhaps even the first—to deserve fame and credit. This means that many if not most histories of collectives are woefully distorted—yet including "the rest" of the collective would destroy the clarity of the timeline.

Inclusion might also contradict the origin at some point—while the timeline might celebrate the political independence of its property-owning male members as "Independence Day," the socioeconomic minority (likely the numerical majority) would reject or counter the marking of this day with their own arch note about their own status at the time of this "independence." Because the origin of this timeline inaugurates a progress history of the collective *as a whole*, the options are untenable: only one group can represent the collective. This does not mean that achievements by women and queers cannot be noted, just that such histories cannot include any events that point to the failure of the history to do what it claims: trace the shared progress of an entire collective.

The third limit to linear progress narratives involves agency, but this pertains only to collectives that originate as an *effect* of others' actions—such as the Middle Passage epistemology's direct reference to the white European and U.S. slave ships that transported millions away from their homes and families. The Middle Passage epistemology has a complicated origin because its theme is not only progress but progress *against* anti-Black racism. Each event on this progress narrative therefore always refers, explicitly or implicitly, to triumph over white racist obstacles, tying Black agency to white racist actions. In other words, Black actions are always *reactions*, making Black agency highly contingent and ambiguous rather than a celebrated given.

To return briefly to Seacole, if one reads her through the Middle Passage epistemology alone, she is almost "ungraphable," because she does not intersect with the struggle that defines its original thematic, nor does she meet or otherwise comment on the personages and events that define it. Yet if we add Epiphenomenal time, Seacole actually connects the Atlantic, from her birthplace in Jamaica to her time in Panama to her eventual home in England—and beyond (the Crimea). She does so, Epiphenomenal time reveals, by virtue of her status as free, widowed, the inheritor of property, and the recipient of an informal education that nonetheless launched her into a successful career as publican and "doctress." Seacole's text is also an Anglophone text that connects the Hispanophone Diaspora to the dominant Atlantic narrative, however briefly, by noting work on the Panama Canal (an enormous source of jobs for Black Caribbean men) and the transport of slaves through South America as well as the commerce between U.S. slave traders and their even more southern counterparts.

While the Middle Passage epistemology uses a linear spacetime, there are scholarly narratives—both emerging and established—that gesture to the need for an alternative spacetime. One such narrative, from Annette Henry, offers a nicely dialogic place to start, because it not only explicitly invokes the need for adopting at least a complication of a single linear spacetime for interpellated Blackness in the United States but also focuses on women, invokes earlier examples of established Middle Passage narratives, and also uses the term *Middle Passage Epistemology* (which, as noted in the introduction, explains my use of the small *e*).

The original use of the term occurred in an article by Henry that makes a powerful call to fellow scholars and educators to consider more seriously adopting lay epistemologies of the Middle Passage that are taught in households by Black parents and guardians to their children. Forced to look on the bright side of coming in second, Henry's definition of *Middle Passage Epistemology* explicitly expresses what many scholarly works only imply. For Henry, this epistemology is very much an informal, quotidian means of negotiation between African American identity and the often passive racism that is taught to all schoolchildren in U.S. schools, both public and private.

In her 2006 article "'There's Saltwater in Our Blood': The 'Middle Passage' Epistemology of Two Black Mothers Regarding the Spiritual Education of Their Daughters,'" Henry, a professor of education, documents the process by which two "Black women educators" seek to offset the effects of a public education through "spiritual practices [that] suggest ambidextrous epistemological terrain."[14] Henry elaborates:

> As I continue to extend Black women teachers' standpoints here
> through these educator-mothers' narratives, I want to suggest
> that the quest for a holistic and spiritual education for their
> daughters situates their "both/and" practices in a conceptual
> Middle Passage or, as [Homi] Bhabha (1994) has theorized, in the
> "spaces in-between" a "both/and" practice is a familiar concept
> for those in the margins, a hybrid perspective resulting from
> lives lived at the intersections of two cultures. Scholars across
> disciplines have challenged the "either/or" thinking in Eurocen-
> tric, patriarchal thought, as modernist thinking categorizes the
> world and all therein in static, binary oppositions (e.g., White/
> Black, man/woman, Standard English/Non-Standard English,
> Christian/heathen). These scholars have illustrated in varying
> ways that consciousness and experience can syncretize some-
> times contradictory angles of vision. As Paul Gilroy (1993) has
> suggested: "Striving to be both European and Black requires
> some specific forms of double consciousness" (p. 1), which he
> describes as "trying to face (at least) two ways at once" (p. 2).
> I shall explore the "both/and" spiritual educational practices
> of Mavis and Samaya as they embraced both a Historical Past
> and a Contemporary Present.[15]

Henry focuses on the need for the Middle Passage epistemology to negotiate or counteract the effects of living as a Black woman or girl in a majority white Western nation-state. This is a preoccupation, she notes, that one can trace back over a century to Du Bois. In Henry's experience as an educator, this timeline is always in some ways doubled, exactly like Du Boisian double-consciousness, in which Black progress is often impeded or even driven back by encounters with an antiprogressive white racism. Moments of stasis and reversal as well as progress occur, depending on the ferocity of the white assault and the depth of Black defiance. Although the actual functioning of the syncretic model remains unnamed here, one can note that *The Souls of Black Folk* does indeed use *moments* of encounter—that is, the shared spacetimes of an Epiphenomenal frame—to analyze Black progress and its enemy in racism.[16]

Henry's invocation of a "historical past and contemporary present" (being and becoming) also intersects with the claims made here in *Physics of Blackness* that one must use two spacetimes to accurately denote the full multiplicity of the dimensionalities of Blackness created in that moment. Henry denotes a "Historical Past" through an Africanist and womanist perspective using a linear continuum of space and time in the form of a collective memory: "Womanist and Black feminist theorists have emphasized the importance of intergenerational knowledge passed down from our foremothers. Both women [Mavis and Samaya] drew from their historical and cultural memory in an attempt to create a pedagogy for the children that would allow them to embrace their heritage and participate fully in their African-American communities and in the wider society."[17] Here Henry departs from the use of both linear and Epiphenomenal spacetimes by defining this epistemology through "progress." In this quote, the contemporary present is not a moment unto itself but squarely part of cause and effect: maternal memory is the culmination of all previous eras and will, it is presumed, grow ever more voluminous through successive generations, beginning with Mavis and Samaya. While the passing down of knowledge from generation to generation is cherished by almost all collectivities, it does not operate as smoothly as most discourses describing it would prefer. As historians can attest, not only are we in the contemporary moment ignorant of many past eras, but our understanding even of many "known" historical periods and movements is imperfect and prone to moderate or even radical revision. If we add to this the hard fact that each generation can never be sure if it understands the true intentions and motivations of its successors or predecessors, the spiritual education Henry describes may or may not be wholly remembered or imbibed by Mavis's or Samaya's daughters. We can at least be sure it will undergo some retranslation as both oral and written histories are wont to do.

This assumption—that progress creates an accumulation of history enjoyed by each contemporary generation—can also be understood as an assumption of the "vertical" over the "horizontal." Mavis's and Samaya's daughters will most likely absorb a great deal of information and opinions on Blackness, and the most lasting and profound may be absorbed not through their vertical relationships with authority figures (parents, teachers, police, etc.) but through "horizontal" or nonhierarchical peer groups who may or may not interpellate or "read themselves through" the Middle Passage epistemology.

In addition to the problem of cause and effect, "Saltwater" also encounters problems with origins. Mavis and Samaya articulate a specific type of Blackness that resonates among many U.S. Blacks but likely would be interpellated by other members of the African Diaspora, especially Africans, as questionable. Mavis and Samaya both argue that they are not "American" but "African"—yet Africa is not a homogeneous nation; it is a vast continent that incorporates a diverse range of nations and cultures—from Libya to Zimbabwe, the People's Republic of the Congo, Morocco, Nigeria, and Sudan—whose populations, borders, fortunes, and roles in world history have changed continually over the centuries. Many Black Africans would balk at this claim and react as perhaps any member of a collective would when listening to or hearing an "outsider" (someone who is unfamiliar with the language, history, cultural practices, or other epistemologies of the collective in question) claim to be a member, as if membership need only be spoken, not achieved.

Within linear spacetime, their claim to this identity is completely logical: they are the direct linear descendants of Africans and of course are defined by that African origin, as linear time requires. Yet ancestral or family trees are the result of heavy pruning—some of it deliberate, some unknowingly committed—so an accurate mapping of any one person's ancestry rapidly becomes a tangled bush. Chances are great that Mavis and Samaya would also find themselves linked to white Europeans, but perhaps also to American Indians, Central and South Americans, early Chinese settlers, Eastern Europeans, Japanese, Vietnamese, and so forth. Through this valence, the role of white racism in the Middle Passage epistemology becomes deeply problematic, as Mavis and Samaya may find they are also the descendants of white slave owners, thus entangling white racist epistemologies with Black progressive ones in troubling ways.

"Saltwater" offers no simple argument, but its focus is not on spacetime interpellations, so its call for a syncretic understanding of the Middle Passage epistemology must be pursued through the texts it cites as inspiration: W. E. B. Du Bois's *Souls*, Henry Louis Gates's *The Signifying Monkey*, and Paul Gilroy's *The Black Atlantic*. In other words, where do these texts offer moments of interpellation for Mavis, Samaya, and their daughters—and where (and why) do they encounter limits? Du Bois begins with all the requisites of the linear progress narrative—a fixed origin, a linear spacetime continuum in the form of collective memory, and a drive for progress achieved through cause and effect. It is also the most famous evocation of the "two-ness" that Henry's article commends for introducing a means of expressing the otherwise contradictory epistemologies that inform the Black subject in the West: "In this merging he wishes neither of the older selves to be lost. He would not Africanize America, for America has too much to teach the world and Africa. He would not bleach his Negro soul in a flood of white Americanism, for he knows that Negro blood has a message for the world. He simply wishes to make it possible for a man to be both a Negro and an American without being spit upon by his fellow, without having the doors of Opportunity closed roughly in his face."[18] Here the origin of the "Negro American" is a merging, with Africa fused to the landscape of "America," creating a new identity that nonetheless seeks to preserve the two "older selves." Unlike traditional Middle Passage narratives that directly trace the African American from Africa to the United States—as we see in "Saltwater"—Du Bois instead envisions Blackness in the United States as a merging of two strands. This might well be Henry's "both/and."

Outside the notion of a "Negro American" that is both doubled and merged with two other progress narratives, visual clarity ends there, and the creative rhetoric that is then used confounds and intrigues. In his writing, Du Bois notes a birthplace in America for this body with "two souls" ("an American, a Negro"), but Africa arrives as a verb ("to Africanize"), a set of practices that could be deployed to change America—reinterpellate Americanness, so to speak, through an alternative epistemology. Because the text states that the "American Negro" would be the agent of this change, Du Bois's rhetoric imagines not a distant homeland but a power to reinterpret and change one's home space.

Spacetime works well as a common denominator here, because it meets Du Bois's dizzying range of descriptions and expressions. Rather than attempt to negotiate the odd gaps that the American Negro occupied in the dominant spacetime of the white U.S. imagination—as an Other from within—this first part of *Souls* produces an identity that is the product of action, agency, and choice, in which identities are verbs and abilities rather than static locations. Blackness is agential here, because it can reinterpellate (a white-controlled) America by "Africanizing" it. At first glance, it seems as if the paragraph finally settles on a biological concept of Blackness ("Negro blood"), but the actions of the blood ("has a message for the world") strongly suggests blood as a synecdoche for the "Negro American," collective because it is difficult to understand "blood" communicating a message when deprived of the rest of the body. Thus even in the blood lurks an agency committed to this epistemology's drive for progress.

The activity assigned to Blackness appears to be purloined directly from the white Western notion of the linear progress narrative as first imagined by Newton and then manifesting at various moments in Enlightenment philosophy as well as proslavery and procolonial Western discourses. Time, like Blackness, moves forward *naturally*, the mechanism that unites the universe. Racism or racist whiteness, of course, attempts to reverse this natural progress and thus is naturally antiprogressive.

This critique of Western epistemologies (beginning first with Du Bois's anecdote of being accosted in the street by boorish white Americans who even in their sympathy cannot help but misunderstand racism as a "Negro problem") certainly aligns with the goals of the Middle Passage epistemology as Mavis's and Samaya's respective offspring are taught to imagine and deploy them. Simple logic dictates that the anti-Black racist discourses they encounter in the United States betray the goals of their own progress, while resistance to racism, including alternative education, moves the Black collective forward.

Yet excluding women from this undeniably linear and progressive trajectory of equality-seeking (or simply being able to open and walk through the "doors of Opportunity") in this first section of *Souls* (the pronouns are all insistently male, in line with the dominant discourses of the time) creates an obstacle, however small, for the two girls if they are to read themselves as *these* "Negro Americans" bravely pushing forward for progress. As Hazel Carby's brilliant critique of *Souls* in her book *Race Men* argues, it is difficult for Black women to read themselves into *Souls's*

Negro American drive for progress. Black women are not excluded from the text or the Middle Passage narrative—they are memorably present, just not as agents of progress; they are victims of racism whom the Middle Passage Black man is sworn to try to rescue or protect. Carby points out that *Souls* does mention African American women, but not in the same agential capacity Du Bois grants to educated "Negro American" men: "Although [Du Bois] declares that he intends to limit his striving 'in so far as that strife is incompatible with others of my brothers and sisters making their lives similar,' beneath the surface of this apparent sacrifice of individual desire to become an intellectual and a race leader is a conceptual framework that is gender-specific; not only does it apply exclusively to men, but it encompasses only those men who enact narrowly and rigidly determined codes of masculinity."[19] If Mavis, Samaya, and their daughters could access traditional Middle Passage narratives today that were free of these masculine assumptions surrounding the cause and effect of Middle Passage progress—resistance, challenge, and combat—this old-fashioned logic might be of little note. Yet our iconic figures of resistance, challenge, and combat are overwhelmingly male: Frederick Douglass, Nat Turner, Martin Delany, Du Bois, Malcolm X, Martin Luther King Jr., Walter White, A. Philip Randolph, and so forth. Our iconic female figures are celebrated for passive, feminine means of resistance that almost seem at first to signify submission rather than subversion: Harriet Jacobs is famous for lying prone in an attic for seven years; Harriet Tubman for traveling by night and also for hiding; Sojourner Truth for insisting that she is, indeed, a woman;[20] and Rosa Parks for sitting down and refusing to stand up.

This is the "vertical" logic that dominates our Western narration of human communities almost worldwide: a narrative according to which all communities can be broken down neatly into heteropatriarchal family units, whether nuclear or extended. If a man is not the primary breadwinner or somehow otherwise the head of household, we have a symptom of a troubled family/community. Oddly and ironically, in protest of an entire people's suffering under racist treatment, *Souls* asks us to see and seek agency in the (heterosexual) male body alone.

This does not mean that *Souls* is unworthy of reading for Mavis and Samaya, but it is to note that they are less likely to thrill in the role of a Du Boisian Black maiden in distress, as in "On the Coming of John" or as sweet, simple Josie. They may instead wish to emulate Alexander Crummel or wonder why Du Bois views the vocational curriculum of Booker

T. Washington's Tuskegee Institute as beneath the dignity of the Talented Tenth but perhaps not that of other Middle Passage Blacks.

The Signifying Monkey is a Middle Passage epistemology par excellence—indeed, outside of *The Black Atlantic* and *Souls*, it is the only one with which scholars outside of Black studies are widely familiar. In the following quote, Gates's arguments contain all three of the fundamental demands for interpellating a collective through a linear progress narrative: it is predicated on a fixed origin (West Africa); an unbroken line of a collective continuum (the practice of "signifying" first through the folktales of the somewhat Ghanaian trickster monkey Esu, then through the creative and artistic productions of contemporary Blackness, which "signify" on racism, whiteness, and so forth); and a progress mechanized by cause and effect because signifying is a performance of resistance:

> The Black Africans who survived the dreaded "Middle Passage" from the west coast of Africa to the New World did not sail alone. Violently and radically abstracted from their civilizations, these Africans nevertheless carried within them to the Western hemisphere aspects of their cultures that were meaningful, that could not be obliterated, and that they chose, by acts of will, not to forget: their music (a mnemonic expression for Bantu and Kaw tonal languages), their myths, their expressive institutional structures, their metaphysical systems of order, and their forms of performance. Common sense, in retrospect, argues that these retained elements of culture should have survived, that their complete annihilation would have been far more remarkable than their preservation. The African, after all, was a traveler, albeit an abrupt, ironic traveler through space and time.[21]

While Gates's introduction states that "*The Signifying Monkey* explores the relation of the Black vernacular tradition to the Afro-American literary tradition," the temporal-geographical scope cited here is the entire Middle Passage from West Africa to all the Americas. Gates undergirds this vast span with a doubling notion that recalls Du Bois's invocation of the Negro American ability to "Africanize" America, albeit a bit more complexly. Whereas for Du Bois the Negro American is a merger of the African and America, here Middle Passage Blacks are the survivors who carry their ancestors with them—or rather, their ancestral epistemologies and practices.

This also dovetails neatly with Mavis's and Samaya's interpellations through the Middle Passage epistemology: as per Gates, they may reject my own critique that they are not in fact "African" and point to a practice with which they are likely familiar—signifying, or "reading," as the colloquial term goes. Gates draws on the famous West African tales of the trickster monkey and links this tendency to create ambivalent meaning in both minority creative discourses and quotidian practices.

However, in such a quotidian practice, they may find themselves, as they do with Du Bois, sidelined by their gender again through the oppressive logic of vertical relationships. In this example of how Black communities perform their identities, women become objects while male actors take the foreground. Gates draws on poet, novelist, and painter Clarence Major's *Dictionary of Afro-American Slang* to identify the "Dirty Dozens" as a performance of signifying, which is defined as "a very elaborate game traditionally played by Black boys, in which the participants insult each other's relatives, especially their mothers. The object of the game is to test emotional strength."[22] On the one hand, it is possible to read the reverence for mothers as explaining why the "Dirty Dozens" can be considered a masculine challenge. At the same time, in turning its denigration of mothers into an art form, it will also always read, especially explicitly, as a humiliation of women. Even further, it suggests that one way to achieve masculinity is through the mastery of a specific form of misogynist discourse.

Matters are not helped by *Signifying*'s interpellation of U.S. activist and writer Alice Walker's bestseller *The Color Purple*, whose unapologetic indictment of Black male violence against women implicitly echoes the vague worries expressed by Mavis and Samaya about the challenges of womanhood that face their daughters. Gates reads the actions of the central female characters—Celie, Shug, Sofia, and Nettie—as making up a successfully resistant Black feminism through their transformation of the domestic space: "Houses confine in *The Color Purple* . . . but Celie, Nettie, [and] Shug . . . all find a form of freedom in houses in which there are no men. The home that Nettie and Celie inherit will include men, but men respectful of the inherent strength and equality of women."[23] Through a Black feminist interpretation of signifying, Gates nicely interprets Walker's feminism here as one that is constructive and productive—seeking to reject misogynist behaviors rather than men as a whole, a very viable approach for Mavis and Samaya.

Yet exactly which men Gates suggests will or will not be allowed into these spaces appears at odds with Walker's text. Gates quotes from a scene between lovers and allies Celie and Shug, in which Shug states, "The problem is not only 'the old *white* man,' but *all* men."[24] While not elaborating on this, *Signifying* does go on to interpret this assertion through Rebecca Cox Jackson's *Gifts of Power*. The last paragraph in the chapter begins and ends with a summary of its argument: "Shug and Celie's conception of God Signifies upon these passages from Jackson. Jackson's 'white man' and Celie's, the speaking interpreter and the silent reader, are identical until Celie, with Shug's help, manages to 'git man off your eyeball'. . . . Walker's text points to a bold new model for a self-defined or internally defined notion of tradition, one Black and female. The first step towards such an end, she tells us, was to eliminate the 'white man' to whom we turn for 'teaching' and the 'giving of understanding.'"[25] Here Gates argues that Shug's indictment of not just old *white* men but *all* men, coupled with a plot teeming with misogynist abuse from fathers and other male mates, can be summed up as advocating the elimination of the white man and his epistemologies. Yet he does not explain how this is achieved, so neither Mavis nor Samaya can take away a Black feminist tradition of signifying in the Middle Passage. While the erasure of any identity from an epistemology risks unproductive distortions, to erase white men from the Black feminist epistemology effectively erases a telling and complicated history of negotiating both physical and sexual violence committed through the privileges of white capitalism. All the same, as in Du Bois's text, here they once again will encounter moments of difficulty, such as these, in which the insulting of Black women is blithely passed over and a famous Black feminist narrative of misogynist violence and physical abuse in Black households is interpreted to bypass its very explicit critique.[26]

Engaging with Paul Gilroy's introduction to *The Black Atlantic* offers an inclusivity that Du Bois and Gates do not. Here, Middle Passage Blackness is read as coming into being at the moment of Western modernity, a defining experience that can encompass those classmates of Mavis's and Samaya's respective offspring who have come into the West through means other than U.S.-based Atlantic slavery. Although they may find themselves as actors in Gates's articulation of Middle Passage epistemology, it is unclear whether Mavis, Samaya, or their daughters can interpellate themselves as agential subjects, because modernity is first something acted on them due to their ancestors' forced removal to the New World. Their negotiations with modernity are not so much voluntary as forced.

Mavis, Samaya, and their daughters will not find themselves theorized at great length in *The Black Atlantic*, nor will their classmates find many explicit references to themselves, as critics such as Simon Gikandi, Natasha Barnes, and Laura Chrisman have observed.[27] Yet adopting Gilroy's focus on space and time to read the Black subject in the Atlantic offers marvelous possibilities. In his first chapter, he elaborates on the "routes and roots" through which Black collectives have literally and figuratively encountered the West:

> I have settled on the image of the ships in motion across the spaces between Europe, America, Africa, and the Caribbean as a central organising symbol for this enterprise and as my starting point. The image of the ship—a living, micro-cultural micro-political system in motion—is especially important for historical and theoretical reasons that I hope will become clearer below. Ships immediately focus attention on the middle passage, on the various projects for redemptive return to an African homeland, on the circulation of ideas and activists as well as the movement of key cultural and political artefacts: tracts, books, gramophone records, and choirs.[28]

When cast against the linear graphing through which *Signifying* organizes itself, here we are almost given a whirlpool: a notion of motion through water, of returning and circulating, a sense of "roots and routes" that effectively links the continent of Africa to the Atlantic (despite the complaints of critics such as Pius Adesanmi).[29] Mavis's and Samaya's daughters will have to do more work here, but they are not faces marked by outright expulsion or a troubled interpellation over the course of the linear progress narrative of the Middle Passage epistemologies offered in *Souls* and *Signifying*.

If we use the linear progress narrative to connect the African continent to Middle Passage Blacks today, we run into a logical problem, because our timeline moves through geography *chronologically*, with enslavement taking place at the beginning, or the past, and the march toward freedom moving through the ages toward the far right end of the line or arrow, which also represents the present. Exactly insofar as Gates's engagement with West Africa is with Africa of the sixteenth century and beyond, and as Du Bois, albeit more obliquely, defines Africa as one of the "past selves" in the beginning of his book, never to mention it again, Africa inadvertently becomes locked in its past—as Dagmawi Woubshet has put it, in "romantic arrest."[30] While this problem will be elaborated on further in the following chapter, here we see a problem that Mavis, Samaya, and their daughters might encounter when attempting to claim "African" identities in dialogue with peers whose parents, or perhaps themselves, were born in an African nation.

Gilroy also proposes, as mentioned in the introduction, a rhizomatic structure for interpellation (e.g., a root-like formation that grows both horizontally and vertically) to counteract the effects of the verticality that is found in some Middle Passage epistemologies: "The first part [of this chapter] addresses some conceptual problems common to English and African-American versions of cultural studies which, I argue, share a nationalistic focus that is antithetical to the rhizomorphic, fractal structure of the transcultural, transnational formation I call the Black Atlantic."[31] While he does not define "nationalistic" in this passage, by characterizing it as the antithesis of the "rhizomorphic, fractal" structure of his own formation of Blackness in the West, one could assume that the former has a more hierarchical, straight-up-and-down vertical formation as opposed to a tangle of horizontal and vertical roots. As he explains a few pages later (and particularly emphasizes in a subsequent work, *Against Race*), Western structures of nationalism, whether imagined as Black, white, or any ethnically or racially bound identity, are "tragic" and based on "especially crude and reductive notions of culture that form the substance of racial politics today."[32]

The Black Atlantic's advocacy of a rhizomorphic structure allows us to pursue this critique of nationalism in a way that opens the text up to explicit links with Black women and queers of the Atlantic world. The nation-state, as Angela Davis (*Women, Race, and Class*), Patricia Hill Collins ("It's All in the Family"), and Iris Marion Young ("The Logic of Masculinist Protection") observe, hierarchizes bodies within a largely gendered logic that "feminizes" the working class and racial minorities by attesting to their irresponsibility, lack of rational behavior, lack of emotional control, and tendency to abuse power in chaotic and destructive ways when such misfortune occurs.[33] This would link Gilroy's *Black Atlantic* with a shared interest in Black and white U.S. feminisms, but of course it also intellectually links postcolonial feminist critiques of the British Empire with the status of the subaltern. Once they are in college or the

workforce, Mavis's and Samaya's daughters could use these links to understand their connections to other classmates/colleagues and see how the
British Empire has produced them as semiliberated subjects of a former
British colony that links their oppression as women in Black and white
communities to that of women under the British Empire, slave women in
the Atlantic, and colonized peoples across the globe.

Gilroy pursues this question of individual liberty under the state
through the theories of Edmund Burke and Raymond Williams before
linking them to Black male intellectuals, primarily from the United States
(Martin Delany, Alexander Crummel, W. E. B. Du Bois, and Richard
Wright). The rhizome, roots and routes, and circulation of Gilroy's structure manifests most often between white and Black Anglophone men,
distorting the true reach of his views and influences. *The Black Atlantic*,
after all, established a means of thinking through Black collectivity in a
way that *did* put us in more effective dialogue with postcolonial, poststructuralist, and postcolonial studies. Yet by focusing mostly on male speakers
from the Anglophone world, Gilroy's rhizome is more of a horizontal stick
or a dynamic whirlpool of dialogue that other voices find difficult to enter.

I want to pursue this question of visualizing conceptual structures
because conceptualizing an integrated structure for Blackness—and
one with agency—is the goal of both *The Black Atlantic* and *Physics of
Blackness*—indeed, of most theorizations of Blackness in the African
Diaspora. The previous quote explains how Gilroy also seeks out a history
of Black agency to curtail the repeated relegation of Blackness in the West
to the "elephants' graveyard" of scholarly consideration.[34] In other words,
his epistemology of the "Black Atlantic" seeks to correct the marginalization of Blackness in (white) Western epistemologies by moving both
horizontally (across peer structures, such as his dialogues between white
and Black male intellectuals) and vertically (with the negative influence of
the nation-state and its racist, sexist, and classist oppressions).

While *The Black Atlantic* explores and analyzes Blackness through a
Middle Passage epistemology, unlike in *Souls* and *Signifying*, the chapter themes do not move chronologically. *The Black Atlantic* begins in the
"now," as a matter of fact, to stage its question, before moving back to revisit
the encounter between slavery and modernity, then passing through a history of Black music, before moving back to Du Bois, on to Richard Wright,
and then to the role of memory and Atlantic slavery within his epistemology. While the narrative is circulatory and rhizomatic, as promised,

the chapters also interpellate their themes through the intellectual and historical moments located in the Middle Passage epistemology—slave insurrections, musical revolutions, sociopolitical dialogues on freedom— producing the epistemology not as a linear timeline but as moments on that linear timeline that are connected to each other horizontally.

Even in this third, most nuanced and rhizomatic iteration, the Middle Passage epistemology implicitly forecloses anything but a male source of agency, further suggesting that even for Black women and queers, narratives by and about Black men and modernity are the most universal. In *Souls*, Mavis, Samaya, and their daughters find themselves represented sympathetically but without agency; in *Signifying*, they find their African connections validated, but their contemporary instantiations are partially veiled through silences on sexist and misogynist violence and behavior in contemporary Black communities; in *The Black Atlantic*, they find themselves valorized as Black Atlantic agents of Western modernity but without a voice in the actual discussions. Whether vertical, diagonal, or more fully horizontal, the linear spacetime of the Middle Passage epistemology— explicitly stated or implicitly constructed through key moments of horizontal circulation—cannot always incorporate all the dimensions of Blackness it seeks or sometimes even claims to represent.[35]

It is admittedly strange, but nonetheless useful, to understand this limitation as one having both physical and metaphysical dimensions. An object in four-dimensional spacetime can be shown in only four dimensions, but the Blackness of the Black Atlantic and the African Diaspora has more dimensions than that to represent multiple geographies within multiple temporal frames (i.e., multiple contemporary moments in distinct spaces, and multiple past moments in distinct spaces), multiple personages, outlooks, viewpoints, and so on. The only spatiotemporal moment that can accommodate all these dimensions is the current moment—not the present, so to speak, but the moment of the *now*, in which the present and the future are conflated and as many past and present moments exist as we can currently discuss, actively linked to Blackness.

These problems of exclusion become even worse when a simplistic emphasis is placed on the rather shaky mechanisms that supposedly constitute, drive, and preserve linear spacetime as our primary mode for understanding space and time. *Souls*, *Signifying*, and *Black Atlantic* are all works of deep erudition that offer notions of origin, a linear spatiotemporal continuum, and cause and effect that in some moments are inclusive due to more nuanced theorizations of these three limitations. In these three books that read Blackness through the Middle Passage epistemology, origins are not so much fixed as understood to be meaningfully transitory passages that point to a past and an unfolding future that is always changing, thus deflecting the paradox of origins (that, when fixed, preclude the existence of earlier and thus truer original). *Souls* and *Signifying* understand that spatiotemporal continuum that squarely links each moment to its antecedent and successor as a practice of multivalent expression that is passed down through the manifestation of performance from generation to generation. *The Black Atlantic* demurs on the question of such an established practice and instead suggests that the phenomenology of being Black in the West is what links and establishes us—that shared experience of negotiating modernity as an ostensible Other. *The Black Atlantic* also demurs on the notion of cause and effect; *Souls* embraces it (small wonder, given its dialectical logic),[36] but *Signifying* is the most adamant about its clear functioning, scoffing at those who dare to question its existence ("Common sense, in retrospect, argues that these retained elements of culture should have survived, that their complete annihilation would have been far more remarkable than their preservation"[37]).

Yet even as nuanced and thoughtful as these discourses are in their exploration of Middle Passage epistemology, there are many others, equally or more influential in their audience share, which make strident claims and assumptions whose illogic is rarely challenged. In the mass media arena, both thoughtful and thoughtless notions of Blackness are manifested together in "real time." Taking an example from mass media here will, however imperfectly, reflect the views of and exchanges between the capitalist class and the working poor, journalists, specialists, and laypersons—however asymmetrically and imperfectly. In these places we also can see Blackness read through the Middle Passage epistemology, and the view is not a little terrifying, recalling Gilroy's admonitions against race-based notions of collectivity in *Against Race*. After all, when we consider Mavis's and Samaya's encounters with discourses on Blackness, we see that not only will they inevitably encounter media discourses but those media discourses may in fact be the primary way in which they engage with discussions on Blackness and through which they are most often inspired to reflect on, define, and speak about Blackness.

In this respect, Mavis and Samaya most likely heard about and discussed, many times over, the candidacy, first election, and presidency of Barack Obama. Debra J. Dickerson's January 22, 2007, article "Colorblind" from Salon.com, which I mentioned in the introduction, casts into stark relief the extremes of the Middle Passage epistemology that have entered public discourse, beginning with the arresting lead, "Barack Obama would be the great Black hope in the next presidential race—if he were actually Black." In a tone that is both caustic and canny, Dickerson begins by noting all the coverage that U.S. senator and 2008 presidential hopeful Barack Obama had been receiving since his speech at the 2004 Democratic Convention (further enhanced by his landslide election to the U.S. Senate in 2006) before going on to comment that "my hopes for Obama are as high as anyone else's [but] I'm of the camp that he isn't quite soup yet." Dickerson then moves on to argue that Obama's ancestry necessarily makes him a new and different candidate from past and present African American power brokers on the political scene (i.e., Jesse Jackson and Al Sharpton), not only regarding his public profile, but also in the nitty-gritty arena of fund-raising:

> Just as the Negro-friendly Bill Clinton had to gamble on retaining that base while reassuring whites he knew how to keep Blacks in line, so Obama has to reassure Blacks he is unafraid to tell whites things that whites decidedly do not want to hear. Never having been "Black for a living" with protest politics or any form of racial oppositionality, he'll need to assure the Black powers that be that he won't dis the politics of Blackness (and, hence, them), however much he might keep it mute. . . . Homie has some rings to kiss and a kente-cloth pocket square to buy.[38]

Dickerson begins the next paragraph by aligning Obama with a white American and then delineating him relative to other prominent Black American political power brokers through his lack of political activism, which allows for an implicit condemnation of his political "bona fides" and, more crucially, also suggests that Obama, although a Democrat, may in fact adhere to a conservative vision in which Black people are the problem rather than anti-Black racism.

Dickerson's characterization of this elitism is shared one year later by Professor Ron Walters at the University of Maryland. In "Barack Obama and the Politics of Blackness," Walters defines those questioning Obama's Blackness as "Black nationalist," such as the journalist Stanley Crouch, who argues that despite Obama's claims in *Dreams from My Father* that he made common cause with African Americans, his lack of "plantation slave ancestry" excludes him from the collective.[39] By contrast, Walters argues that Obama's Blackness should not be questioned purely through "cultural markers," first stating that recent debates on affirmative action admissions for "non-Middle Passage Blacks" to U.S. colleges and universities runs against the intent of the original legislation, which was to secure proportionate representation of "Americans of African descent." Obama's need to capture the center of the electorate, Walters opines, requires that Obama not speak from an *explicitly* Black point of view. Applying a more horizontal interpellation of the "Black community," he reasons that what should matter most for African Americans is not someone's skin color or ethnic origin but that person's politics—in other words, that she or he will champion platforms that benefit the Black community, even if not in name. Antipoverty programs, reproductive rights for women, equal treatment under the justice system, raising the minimum wage—these are issues that impact Blacks but not only them: they are also national issues. On these issues, Walters sums up, "The record shows that beyond his physiognomy, Obama has established a credible record of both assimilation into the Black community and political representation, which stands as a credible claim for Black political support. However, his 'Blackness' is weakened by his tendency to exercise considerable caution with respect to strong support of symbols and issues of Blackness."[40] By framing Obama's Blackness wholly within the terms of appealing to a majority of the U.S. Black electorate, defining the "strong assets" of his "cultural presentation" as "of African descent, he married a Black woman, he belongs to a Black church, and he lives in a racially integrated community," Walters offers a new avenue into Middle Passage Blackness, albeit one that sits on a sliding scale (at least in the political arena), in which one's Blackness is "weakened," like Obama's, by failing to engage with certain issues. While suggesting that he views Black nationalists such as Stanley Crouch as too partisan, he does in fact adopt the view of Pan-Africanists and Black nationalists that Black people share a common cause that is not limited to, but is wholly inclusive of, that of the descendants of the Atlantic slave trade. Middle Passage membership is thus expanded, but the requisite ideology, or political perspective, becomes all the more important. In short, both Walters and Dickerson vet Obama's imagined application for membership through what they understand as an authentically "Black" notion of socioeconomic and political progress.

Who decides these politics? Walters admits that his list of Obama's political views and actions are defined as tenets of the liberal platform even though he argues that Obama is speaking from the center. Yet even within the confines of political identity, collapsing U.S. liberal platforms with "Black" political platforms means that conservative Blacks are not "Black." Because Walters notes the importance (but argues against the centrality) of family ties in asserting one's membership in the Black collective, one would suppose that Clarence Thomas would be Black by ancestry and family ties (excluding marriage, it seems) but not by politics. The notion that some bodies are able to claim a "stronger" Blackness over others is troubling even if limited to the political sphere, not least because Walters identifies that sphere as not specifically Black. Political Blackness thus becomes a subset of the U.S. centrist left wing. Even further, African Americans of more recent African descent are expected to make common cause with these platforms in order to "strengthen" their (political) Blackness.

Despite his disagreement, then, Walters's analysis largely dovetails with Dickerson's. By framing the notion of "Blackness" within a sociopolitical argument, specifically the continuing protest and denunciation of institutional racism practiced by members of the Congressional Black Caucus, Dickerson is specifically separating an "illegitimate Blackness" symbolized by "Ebonics" and Kente cloth from an "authentic Blackness" constituted by a social and political awareness of institutional racism. Here, the Middle Passage epistemology is used to exclude those who seek to read themselves through it by intersecting at certain key moments. Here is an extended version of the rather loaded Dickerson quote I included in the introduction:

> "Black," in our political and social reality, means those descended from West African slaves. Voluntary immigrants of African descent (even those descended from West Indian slaves) are just that, voluntary immigrants of African descent with markedly different outlooks on the role of race in their lives and in politics. At a minimum, it can't be assumed that a Nigerian cabdriver and a third-generation Harlemite have more in common than the fact a cop won't bother to make the distinction. They're both "Black" as a matter of skin color and DNA, but only the Harlemite, for better or worse, is politically and culturally Black, as we use the term.

We know a great deal about Black people. We know next to nothing about immigrants of African descent (woe be unto Blacks when the latter groups find their voice and start saying all kinds of things we don't want said). That rank-and-file Black voters might not bother to make this distinction as long as Obama acts Black and does us proud makes them no less complicit in this shell game we're playing because everybody wins. (For all the hoopla over Obama, though, most Blacks still support Sen. Clinton, with her long relationships in the community and the spillover from President Clinton's wide popularity.)[41]

While Dickerson and Walters cohere with Gilroy in reading Blackness as the moment of negotiation with the West informed by the Middle Passage epistemology, they strike out in a wholly different direction by insisting on the existence, as in *Signifying*, of an enduring collective memory of preserved and accumulating experiences caused by the effects of slavery and the attendant forms of racist harm and exclusion that followed in Western nation-states.

Before looking more closely at this assertion of a linear collective memory as the product of cause and effect, there are two other distinctions that separate Dickerson (and Walters, but only somewhat) from the Middle Passage epistemologies found in *Souls*, *Signifying*, and *Black Atlantic*. The first distinction depends on understanding Blackness as geographically diverse, even when located within a shared moment in the United States. Rejecting intersection with other Black communities who share similar moments (Dickerson argues this explicitly by insisting that U.S. Blacks of U.S. Middle Passage ancestry experience racism differently from the "Nigerian cab driver") ahistorically occludes the vast majority of Blacks in the African Diaspora who possess ancestries that came into the West. This narrow expression of Blackness will, of course, come into immediate conflict with the bevy of Black Americans, African Americans, who are quite literally from both the United States and the Americas or Africa. Yet within the perverse logic of a linear spacetime, it must be pointed out that Dickerson is purely Newtonian in her assumptions—that any Black collective that moves generationally through the Middle Passage timeline is the cumulative product of a series of linear causes and effects (enslavement, Emancipation, Jim Crow, the world wars, Civil Rights, Black Power, the rejuvenation of white conservatism in the nation-state, etc.). As such, such a collective is a specific product of a linear set of generational experiences that do not intersect with those of other collectives who may share many of the same historical moments—and here at least seventy million Black Brazilians should be of note.[42] Walters allows for intersection through marriage and the production of children (a vertical alignment) but does not elaborate as to whether there are other ways than marrying and reproducing to intersect with the Middle Passage epistemology.

Both Dickerson and Walters fudge on the second concern—Black agency, something foregrounded in the three academic texts (albeit imperfectly so). For Dickerson, suffering is the effect of the causes of the Middle Passage epistemology, where Blackness is squarely located in slavery and racism, and lack of agency is what marks the Black subject. For Walters, suffering is also the basis for Middle Passage consciousness, but his allowance for intersection and understanding of suffering and his horizontal reading of the Black community open up the possibility of Epiphenomenal time and therefore agency. By forging elective affinities with other subaltern groups (rather than wholly focusing vertically on the white oppressor) and sharing identification of common obstacles (if not the same one), Blackness becomes an identity that faces obstacles, but Blackness itself is not an obstacle. This is only a possibility, however, as Walters's focus, like Dickerson's, is on Blackness as a subaltern status.

Agency bedevils the Middle Passage epistemology because, unlike the white Western epistemology of its history of civilization, it begins with Blackness as an object of white oppression (or Black African slave traders and leaders of African slave-trading nations). On a linear progress narrative driven by cause and effect (based on Newton's three laws of motion and gravity), to enter as an object without motion means that one's path has always already been determined by another moving object—or as philosophy would term it, one who creates changes, an agent. Indeed, it is worth considering whether scholars such as Mary Lefkowitz refute the researched claims of Egyptian and Levantine influences on ancient Greece and other parts of Europe by Martin Bernal and Ivan Van Sertima, because they enable a reading of whiteness that is always indebted to Blackness, always "colored" by it, pun intended.[43]

This analysis of the linear progress narrative that structures the Middle Passage epistemology concludes by returning to a media discourse that represents the views of two academics, Henry Louis Gates Jr. and celebrated legal scholar Lani Guinier, to show how Dickerson's exclusions are

shared in other moments when Blackness is read through a strictly lin-
ear Middle Passage epistemology. In the introduction to a June 24, 2004,
New York Times interview with Gates and Guinier, both faculty at Harvard
University, the interviewer notes,

> While about 8 percent, or about 530, of Harvard's undergradu-
> ates were Black, Lani Guinier, a Harvard law professor, and Henry
> Louis Gates Jr., the chairman of Harvard's African and African-
> American studies department, pointed out that the majority of
> them—perhaps as many as two-thirds—were West Indian and
> African immigrants or their children, or to a lesser extent, children
> of biracial couples.[44]
>
> They said that only about a third of the students were from
> families in which all four grandparents were born in this coun-
> try, descendants of slaves. Many argue that it was students like
> these, disadvantaged by the legacy of Jim Crow laws, segregation
> and decades of racism, poverty and inferior schools, who were
> intended as principal beneficiaries of affirmative action in univer-
> sity admissions.
>
> What concerned the two professors, they said, was that in the
> high-stakes world of admissions to the most selective colleges—
> and with it, entry into the country's inner circles of power, wealth
> and influence—African-American students whose families have
> been in America for generations were being left behind.
>
> "I just want people to be honest enough to talk about it," Profes-
> sor Gates, the Yale-educated son of a West Virginia paper-mill
> worker, said recently, reiterating the questions he has been raising
> since the Black alumni weekend last fall. "What are the implica-
> tions of this?"
>
> Both Professor Gates and Professor Guinier emphasize that this
> is not about excluding immigrants, whom sociologists describe as a
> highly motivated, self-selected group. Blacks, who make up 13 per-
> cent of the United States population, are still underrepresented at
> Harvard and other selective colleges, they said.[45]

While admittedly Dickerson's ultimate agenda is to attract and increase
her readership, Gates and Guinier nonetheless share a common goal with
her in that both seek to distinguish "Middle Passage" Black Americans

from "other" Black Americans. Whereas Dickerson jumps from argument to argument, never quite resting on any one argument long enough to tip her hand toward either pure mockery or sober assertion,[46] the Harvard professors are quite serious—and at pains to avoid being viewed as neosegregationists. So while Walters vacillates between a liberal political platform and family ties, and Dickerson plays with ancestry, history, activism, and white liberal guilt, Gates and Guinier establish a relatively constant delineation between those Black Americans for whom "all four grandparents were born in [the United States], the descendants of slaves" and "West Indian and African immigrants or their children [and] children of biracial couples."[47]

Unlike Dickerson, Gates and Guinier are careful in their enunciations, yet their determinant seems, at first glance, even more provocative than Dickerson's. At once a fanciful inversion (and therefore, inevitably, a reiteration) of the One Drop Rule (whereby slaves possessing at least 1/16 "Negro blood" were deemed Black and thus likely candidates for enslavement or at least racist discrimination) and similarly reminiscent of the Nazi mathematics that informed their Nuremberg Laws (in which the equation of a contemporary "Jew" was broken down into grandparent-components),[48] their definitions recall historical eras in which minority groups were solemnly separated from one another to determine anything from punishment to enslavement to extermination.

What supplies the troubling cast to their formulations is, ironically, the desire for accuracy—even Walters's desire to include Obama requires establishing boundaries to which there are alarming exceptions. Walters's stipulation of blood ties to African Americans, even according to its own logic, recalls a false but forceful discourse that binds all African Americans to biology. "The Politics of Blackness" somewhat circumvents this by adding cultural interaction, yet that still leaves out Black U.S. citizens who are recently arrived from Africa or other parts of the Diaspora. Walters includes Black immigrants to refute Dickerson's exclusivity, yet his conclusive definition leaves out those who are not meaningfully linked to "Middle Passage" Black communities. There is a deeply frustrating truth here: any fixed stipulation for membership, whether national, biological, cultural, political, social, or otherwise, initiates a simplistic framework with essentialist consequences.

Dickerson's desire to prevent her terms from backfiring on her argument (such as avoiding the term *African American*) allows her to skirt the larger issue of attempting to design generic categories that can be imposed on individual personalities and histories. After all, this is what makes "Blackness" so very different from "whiteness" in the United States (and, in certain contexts, also from other Anglophone nations such as Australia, England, Jamaica, and New Zealand), because the former spreads a much wider net than the latter thanks to the One Drop Rule. To that end, at least in the Anglophone world, Black communities have always boasted a wealth of ancestries that whiteness, by its own rules, simply cannot tolerate—in all meanings of the word.[49]

Gates and Guinier's evocation of grandparents is a telling reflection on this—they cannot draw a broad distinguishing line between "pure" African ancestry and "mixed" race Blacks because the overwhelming majority of, if not all, peoples of African descent in the United States and Caribbean have non-African ancestors.[50] So in denoting "four Black grandparents" as their minimum standard to be categorized as "Black" (the same term Dickerson uses, we should note), the odd aspect to this equation is that those grandparents could in fact all be mixed—and probably all are to one extent or another (at the very least, it is doubtful that more than one could honestly claim "pure" African ancestry).[51] As in Dickerson's piece, time plays a key role here: if the grandparent in question, say, possesses three Black grandparents of his or her own, then according to Gates and Guinier, they are Black now, but their grandchild of the exact same "grandparent-component" is *not* Black.[52] Even more intriguing, under these Gates-Guinier categories Frederick Douglass, W. E. B. Du Bois, Malcolm X, and Sasha and Malia Obama today would be classified as "not Black," as all had one or more white grandparents.

This contestation, however, is too superficial, because the temporal qualification Gates and Guinier bring to bear is not unplanned. Whereas Dickerson invokes "Middle Passage Blackness" by discussing a particular mind-set that marks those who possess this ancestry, Gates and Guinier invoke a historiography of Blackness—that is, what it meant to be Black in earlier eras as opposed to today. Under this logic, an African American who today we would call "biracial" would not on this basis have been exempted in the antebellum South from the same kinds of treatment that befell other Blacks.[53] There is a problem, however: a biracial Black American is not immune from racist treatment today and certainly can't be assumed not to have been "disadvantaged by the legacy of Jim Crow laws, segregation and decades of poverty and inferior schools"—that is, biracial Black Americans should be included among those whom Gates and Guinier argue are meant to be the "principal beneficiaries of affirmative action in university admissions." This glaring fact may explain the qualification the Harvard professors add to this category ("to a lesser extent"), but it does not wholly erase its problematic assumption: that by having a white parent (the term *biracial* is often incorrectly limited to Americans with one white and one Black parent), a Black American is no longer Black because he or she is likely to have had led a life free from racist treatment and at the very least remains unmarked by the history "Middle Passage Blackness" narrates (e.g., slavery, Jim Crow, segregation, institutionalized racism).

Indeed, what is intriguing here is the obvious elision Gates and Guinier are making: in attempting to delineate which Blacks are most likely the victims of socioeconomic discrimination, the category of economic power remains absent. As such, they are rewriting a broad and odd history in which "West Indian and African immigrants or their children" endured neither the Middle Passage (in the case of the former) nor colonialism. Yet directly following this categorization, Gates and Guinier qualify it further by redefining their "four Black grandparents" group as "African American students whose families have been in America for generations"—in short, nonimmigrants, which of course recalls over a century of ugly anti-immigrant rhetoric one usually attaches to white Americans.

The Harvard professors hasten to note that their observations are "not about excluding immigrants"—unfortunately, a surefire way to convince your skeptical listener or reader that that is indeed what you are seeking to do. At the same time, it would be highly problematic to align Gates and Guinier—both noted for careers rooted in combating racism and seeking to destroy racist barriers—with the anti-immigrant lobby, which often revolves around the same logic of racial Others that the former seek to destroy. As Blacks in America, Gates and Guinier, despite their lofty status, still belong to a minority group that many non-Black Americans believe to be lazy and lacking in intelligence. Indeed, an ugly reminder of this is the *New York Times* reporter's own phrasing, which tellingly inserts into the discussion the idea that immigrants are described by sociologists as a "highly motivated, self-selected group." Agency, it seems, is suspect in conservative readings of the Middle Passage epistemology as a progress narrative.

Linear progress narratives are essential, necessary, and useful for reading Blackness as a collective identity in the West: they inspire and make up the bulk of what we know about Blackness throughout Western history, and they quite often retrieve Black individual and collective identities in the West of which historical discourses previously had no knowledge or had forgotten. At the same time (literally and figuratively), they are best empowered and enabled when read through the Epiphenomenal moment of the now, which, not unlike Gilroy's moments of circulation, his roots and routes, produce Blackness as a negotiation through active dialogue. It is not unlike driving a car (as my dear friend calmly reminded me the second time I ever practiced): you cannot direct the car from the position you occupy; you must imagine a straight line ahead (or a diagonal one for a curve, but straight nonetheless), because by the time you make your speed and direction adjustments, you have already left the place from which you were originally navigating. Our present moment is conflated with the future, a "now" that requires a direction forward even as it must take into account encounters in the now (in our driving metaphor, the pedestrian at the corner who looks as if she is going to run into the street just as we pass, or the annoying tailgater who seems to be accelerating at an alarming rate).[54]

In those moments when Mavis, Samaya, and/or their daughters cannot interpellate themselves through a Middle Passage epistemology, Epiphenomenal time can help. Such a framework can, first, remove the latter from their subaltern status as "children" rather than adults in this progress narrative, which reads children as Subjects in the making and therefore unworthy of extensive study until adulthood is achieved. Rather than daughters, or more specifically Black females whose mothers have not yet taught them the entirety of the Middle Passage epistemology, Mavis's and Samaya's respective offspring can claim full subjecthood, full dimensionality in the "now."

Because they read themselves in the "now" moment, Mavis and Samaya need not worry about countering those who disagree about their identities as Africans. Because the Epiphenomenal structure uses the now to connect with a variety of collectives in various and shared spacetimes, there is no origin but instead a series of intersections. To interpellate oneself through a broad variety of collectives based on the physical, emotional, and intellectual stimuli creating the interpellation in that moment is to be agential: one defines oneself. Ideally, especially under the conditions of the postwar epistemology, in which Black agency is predicated through its interpellation in the "now," Mavis's and Samaya's daughters would be directly quoted;

because we do not have that, we can instead interpellate them as we do the following: as postwar Subjects who necessarily intersect with a variety of identities across the globe (e.g., as young global Internet users).

If we read Mavis, Samaya, and their respective offspring in this moment, they can produce the multifarious aspects of their Blackness—as mothers and young women, as urban dwellers, as two generations, as teachers and students, as denizens of a neighborhood, and so forth. By reading themselves in the "now," through encounters with their different peer groups, this foursome can interpellate a postwar Blackness that intersects with a broad variety of Western and perhaps even global experiences.

Although this chapter has outlined the three limits of linear space-time and has explored how, where, and why they inhibit more inclusive interpellations of Blackness, there is another aspect to the Middle Passage epistemology that can also produce interpellative limits that has only been touched on here: the act of return. Because the Middle Passage epistemology is often understood as diasporic—that is, containing not just a thematic but some aspect of a physical or spiritual need to return to "origins"—I examine the act of return through a linear progress narrative in chapter 2.

2

The Problem of Return in the African Diaspora

Its implied diasporic scope complicates the Middle Passage epistemology, thereby suggesting that the question of returning, whether physically or metaphysically, to the collective's point of origin inevitably arises. Rendered in its most basic form, a linear progress narrative struggles to be diasporic, because the notion of return suggests a reversal of the progressive direction from the narrative's origin to the present day/era. Nondiasporic epistemologies accommodate the idea of return more easily—they chart an (uncritical) march forward through progress, but they do look back. Indeed, the problem of return and the paradoxes it entails attend any linear progress narrative: to ground oneself in an origin means that the collective, at any moment, must always be able to define itself through a direct connection to the etiology that first defines and necessarily frames that collective. In other words, nondiasporic epistemologies may indeed notate themselves as always already moving forward, but there are many, many backward glances and fantasies of return. Within epistemologies of Western civilization, ancient Greece and Rome (not to mention the Enlightenment) are often asserted as origins without, it seems, widespread reflection on this progress narrative that is somehow always looking backward.

In contrast, diasporic theorizing of return in the Middle Passage epistemology tends to be far more self-aware: the past is often engaged ambivalently and understood as having ambiguous effects; progress is often deconstructed (especially white Western claims of progress); origins are often shifted and rendered fluid (between Atlantic slavery and the West African departure from the Door of No Return); and agency and Otherness often haunt textual expression, obliquely or directly. In creative discourse, it is Black speculative fiction that most often takes on these questions and problems of return brought about by a Middle Passage epistemology, sometimes to surprising effect.

These ambivalences, I argue, are the result of the limits of Newtonian spacetime (i.e., that space and time always flow forward in linear fashion).

These limits are highlighted in creative discourses that compare and contrast imagined Black identities in the past, present, and future by featuring scenes and characters that underscore the importance of horizontal *as well as* vertical connections when exploring Blackness through time. The argument is not that the discourses I discuss in this chapter use Epiphenomenal spacetime as a "solution" to the limits they highlight. Instead, this chapter demonstrates that, taken together, these texts reveal how using both linear and Epiphenomenal time to analyze the limits they encounter and explore can provide a more cogent, cohesive, and inclusive analysis of Blackness than the former spacetime alone.

When I speak of vertical connections, I have in mind identity categories that emphasize hierarchy (fathers/sons, leaders/followers), whereas horizontal categories *allow for*, if not always constitute, more equal, or peer, relations (friends, cousins). Unfortunately, hierarchies can also be established in those relationships categorized as "peer"; this is why one can find only structures that allow for, rather than establish, a relationship negotiated between equal identities. As this chapter will show, the vertical assumptions that may accompany uncritical interpellations of Blackness through a linear spacetime are hobbled by limitations and logical paradoxes predetermined by the linear narrative. In addition, I will show how the most successful critiques—those that provide broader and more inclusive readings of Blackness—also emphasize the presence of Epiphenomenal time, a time frame in which return is a matter of not simply backtracking along the progress narrative but recognizing that one is manifesting the past in the present moment.

This chapter begins by showing exactly how and where the idea of Newtonian linear spacetime breaks down and finds itself limited through Newton's four laws of motion and gravity. It then reveals five influential discourses on return and the Black relationship to the past in Middle Passage discourses. The first analyses come from the first two decades of Black/African Diaspora studies: Hortense Spillers's 1987 "Mama's Baby, Papa's Maybe," Octavia Butler's 1979 time-traveling novel *Kindred*, and Maryse Condé's 1983 *Heremakhonon*. This chapter concludes by discussing more recent but also acclaimed discourses in Saidiya Hartman's 2007 *Lose Your Mother* and Mat Johnson's 2010 *New York Times* best seller *Pym* to assert that they, too, critique the limits of linear spacetime but also incorporate successful "horizontal" or peer identity relations that in fact dominate their texts and produce diverse, inclusive models for exploring Blackness.

Physicists joke that time travel is in fact possible—we are doing it now—because nanosecond by nanosecond, minute by minute, hour by hour, day by day, year by year, we are traveling into the future. However, it is the temptation to travel back into the past (the directional assumption on which the joke is premised) that appears impossible—or at least it appears impossible in the real world; "on paper" (or whiteboard, computer screen, etc.) the equations for time and space actually allow time to move both "backward" and "forward."

Moving *"forward"* is itself a concept that takes a bit of unraveling: what exactly constitutes "forward" on a planet, a spherical solid occupying a space that is largely symmetrical, that itself does not appear to privilege any single direction of movement within that space? Yet many endogamous and exogamous bigotries across the globe assume "Northern" regions, cities, and nations as more civilized—as regions that have advanced further forward in the progress narrative than their "Southern" counterparts, who are "backward," lazy, bigoted, and so forth. This logic operates in bigoted discourses in the United States, Europe, and Africa (in the latter specifically anti-immigration discourses in North and East African nations such as Morocco and Egypt). Considering organic matter (ourselves, animals, plant life), we of course do observe movement over time: babies, puppies, and bamboo shoots grow "out" and "up" as they grow older. Yet even as such things *do* appear to move "naturally" through time, this movement is not exactly "forward" but is more aptly described as "out" and "up." Furthermore, science does not help to clarify this phenomenological conundrum—the mathematical notation for time actually allows for time to also move in reverse. As far as physics is concerned, the old man *can* become a baby, the dog *can* become a pup, and so forth, even if we never observe such phenomena, without violating any laws of nature.

This paradox is known as the "arrow of time," and lay discourses by physicists (such as Sean Carroll, quoted following) profess that physicists are still baffled by exactly what it is:

> The arrow of time, then, is a brute fact about our universe. Arguably *the* brute fact about our universe; the fact that things happen in one order and not in the reverse order is deeply ingrained in how we live in the world.
>
> Why is it like that?

The answer lies in the concept of "entropy"... Like energy or temperature, entropy tells us something about the particular state of a physical system; specifically, it measures how disorderly the system is. A collection of papers stacked neatly on top of one another has a low entropy; the same collection, scattered haphazardly on a desktop, has a high entropy. The entropy of a cup of coffee along with a separate teaspoon of milk is low, because there is a particular orderly segregation of the molecules into "milk" and "coffee," while the entropy of the two mixed together is comparatively large. All of the irreversible processes that reflect time's arrow—we can turn eggs into omelets but not omelets into eggs, perfume disperses through a room but never collects back into the bottle, ice cubes in water melt but glasses of warm water don't spontaneously form ice cubes—share a common feature: entropy *increases* throughout, as the system progresses from order to disorder. Whenever we disturb the universe, we tend to increase its entropy.[1]

On paper, entropy/time *can* "go backward"—there are no properties that physically prevent this. Yet as Sean Carroll observes, we have never seen the arrow of time reverse itself. When one begins to imagine an object moving back in time—such as an omelet into an egg—our concept of time as linear is immediately betrayed. All those mixed pieces of egg have to uncook and reseparate into their beaten mixture within the bowl before swirling about to reformulate clearly delineated white and yolk in a cracked and then whole shell. This is a not a neat, linear repacking of chaos but a series of distinct movements literally, physically taking place as that omelet recollects itself as a single egg. The same nonlinear obstacles occur if we attempt to reverse the course of history—or even just one day in one individual's life. This is because there is not much linear movement in daily activities—one rises from sleep, from the ground or bed or pallet, and then *circulates* about the living space and so forth throughout the day. Even when engaged in a task we think of as strictly cause and effect (and therefore linear in concept, with cause followed by effect, that effect causing a further effect, etc.), such as building a wall, many of the movements involved in the activity (such as unplanned pauses, interruptions, hesitations, mistakes, or accidents) will appear extraneous and therefore nonlinear.

This is simply to state that the thought of traveling back through time in a linear progress narrative is inherently limited, because physics shows that our movements "forward" are entropic, not linear. Imagining a reverse entropy not only is startling and astonishing (to anyone who has ever seen a film run in reverse to show a transition from high to low entropy, such as a splattered watermelon regathering itself) but also thwarts our attempts to imagine *humans* traveling back through time.[2]

This difficulty in imagining more than one spacetime (one that moves both "backward" and "forward") in a linear progress narrative has not stopped Western discourses on racial difference—or their diasporic counterdiscursive interlocutors—from critiquing and recommending peoples, civilizations, ideas, and behaviors variously as "backward" or "progressive." As *Becoming Black* has argued—and as has been shown in a far broader and more diverse context in Dipesh Chakrabarty's *Provincializing Europe*—anticolonial, antiracist, and postcolonial counterdiscourses that frame racism as antiprogressive (and the fight against it as correspondingly progressive) can be not only compelling but also popular and effective strategies. At the same time, readers from dominant groups appear to respond to this critique through spatiotemporal segregation that deflects blame and responsibility for an antiprogressive past. In the United States, for example, liberal white discourse often enjoys assigning labels such as "white trash" and "rednecks" to Southerners who live "below" the Mason-Dixon Line in rural areas and in "backward" ways—that is, in another space and time altogether.

Perhaps one of the most prominent and compelling arguments that offers a sustained focus on Blackness as "stuck" in a racist West that irrationally and viciously denies it progress is Hortense Spillers's 1987 "Mama's Baby, Papa's Maybe: An American Grammar Book." After all, it was Spillers, in her now-canonical article originally published in *Diacritics*, who famously provided a new theoretical landscape through which one might interpellate an epistemology as a mediated ontology—that is, the Black body as a (performative) site of knowing.[3] Auspiciously published at the same time as Toni Morrison's *Beloved*, the scholarly argument and the blockbusting novel both sought to show how slavery was not a neatly delineated "past" episode with little relevance to contemporary African American subjects. Spillers reworks Lacan's statement that the unconscious is structured like language, arguing here that a "symbolic grammar" inherited from the slave codes still informs the ways in which Black subjects are interpellated by white Americans. In this way, "Mama's Baby" posits a collapse of time and space that not only anticipates Avery Gordon's and Saidiya Hartman's tropes of "haunting" and "social death" (in *Ghostly Matters: Haunting and the Sociological Imagination* and *Scenes of Subjection*, respectively) but remains an unaccredited influence on works of the African Diaspora that explore Black subjectivity and agency through the Middle Passage, including my own.

"Mama's Baby" begins by privileging the body over other forms of retrieval. "Let's face it," Spillers begins, "I am a marked woman,"[4] memorably combining the ontology of (Black) female identity with the signification of U.S. white racist discourse.[5] After reading the title, the signification of being "marked" can take on three immediate valences. The first is the most striking, because it suggests that Spillers is "marked" by some authority or malevolent body for punishment or perhaps even death. The phrase "marked woman" may also suggest a body that is seen as having defied heteropatriarchal norms, or it may remind us that to be marked in an "(American) *Grammar* Book" may suggest a special notation, an important exception to the rule.

Yet Spillers reveals that her marking also involves a specific spatiotemporal status. The first three name-tropes she invokes, "Peaches," "Brown Sugar," and "Sapphire," manifest variously from an interracial epistemology in which both Black and white U.S. discourses on the Black female, racist *and* antiracist, produce her as sexually luscious, sexually promiscuous, and a shrew (respectively). By contrast, her use of "Auntie" and "Grannie" carry specific U.S. connotations because they were patronizing pet names given to enslaved or otherwise exploited Black female caregivers by their white wards, owners, or employers. These marks-cum-epithets become more elaborate over the course of the article, shifting from their antebellum connotations to phrases that suggest that even a professional Black woman must now endure the same racist attitudes from whites— and perhaps from her fellow Blacks as well: "Miss Ebony First" and "Black Woman at the Podium." Here, "Miss Ebony First" denotes achievement (being the first to do something) tainted by the perception that one's minority status simply relegates one to being, as it were, the best of the worst. At first glance, "Black Woman at the Podium" strikes one seemingly as a statement of fact, yet it does the same kind of racist work on the Black female body: simply mentioning the fact of Blackness deprives the speaker of her celebrated individual role and returns her to the collective.[6]

Being "marked," then, is both a grappling hook and an impossible weight. It is the latter in refusing Spillers's contemporary interpellations—her status as a Black female grounds her, in a fully negative sense, within the imagined slave past. Yet the former yanks her at her moment of agency (the act of speaking): she might remain at the podium physically, but the white gaze interpellates her attempt to move outside of the spatiotemporal cage of her (enslaved) antebellum status as the Black female Other. "My country needs me," Spillers ironically notes at the end of the first paragraph, "and if I were not here, I would have to be invented,"[7] exposing the heart of a bigot's logic—in order to feel superior, the bigot must find someone inferior. Inferiority is thus always already located on the social body that lacks the same power or access to power as the dominant body.

"Mama's Baby, Papa's Maybe" fully intends to be devastating. Perhaps the term that is squashed between all the others should command our attention first: "God's 'Holy Fool,'"[8] an old trope of the West suggesting that those who are most divine are most often misunderstood, implying that the harshness of their truths must be cloaked, perhaps by acting as a beggar, or the king's fool, as in *King Lear*. One becomes the "Holy Fool" to escape becoming a Cassandra, the mocked prophet whose warnings of doom are fated to go unheeded. The truth Spillers seeks to show us becomes partially revealed as she explains that these names are examples of how deeply the Black female figure is overdetermined by white U.S. society; indeed, the racist-misogynist discourse is layered on so thick and these "markers are so loaded with mythical prepossession that there is no easy way for the agents buried beneath them to come clean."[9]

Importantly, Spillers defines the buried Black female body as an agent despite facing overwhelming objecthood, thus distinguishing between what the United States would *like* the Black woman to be and what she *is*. Yet in order to activate that agency, à la Hegel, a great deal of effort must be made: "In order for me to speak a truer word concerning myself, I must strip down through layers of attenuated meanings, made an excess in time, over time, assigned by a particular historical order, and there await whatever marvels of my own inventiveness . . . the personal pronouns are offered in the service of a collective function."[10] She may be an agent, but she is first and foremost one who reacts rather than acts.

It is clear that Spillers must unwrap and exhume herself, unraveling the patterns of "historical order" (i.e., the dominant discourse's linear progress narrative), but what is unclear are her own "marvels of inventiveness" that, seemingly, will finally spring her from this prison of time and racist discourse. A potentially problematic synecdoche is also at work here: Spiller's

"I" that explicitly speaks for all Black women complicates matters—how does one unravel the untruths of a racist history by using one person to represent the entirety of that history?

We can connect Spillers's synecdochal use of herself with the Middle Passage epistemology's use of collective memory and the linear progress narrative—in other words, "Mama's Baby" is indeed using this epistemology to define the Black collective and the racist obstacles they have faced in the United States since their ancestors first landed. By understanding herself as representative of a Middle Passage Black female collective, Spillers is using a "vertical" logic of collective representation, a common property of collective linear histories. In one of the aforementioned quotes, Spillers also uses the concept of meaning made by an "excess in time." This concept of knowledge as a quantity that increases through progress is also a property of most collective epistemologies that deploy a linear notion of spacetime marked by progress.

As Spillers ironically notes, such an accumulation buries her further beneath the weight of her anachronistic notation, and an interesting visual figure comes into play—that of a white force moving forward as its acceleration creates an accumulation that eventually reaches far enough back to further bury the Black woman in her imagined stasis. While dominant groups traditionally imagine their progress as positively accumulative (sometimes imagining that this progress also brings the "less fortunate" alongside them), Spillers argues that the antebellum stereotypes that threaten to bury her are part of this accumulation. In other words, that very Western progress is at least partially based in the continuing oppression of U.S. Blacks.

We have already seen that Spillers's article uses a vertical logic of representation (in which her body stands in for all women) and suggests the possibility of agency (in the resistance of unraveling the grammar that stereotypes her). Yet how are origins defined and deployed (if at all) in this article? This is perhaps the most pressing question, because Middle Passage narratives of return logically require an origin, a spacetime to which one can "return."

"Mama's Baby" seeks to answer this question through the lenses of gender and sexuality: part of the resistance, it insists, to white racist caricatures deployed against Black women involves returning to the heteronormative gender and sexuality roles that preceded enslavement. Spillers explains her logic by reading Lacan via the Moynihan Report, which asserts that the matriarchal "Negro" household lacks authentic (male) leadership and therefore lacks the means to interpellate itself through the dominant epistemology of U.S. normalcy, or what the report terms the "American society." Spillers notes that in this reading she also locates herself (in service of the "collective," she writes) within the wholly Western tradition of "patrimony"—that is, of vertical identity relations.[11] As such, she notes that the masculinization of the Black female mother in "American Grammar" (here represented by the Moynihan Report) perversely creates a "stunning reversal of the castration thematic, displacing the Name and the Law of the Father to the territory of the Mother and Daughter, becom[ing] an aspect of the African-American female's misnaming."[12]

More specifically, "Mama's Baby" continues, "'Sapphire' enacts her 'Old Man' in drag, just as her 'Old Man' becomes 'Sapphire' in outrageous caricature."[13] While a Black queer theorist might, in another context, argue that this mutual drag performance is at least subversive if not liberatory, Spillers posits that this is instead a *prescribed* internecine degradation" (Spillers's emphasis). In other words, according to Spillers, this performance is foisted on us by state-sanctioned/created racist-misogynist discourses. This forced mutual performance of Black drag between father and daughter is most damaging because it "adhere[s] to no symbolic integrity," but the origin or basis of that integrity is not named here. Rather than evoking biological purity, Spillers's use of "integrity" seems to denote the repetition of tradition as the "class of symbolic paradigms" spoken, believed in, and perhaps most crucially *performed* by dominant Western subjects. "Integrity" becomes that which fits in with the behemoth of Western tradition—and *both* the African American female and African American male do not. At the end of the day, interpellating Blackness through vertical relations will harm the entire collective, Spillers argues, because Black men are eventually subsumed by a white racist patrimony.

Spillers herself is not unaware of the implications of her call for a return to "traditional" gender roles, especially at a time when, as she notes, queer theorists are celebrating the subversion of these very roles. Yet, she argues, "undressing these conflations of meaning, as they appear under the rule of dominance, would restore, as figurative possibility, not only Power to the Female (for Maternity) but also Power to the Male (for Paternity)."[14] In other words, in creating tradition, the weight of time and repeated performance also creates a "Power," but Spillers does not go on to explain a logical corollary of this equation: what should we do with those subjects who do not/cannot find power in their reproductive abilities (paternal or maternal), figuratively or literally? For the Spillers of "Mama's Baby," the fixed nature of "ethnicity" ("fixed in time and space") is what allowed the slave trade not only to endure but to flourish, and it disfigures the written history of the trade with an indelible mark of horror. Bills of lading, slave codes, and new laws and debates among merchants, newspaper editors, and legislators chillingly show what can happen to human beings when their subjecthood has been crushed into objecthood. However, the Spillers of "Whatcha Gonna Do?: Revisiting 'Mama's Baby, Papa's Maybe: An American Grammar Book'" sees the limitations in this older article and the need for some reinterpretation:

> I think that is what I was trying to do, at the same time that I wanted to point out what is problematic about Black women stopping at the gender question because the refusal of certain gender privileges to Black women historically was part of the problem. At the same time, that you have to sort of see that and get beyond it and get to something else, because you are trying to go through gender to get to something wider. . . . If there is any such thing as a kind of symbiotic blend of melding between our human categories, in this case of the diasporic African, then this is the occasion for it.[15]

Physics of Blackness argues that there is in fact a "symbiotic blend of melding between our human categories" that can be achieved to explore diasporic Blackness, but one first must remove the interpellative limits that are fixed in the properties of linear spacetime. In "Mama's Baby," Spillers seeks to overturn the fatal effects of the American grammar that fix the Black woman in the past with a counternarrative that reimagines a Black African origin in which "traditional" (and of course) heteropatriarchal societies were the norm.

Yet as first-time travelers clutching our guidebooks, we do not know what to expect of the past and therefore can only project onto it whatever questions, ideas, and information occur to *us* in the present moment. Unlike my analogical traveler, who (goodness willing) will reach the desired destination, we can only summon our version of the past, not actually travel back to it. As a result, when we construct a marker of identity, such as the traumatic continuum for U.S. Black women who have Middle Passage ancestry, we begin with our assumptions: that sexuality is a category-friendly set of behaviors in which "heterosexuality" is the default (and therefore barely a category of analysis, more an implicit norm) and other types of sexuality did not exist.[16] Nonheteronormative sexualities existed long before the birth of Europe, of course, and our actual histories are also far less linear and monochromatic; "Middle Passage Blacks" can trace themselves back to Africa, yes, but also to Europe, to Asia, and to South America—not to mention to the first peoples of North America. Even more confusingly, our ancestral lines comprised not just victims but their victimizers as well: we are the result of trauma but also of many other actions—triumphant, cowardly, dastardly, ingenious, predictable, astonishing, and so forth. The trauma continuum does not shine brightly against the background of our past but is a carefully sculpted notion, with many poignant histories chiseled and smoothed away—and thus needing to be found "elsewhere."[17]

The simple linear progress narrative of the Middle Passage epistemology seems so easy at first glance, but its need for return requires both the collapse of time and space and the use of both a scalpel and a shovel to rid itself of the messy overlaps of peoples, places, and times that fully constitute the histories of most U.S. Blacks, not to mention Blacks across the Diaspora. In other words, we cannot travel back through linear time as a collective, because our pasts comprise not one line but innumerable strands. By seeking to retrace our steps directly to "West Africa" and to it alone, we produce a past that perhaps reflects more on our present imaginings.

This means that the site of trauma is often displaced in the act of linear return. The manifold spacetimes of the Middle Passage past specifically remain unimagined in favor of an oversimplified past in which unmediated Blackness moves from Africa to the Americas and then back again. One can see the pull of this illogic: if contemporary Black subjects imagine themselves as racially "mixed," containing threads of other peoples and places, they might well understand themselves as less "pure" than those Black Africans who (supposedly) remain "unchanged." The assumptions that often define the differences between Black Diasporas and Black Africans are linear and in fact deeply racist but also ubiquitous to any contrasting of diasporic peoples with those who occupy the "homeland." Because "home" is also the origin in a linear spacetime epistemology of a collective, it becomes fixed in time, untouched by change, but only theoretically: the continent of Africa, like every other continent, is always changing and never static.

While Spillers seeks resolution by returning to an origin that predates Atlantic slavery, Octavia Butler's speculative novel *Kindred* draws the past and the present into a comparative parallel where each appears to inform the other. The protagonist of *Kindred*, Dana, speaks an ambivalent foreshadowing of her violent travel back to slavery in her introductory descriptions of her courtship and marriage to her white husband, Kevin. Dana describes the employment agency where they meet as a "slave market" and not much later relates Kevin's intense anger over her continuing refusal to type his manuscripts for him—even though, she notes, they are both professional writers. Dana's initial description of figuratively being a slave, paired with her mention of Kevin's forceful suggestion that she should understand her labor as due in the first instance to him, reveals how Dana interpellates her contemporary moment as a strictly Middle Passage interpellation—that is, its thematic origin of enslavement by white Americans.[18] Seeking a job as a writer and being married to a white man both invoke the ancestral experience of slavery.

Neither of these instances would attract especial notice if this were not the story of a Black woman who fantastically and repeatedly is "pulled back" in time and in one instance must pretend to be Kevin's slave in the antebellum South. After her second sudden and physically punishing "yank" through time, Dana quickly becomes convinced that the cause of her travel is Rufus, the young Southern white boy who appears to "call" her when he encounters moments of extreme physical distress. Upon learning that this is indeed her white slave-owning ancestor, she assumes the reason for her time travel must be to ensure Rufus's survival—or, at least, to keep him alive long enough to father what will become her family tree.[19] In other words, Dana assumes a vertical relation of identities between herself and Rufus despite the fact that she and Rufus are produced through very different spacetimes; as she explains to her skeptical husband after returning from her second spacetime trip, she has been "called back" into enslaved service. Here the text lays bare for us a perverse logic of the linear progress narrative in a Middle Passage epistemology when defining contemporary Blackness through a fixed past.

Dana's logic (and, likely, the readers' own, as the trope is a common one in science and speculative fiction) is purely Newtonian: that history is a series of cause and effect events, and some force has recalled her to the past to fix a "mistake"—some hiccup that now derails, has derailed, and/or will derail the straight track that connects the past to the present.

While this premise is entertaining in a story such as *Back to the Future*, it carries more serious significations in the logic of a Middle Passage epistemology. Because the rape of Black women was so prevalent during slavery, reading oneself as the product of the past means one is also the product of rape—a violence one condemns and yet . . . would anyone sacrifice his or her existence in order to undo these rapes that exist in the antebellum family tree?

This leaves a question for Dana—to what degree is she a coconspirator in rape and other forms of brutalization?—a question that is easily extended to almost all individuals on this planet by moving far back enough on a family tree. The history of world civilization is also the history of violent overthrow, conquering armies, and attendant rape; one would be hard put to find anyone, even the descendants of royalty (or perhaps, considering all the forced marriages, them *least* of all), whose entire family tree is free of involuntary procreation.

Yet this question of culpability achieves shape only through the moment into which Dana is yanked back—one can just as easily locate the "beginning" of her family tree in West Africa in earlier decades, centuries, and so forth. In other words, the whole concept of culpability exists only through the Middle Passage epistemology because of the origin it chooses as well as the cause-and-effect logic that drives its motion forward. Dana's family tree can be seen as "starting" anywhere because it is like all other family trees: intensely pruned so as to define a more recent generation through a particular set of interpellations. The question of Dana's agency and culpability in her enslaved past is created by Dana because she chooses to honor a perverse heteropatriarchal logic that locates and defines a white slave owner as her forefather. In other words, why is *this* great-great-grandfather, out of the eight that she possibly can claim, the one whose survival compels her collusion? It is because Dana's time travel is informed by the text's spatiotemporal epistemology (or, as Spillers would term it, the perverse logic of our "American Grammar") that it can manifest in such a circumstance.

In "Speculative Fictions of Slavery," Madhu Dubey argues that a conundrum such as Dana's occurs because "speculative fictions of slavery attempt to know the past as something other or more than history."[20] Describing history as a "register," Dubey suggests that, at least in the U.S. imagination, "history" is both enduring and evanescent—always present but ghostly and ultimately inaccessible:

Common to all these works is the phenomenon of an actual rather than figurative return to slavery, and the fact that return always results in an involuntary but powerful identification—not connection, but identification—of the present-day African American subject with a slave. . . . If historical knowledge involves a distanciated relation to a past that is no longer available as direct experience, the devices of return to slavery in novels such as *Kindred* . . . make possible an unmediated relation to the past as something that has not quite passed into the realm of history. To really know slavery in [these] novels . . . is to know it subjectively, to know it as something other than the characteristically remote object of historical knowledge.[21]

Dubey lays out the complexity of Black speculative fiction's engagement with the past. It is impossible to reconcile with the linear progress narrative's notion of a fixed origin that is static, locked in time, and far away, and it does so by underscoring the slave past less as an epistemology (a form of knowledge) and more as an ontology—a form of being, the "visceral experience of slavery." Reading through Dubey, we can see how the theme of return in this genre's tradition is used to highlight another paradox of return through linear spacetime: that if the collective must always be defined through its origin, then the origin cannot be fixed—or cannot *only* be fixed. As I argued in chapter 1, origins in a linear progress narrative must dominate the narrative, and each event that follows its predecessor must be linked clearly to the origin. In other words, origins must operate in at least two spacetimes—the fixed past and the fluid present.

Kindred, I would argue, does indeed come to this conclusion through its final metaphor when Dana returns from her final journey, having killed her increasingly oppressive and monstrous ancestor, but with one of her arms apparently fused into the wall of her home. Dana is alive and well, but her arm is elsewhere. If we read this moment through Dubey's "Speculative Fictions," this deeply injurious encounter with the past has taken part of her body and left it as fixed, fused, and immobile as an artifact of a linear past.

Whether one argues for the validity of the Middle Passage epistemology's progress narrative or asserts an Afro-pessimist interpretation (that progress has been denied and the Black collective still inhabits an oppressive stasis), it is the problem of origins that leads to this impasse. Because the Middle Passage epistemology begins with white actions and Black reactions (not as a historical but as an ideological "fact"), it produces a Black collective identity that is not only predicated on white agency; it is a specifically malevolent white agency that brings the fact of Blackness into being. As a result, even within a progress narrative the question of a nonreactive agency arises: at what point can African Americans define themselves outside of white anti-Black racism, or, as Dubey puts it, "possible futures unbound by the racial scripts of the past"?[22]

In "Mama's Baby," Spillers seeks agency against a tsunami of overdetermined signifiers that interpellate the Black female as Other by seeking alignment with a heteropatriarchal Black African past. As noted earlier, Butler's *Kindred* initiates Dana's journey into the past when she herself interpellates her present moment through signifiers of Middle Passage slavery—but both Dana and the narrative argue that the *actual* time travel is caused by Rufus.

Throughout *Kindred*, the question of agency is complicated by the fact that some of its most profound plot twists are based in knee-jerk, instinctive, or even wholly unconscious reactions from all characters, but most meaningfully from Dana and Rufus—the time traveler and her ignition key, as it were. While Dana and Rufus often state their intentions, those intentions are changed and waylaid by both themselves and others. Rufus, for example, both exploits and is constrained by the strict and perverse mores of Southern slavery, which limit his options and choices; Dana decides that she must variously enable and disable her racist slave-owning ancestor in order to ensure her "future" birth. While *Kindred*'s construction of return is traditionally linear, its understanding of the individual as intersubjective and operating on a number of conscious and unconscious levels of behavior logically defies that epistemology's understanding of slavery as a spacetime of fixed vertical relations. Instead, because the narrative produces slaves who make choices and whose resistance and negotiation is sometimes successful and produces white owners who are fallible and incapable of being omnipresent and thus omniscient, the outcome of all conflicts between slave and slave owner is *not* foregone. Instead, we see how even in a strictly vertical or hierarchical system horizontal relations can have their sway.

To use a more familiar model of power relations—Hegel's master–slave dialectic—*Kindred* provides moments when the slave does not recognize the master as a master but as a human being who is vulnerable in specific contexts or circumstances. In doing so, *Kindred* does not deny or downplay the whippings, beatings, murders, and everyday ubiquitous tortures that attend enslavement—that is, the vertical relations—but it also argues for the existence of the horizontal. When agency is "released" from wholly vertical identity relations, moral fixity may also evanesce—in other words, the Black subject can and will act selfishly as well as selflessly.

Seen through this lens, Maryse Condé's 1982 novel *Heremakhonon* can be understood as combining Spillers's later move in seeking horizontal relations for the Black (female Subject) with Octavia Butler's exploration of the Black female subject at the intersection of horizontal *and* vertical relations. Condé's novel is often read by leading literary theorists such as François Lionnet and, more specifically, Susan Z. Andrade in "'The Nigger of the Narcissist'" as a pessimistic reminder of intertextuality, because it shows how the Black Subject suffers multiple alienations due to her subaltern identities as Black, female, and Black female: "*Heremakhonon* confronts its male predecessor on racial/sexual issues and the position of black women in the Antillean context while upholding aspects of his ideology which do not address gender, thereby exhibiting its feminist stance and larger political interests. . . . Veronica's ideological perspective makes her, in Lionnet's words, 'a victim of her own alienations and mimetic allusions.' Her location in the novel, however, generates a rich and complex field of response to the problems of the construction of history, sexuality and political identity that subtend Caribbean discourse."[23] As Andrade makes clear, *Heremakhonon* locates its protagonist Veronica within "larger political interests" that may intersect with, but are not limited to, her race and gender.

In Condé's novel, Veronica Mercier is a resident of Paris funded by her Guadeloupian family's bourgeois fortunes who "returns" to Africa for reasons that are largely unclear to her. A painful and seemingly pessimistic narrative of selfishness, violence, and betrayal ensues, as her desire to retain autonomy while making friends and lovers within the heteropatriarchal collective in the fictional West African dictatorship ends in rape and psychological violence. Yet the keys to Veronica's survival and, as Andrade asserts, the text's role as "more than a bleak commentary on post-colonial nomadism" are indicated from the first paragraph, which opens with Veronica en route from Paris to an unnamed West African nation:

Honestly! You'd think I'm going because it is the in thing to do. Africa is very much the thing to do lately. Europeans and a good many others are writing volumes on the subject. Arts and crafts centers are opening all over the Left Bank. Blondes are dying their lips with henna and running to the open market on the rue Mouffetard for their peppers and okra.

Well, I'm not! Seven hours on a DC-10. On my left, an African desperately trying to make small talk. Behind me, a French couple as average as they come. Why am I doing this? At the moment, everything is a mess, and this whole idea seems absurd. I can see them now. My mother, sighing as usual. My father pinching his thin lips.[24]

The first collective through which Veronica interpellates herself is that of Parisians, a category that actually unites rather than divides her identities (as Lionnet suggests). This bourgeois Parisian attempts to separate herself from her fellow passengers by mocking the white French cultural tourists as purely superficial and the Black African man beside her as annoying and thus an unworthy companion. Her knowledge of how, why, and where white Parisians indulge in their Afrophilia links her, in many ways, to this collective, but her uninformed and unexplained assumption that the African passenger is sexually interested in her foreshadows Veronica's alienation from West African identities. The imagined disapproval of her parents interpellates her as a disobedient Guadeloupian daughter, and her ability to simply visit West Africa without worrying about time and funding places her high in the air—in this case quite literally in the airplane. By the end of the quote, the text has effectively reinterpellated its opening lines— Veronica's exasperation is more like enervation, we now know, informed by her interpellations of herself as an authentic Black Parisian native / savvy Black European / disobedient daughter of wealthy Guadeloupians / Black cultural tourist / Black Diasporan at a moment of existential crisis.

Veronica is in many ways an antiheroine, and in teaching this novel to my classes, graduate students often complain about her "negative" and "chatty" narrative voice. Her various identities and the differences and alliances they create in various moments throughout the narrative cast Veronica as amoral, unethical, and, as Andrade notes, deeply selfish. Yet novels, of course, are not always meant to serve as moral guides but are sometimes meant to explore the multidimensionality of the individual within his, her, or their collectives and the complexity of life. If Condé's Veronica does not tell us how to navigate cruelty and violence in the African Diaspora, her reflections also do not shy away from it. Inasmuch as this is a first-person narrative, Veronica also shows us her own questionable behavior alongside the corruption and oppression she both witnesses and hears—as a woman who at times must suffer misogynist treatment (often at the hands of her sadistic lover, rapist, and local tyro, Ibrahim Sory) but also as a moneyed woman who is sometimes extended greater courtesies and access as a wealthy outsider, as a Black woman and a cultural tourist, and as a Black Diasporan who is confused and torn by opinions, behaviors, and activities for which her hazy understanding of "Africa" had left her wholly unprepared. Outside of Paris she encounters no unified and noble collective but the complex web of a postcolonial West Africa engaging with a broad variety of influences and spacetimes: colonial, postcolonial, diasporic, precolonial, and "traditional."

In her final thoughts of the narrative, Veronica concludes, "I'm leaving because it would be too easy to stay" and, if she had done so, "I'd continue to shuttle back and forth between Heremakhonon [Sory's compound] and the town.[25] Until one of us got tired, you the first, of course." Inexplicably, she then claims to have "helped kill him" even though Sory is alive and well, as she admits when hypothesizing that *if* the town *had* revolted, she would have joined them.

Her last thought of Sory, whether actually spoken by him or not, remains an odd comment: "It's spring now in Paris." This moves her reflections from a hypothetical scenario of departure to an anticipated arrival:

> Spring? The streetcleaner on the Rue de L'Université will have
> taken off his thick, blue turtleneck sweater that shows under his
> overalls. Will he have noticed my absence? How will he welcome
> me back? Yet another flight! One day I'll have to break the silence.
> I'll have to explain. What? This mistake, this tragic mistake I
> couldn't help making, being what I am. My ancestors led me on.
> What more can I say? I looked for myself in the wrong place. In
> the arms of an assassin. Come now, don't use big words. Always
> dramatizing.
> Spring? Yes, it's spring in Paris.[26]

Heremakhonon defies the Middle Passage epistemology's interpellation of return by ending the novel with the "real" return for Veronica, the return to Paris, thus shattering a neat return to African origin. The text separates the spacetime of return from that of origin, making clear that Veronica was born and raised in Guadeloupe and appears to make sexual choices in defiance of her upper-class family's strict mores (bourgeois women should be chaste and certainly not choose lovers from a class "beneath" their own). In Guadeloupe, Veronica notoriously took the family's gardener as her lover, a combination of horizontal and vertical relations (pun intended). In West Africa,[27] however, she learns that her relationship with Sory was purely vertical—his casually brutal and unapologetic rape underscores his interpellation of her. By imagining a likely and justifiable overthrow of Sory, Veronica interpellates her agency through a hypothetical past, allowing her to imagine Sory as both defeated and an interlocutor straight out of a classic *film noir* (no pun intended).

Paris (imagined as first spoken by Sory in this conclusion) becomes a space in which Veronica interpellates herself alternately vertically and horizontally. She fondly recalls the street cleaner, suggesting an intimate peer relationship, but the fact that she doesn't know his name, and only encounters him as he cleans the streets for citizens such as her, returns us to vertical relations. With her observation that mistaking her journey to West Africa as a return was a "tragic mistake," the final lines of Condé's first novel connect almost seamlessly to the interpellations of an ambivalently agential Black female subject that this distinguished writer later manifests in such as classics as *I, Tituba*, *Colonie du Nouveau monde* (as yet untranslated), and *Segu*.

Veronica blames verticality—that is, those "ancestors" who preceded her and lured her "back" to West Africa. Yet she also blames herself—for looking in the wrong place, daringly implying a parallel between West Africa and the "arms of an assassin." At the same time, she recognizes (and is likely often empowered by) the spacetimes of "return" and her relationship with Sory as those of her own choosing. Veronica is neither heroine nor villain; in deliberately departing from the fixed vertical interpellation of Middle Passage linear spacetime, Condé provides us with an interpretation of the Black female subject in the Diaspora that is instructive: some Black women enjoy privileges located in vertical identity relations, and when one fails to acknowledge one's own privilege and its contextual basis, moving into alternate spacetimes can lead to "tragic mistakes"—here, disillusionment and violence.

It is not coincidental that almost all the authors under discussion here intervene through Black feminist concerns, possessing bodies that must struggle to be represented within the linear logic of the progress narrative. Most overarching mainstream histories that understand and title themselves as representative of the Black collective use a vertical synecdoche: leaders represent the collective as a whole, and the effects of their words and actions are explored by those "below" and "above" them on the hierarchy. Dominant discourses in Black studies, as in most other academic disciplines across the globe, assume a heteropatriarchal model for this verticality; its leaders and workers are represented as overwhelmingly male.

As one might imagine, then, it is often easier for heteronormative male narratives to embrace a linear return to African origins and an African past—and these narratives do indeed typically end on clear, happy notes of inclusion and recovery.[28] Indeed, by seeking brotherhood in heteropatriarchy, Black male travelers can find a socioeconomically empowered horizontal interpellation that Black women cannot, as "sisters" are meant to tend primarily to their families rather than sisterhood. This is because the explicit peer relationship premised by the term *brotherhood* is also horizontally interpellated in heteropatriarchy: men mentor, aid, and enable one another (or defeat one another) as leaders in the community. Its complement sisterhood is pulled vertically in heteropatriarchy: sisters are first read as mothers, daughters, or wives before they are (if at all) accorded the figurative and literal spacetime to perform peer relationships.

For the majority of male protagonists engaged in diasporic return, a melding occurs, and while in most cases the history of the Middle Passage is not erased, it is largely attenuated because the diasporic goal has been achieved: a spiritual (and often political, possibly cultural) "return" to one's African roots. The journey for those Subjects who do not meet these criteria is considerably less clear and considerably more ambiguous.

One of the central points of "Mama's Baby," of course, and its lasting value to Black feminist and womanist theory, is the intervention it makes by theorizing return and the relationship to the past for the Black (female) Subject, locating her, in short, within this epistemology as a central subject and object (of racist stasis). As Spillers notes, her earlier enjoinder that a heteronormative practice was needed to overcome this racist "queering" is of limited strategic use. Within the concerns of spacetime, this limitation is due to its final embrace of verticality—that is, seeking to reassert the normative social roles within a vibrant and healthy Black heteropatriarchal community. After having made the Black female visible, "Mama's

Baby" then seeks to align her with dominant representations and thus begins to cloak her—albeit with reservations.

However ambiguous its conclusion, "Mama's Baby" provides us with a theory of the Black female subject that continually (re)informs us in our ongoing moments of theorizing Black female subject status, Black subject status and subject status writ large. Replying to Spillers's hopes for the contemporary generation, which she encourages to "broaden" the implications of her work, Saidiya Hartman's *Lose Your Mother* does just that.

Lose Your Mother, a highly celebrated and layered first-person account of a Middle Passage "return," emphasizes negotiations that must be made between existing in the present and imagining the past and the importance of interpellating oneself through peer, rather than hierarchical, groups. Rather than structure her journey as a linear retracing back to her origins, *Lose Your Mother* offers moments marked by several types of interpellations, especially with peers. In doing so, Hartman's account opens up possibilities, particularly involving the dynamic space of imagining the past in the present by trying to understand what the past was when it was the present. That is, her narrative is always imagining an intersection between two spacetimes, neither of which is fixed: the past-in-the-present and the present-in-the-past. More simply put, Hartman is applying Epiphenomenal time to her consideration of return through Middle Passage epistemology.

One would not necessarily assume this from the opening lines of *Lose Your Mother*, which at first glance may strike the reader as limiting: "As I disembarked from the bus in Elmina, I heard it. It was sharp and clear, as it rang in the air, and clattered in my ear making me recoil. *Obruni*. A stranger. A foreigner from across the sea."[29] It is noticeable that the first verb used to introduce this journey of return is "disembarked" rather than "arrived," "entered," or "returned," which interpellates movement from the point the traveler has just left. This shifts the focus of the reader to the traveler so we are reminded that the narration is not "objective" but inevitably subjective. Of course, it is more memorable that, rather than depicting the experience as offering at least the promise and potential of the journey's becoming a homecoming, Hartman reacts, as if to a gun's firing, to her negative hailing as an outsider. At the same time, she is not wholly an outsider, as she is partially connected—after all, she is familiar with the term "*obruni*" (which ranges from a pejorative to a nagging tease). Complicating the moment further, the source of the cruel taunting is then revealed—it is children, and, she elaborates, "They summoned me, '*obruni, obruni*,' as if it were a form of *akwaaba* (welcome) reserved just for me."

Through these contrastive juxtapositions, the first words of return in this narrative complicate the very notion of the concept itself. Hartman is a welcomed foreigner, at once intimate and estranged. She is able to interpellate herself through the children's greeting by understanding their signifier of herself as a foreigner and its ability to achieve nuance in the moment of performance. This type of moment is consistent throughout the text, in which moments of insight and intimacy are mediated through the status of an outsider.

While this critique may sound harsh and almost pessimistic, this is so only if one interpellates the status of outsider through a wholly vertical understanding of identity relations. In a hierarchical structure, the outsider is farther away from the center, the most important part of a vertical Diaspora. Given this automatic remove to a subaltern position, one can understand those travel narratives that interpellate outsiders into the center of a largely heteropatriarchal order, thus signaling the end of their estrangement and their successful acceptance and merger into the collective.

If, however, one understands an outsider through the horizontal or peer groups he, she, or they encounter—as, I will argue, Hartman does—"outsiders" can interpellate themselves as agents rather than subalterns. In this opening scene, Hartman develops a peer relationship by choosing an encounter in which it is children who welcome her as *obruni*. Here she occupies the dynamic space of a welcomed stranger, and because her interlocutors neither hold power over her nor are submissive (they are fluent in this landscape and its languages while she is not), the engagement is an *exchange* rather than a forced interpellation.[30] Here, the age difference allows Hartman and the children to achieve a moment of peer relation.

Throughout this yearlong journey—admittedly longer than most diasporic sojourns "back" to West Africa—Hartman's narrative continually produces similarly complex moments in which her status as *obruni* produces multidimensional, rather than wholly subaltern, interpellations. Rather than producing a bildungsroman, perhaps the most famous of creative linear progress narratives, *Lose Your Mother* produces a variety of moments in which distinctive insights and dimensions are achieved. A great summing up, a grand conclusion, is simply not possible, because different moments manifest different meanings; these spacetimes can be intersected with one another, but they cannot be subsumed by one spacetime alone.

Hartman imagines what the children must see, oddly recalling *Notebook of a Return to My Native Land*'s famous moment of ventriloquizing the whispers and giggles of two white French women. Yet here it is Ghanaian children whom Hartman identifies for her "intimately estranging" interlocutors; rather than producing herself in the imagination of the Black Other, as Césaire's narrator does, something quite individually essential yet also *unfamiliar* is achieved:

> I imagined myself in their eyes: an alien tightly wrapped in the skin of a blue rain slicker, the big head bursting from its navy pod. . . . My customs belonged to another country: my too-fast gait best suited to navigating the streets of Manhattan, my unfashionable German walking shoes, my unruly tufts twisted into two French braids, fuzzy and unfurling in the humid air. Old and new worlds stamped on my face, a blend of peoples and nations and masters and slaves long forgotten. In the jumble of my features, no certain line of origin could be traced. Clearly, I was not Fanti, or Ashanti, or Ewe, or Ga.[31]

Hartman's sentences move from the more open signifiers of a horizontal interpellation to one that is painfully vertical. The passage begins with our "outsider" in racial, sexual, and gender ambiguity (and also altogether outside of these categories), a horizontally "big-headed" and "blue alien" (horizontal because it does not denote any sort of immediate hierarchal status), then shifts here into essentialist identities that are static and unchanged through time—"original" in the strictest linear sense. As the Elmina coastal air actively untangles one of Black women's literatures most famous metaphors for both roots and change, Hartman's body is suddenly "stamped" (a violently vertical movement) with a mixture of spacetimes ("old and new worlds") that are specifically unrooted from a linear progress narrative because they are forgotten, and because "no certain line of origin could be traced." Here we see the fears of the outsider and the introduction of hierarchical difference in combination with the summoning of the verticality of origins and fixed biology.

Importantly, Black African authenticity is also a performance, a nuanced theater that draws on both knowledge and assumptions of its diasporic audience—the desire of so many travelers to be declared honorary natives. For Blacks born far away from their West African ancestors, of course, this desire is no simplistic "going native" but is often consistently informed by the traumatic history of the Atlantic slave trade. Yet an unintended insult lurks here. Within the logic of linear spacetime, Africa is a land of fixed origin problematically imagined as unchanging—an observation that could not be less true, especially given humanity's African roots, not to mention its centuries of economic trade and military conflict with European and Middle Eastern civilizations (in addition to its own). By moving to a set of biological metaphors in which historical experience and belonging are stamped on the body, and then interpellating this difference through linear spacetime, this passage shows the costs of reading return through linear spacetime alone. While the Middle Passage epistemology allows for an interpellation imagined through a heteropatriarchal Black African collective identity, this option does not do much for Hartman.

Because *Lose Your Mother* moves from moment to moment, this interpellation is not fixed in the book but instead becomes one type of interpellation that (inevitably) accompanies the traveler. Informatively, at the end of the text, Hartman reflects on who she is now after her journey, and this conclusion does not manifest itself through a linear progressive narrative. She writes that after a year in Ghana "I could still call myself African American." At the end of this paragraph, a move is made toward the horizontal and away from a wholly vertical set of identity relations for herself: "The legacy that I chose to claim . . . didn't require me to wait on bended knee for a great emancipator. It wasn't the dream of a White House, even if it was in Harlem, but of a free territory. It was a dream of autonomy rather than nationhood. It was the dream of an elsewhere, with all of its promises and dangers, where the stateless might, as last, thrive."[32] Rather than contemplating integration into a hierarchical structure in which space and time are not her own (to "wait on bended knee"), the quote rejects "Great Man" history as well as nationalism and even most imaginings of the Black Diaspora as a transnational heteropatriarchy instilled with "traditional African" values. Hartman interpellates her currently desired future through selfhood. She notes that there is no promised utopia but the joy of an agency where verticality does not define one's primary relations—"where the stateless might . . . thrive." The final word of the quote is instructive—as opposed to terms such as *succeed* or *overcome* or *prevail* and so forth, "thrive" is not immediately vertical (which is to say it can, in another context, be deployed as vertical). Not unlike Condé's stated intention for *Heremakhonon*, which is to denote the danger of the Black female subject attempting to embrace a Black African nation state (or states) as home (the word *Heremakhonon* is meant to symbolize "the illusions fostered by the newly independent African nations"), Hartman decisively steps outside of the traditional type of return imagined in most diasporic collective identities that deploy a linear progress narrative. Whether figuratively or literally, she eschews seeking agency through the nation-state and begins her explanation by underscoring the perils of submitting to a vertical set of identity relations in both time ("to wait" as suspended time) and space (to be positioned on "bended knee" and thus below the "great emancipator").

The cover of Hartman's book, combined with its title, suggests that the act of return—specifically through the slave holds at Elmina Castle—is accompanied by immediate loss, specifically of one's mother. The subtitle, *A Journey along the Atlantic Coast*, rather than suggesting travel back through time, places the reader in a contemporary moment in which the past cannot be regained. The act of return here underscores the fact of loss, not recuperation. According to Hartman, to return is to signify that one has lost something; strikingly, however, because the loss is in the moment of return, it is one that did not necessarily exist in other moments. The title, after all, is in the imperative (and is also perhaps a warning): *Lose.* Hartman notes that she "*could still* call herself African American" (my emphasis), denoting loss in a counterintuitive manner. To return entails gain and insight, but it also produces or underscores a loss because one may encounter a moment, as Hartman appears to do, in which the (re)claiming of African American identity is a boon, not a burden. It is a desire rather than an unwanted burden, and perhaps this is the one significant difference between earlier and later moments in the text. As the text moves through moments of encounters with other Black travelers and a range of Black Africans, Hartman worries less about seeming alien and recognizes that she possesses a number of identities in any given moment.

Lose Your Mother's emphasis on Epiphenomenal time as its narrative structure—to interpellate and locate oneself in the "now"—radically changes how we might imagine the moment of return within the Middle Passage epistemology. Hartman's narrative is creative nonfiction, and under a wholly creative lens one can see how a consistent framing of the past through the "now" also creates a wholly unanticipated set of experiences of return. Mat Johnson's 2010 intertextual satire *Pym* frames its entire narrative on this premise, offering the most detailed exploration of the use value of using Epiphenomenal time as a critique that identifies the pitfalls of relying on a wholly vertical interpellation of a Middle Passage epistemology in determining a Black identity—in this case for the Black male subject, yet one who is nuanced enough to continually encounter both horizontal and vertical identity relations.

Pym is confusing to read because it is heavily intertextual, a contemporary African American riff on an actual unfinished novella by Edgar Allan Poe. Poe's novella, *The Narrative of Arthur Gordon Pym of Nantucket*, is a first-person narrative of a fantastic adventure that its protagonist, Arthur Gordon Pym, swears to be absolutely true. Johnson's *Pym* twists its plot around Poe's strange book even further: in addition to making its protagonist Chris Jaynes a Poe enthusiast, Jaynes informs us that Poe's novel is no fiction but *real*—and he is the direct descendant of one of its "characters." Now feeling even closer to *The Narrative*, Jaynes organizes a crew and sets sail to discover the fantastic lands that Arthur Gordon Pym supposedly discovered: the "Black" island of Tslalia and the "white" frozen cliffs of Tekelia.

In *Pym*, it is not just that the protagonist, Chris Jaynes, "returns" to bizarre alien lands where he and his crew end up committing crimes against humanity (or, more accurately, against fellow sentient beings); it is that this absurd past is entwined in and informed by Poe's reflection of this *white* American absurdist past that is equally ambivalent in its fits and starts of racism and antiracist amnesia. In this way, *Pym* manifests a model of Epiphenomenal time more completely than *Lose Your Mother* by pursuing some of the themes offered in "Mama's Baby" and *Kindred* through the role of the *white Other* in the Middle Passage epistemology's imagining of return and our relationship to the past.

Poe's *Narrative of Arthur Gordon Pym of Nantucket* is a fascinating study in its own right, but under Johnson's intertextual engagement, its simultaneously deeply subversive and also traditionally racist nineteenth-century adventure tale can only encourage endless reinterpretation of its meanings. This intertextuality is at once so seamless and yet so dynamic that Johnson's *Pym* is really two tales. One is Poe's unfinished novel, which is an exemplar, as Toni Morrison's *Playing in the Dark: Whiteness and the Literary Imagination* has noted, that relies heavily on its construction of a Black Other to produce white heroics in the face of fantastically primitive savagery. The second narrative in *Pym* is a far less examined thematic, which makes the contemporary satire all the more valuable: how whiteness often operates centrally in the Middle Passage imagination by defining Blackness through assertions of fixed difference.

Pym does not go back into the historical racial past as the Middle Passage or any other linear spacetime epistemology would recognize it. Instead, it imitates Poe's *Narrative* as a fantastic voyage heavy with racist metaphor and distinctly bounded geographies. While seemingly improvising on a broad spread of racial misperceptions and anxieties, the satire's running joke is that twenty-first-century Black fantasies about the white Other can be just as fervently distorted as Poe's fevered fiction about undiscovered territories of the earth effectively locked in the past, where people are wholly products of their environments. *Pym* satirizes the attempt to return to the past through the linear Middle Passage epistemology taken to the extreme to underscore the point that returns to the past are always already voyages made in the present.

Poe's *Arthur Gordon Pym of Nantucket* is contemporary with the racist adventure fiction of the time: the savage Africa of Germany's Carl Peters's series of novels (and later Nazi films)[33] and Rider Haggard's various forays into the forbidding and cruel terrains of hidden islands and valleys running amok with violent Amazonian matriarchies and savage cannibals.[34] To quote Toni Morrison's *Playing in the Dark*, this genre's "dehistoricizing allegory . . . produces foreclosure rather than disclosure. If difference is made so vast that the civilizing process becomes indefinite—taking place across an unspecified infinite amount of time—history, as a process of becoming, is excluded from the literary encounter." Morrison elucidates, "Poe deploys allegorical mechanisms in *Pym* not to confront and explore, as Melville does, but to evade and simultaneously register the cul-de-sac, the estrangement, the non-sequitur that is entailed in racial difference."[35]

Pym does in fact use Poe's structure of a fantastic voyage to confront and explore Blackness and whiteness, at least on the surface reversing Poe's white/black symbolism but then complicating that divide in provocative ways. While Poe's protagonist, Arthur Pym, could be considered a typical white male hero—young, brave, and adventurous—Mat Johnson effectively confronts the reader with his version of an antihero who fails to embody a stereotypical Middle Passage Blackness. Professor Chris Jaynes's features and skin color would allow him to "pass"; he is fighting to *not* teach and research his Middle Passage literature and is punished by white administrators for doing so. Jaynes explains that he loves the work of Edgar Allan Poe even though he is exquisitely aware of the author's racism (and in fact provides a racial critique of the *Narrative* that elegantly coheres with Morrison's thesis).

The desire for return through a Middle Passage linear spacetime haunts Jaynes, perhaps especially when he attempts to deride the importance of this trope in his narrative. In volume three of *Pym*, in which Jaynes and his crew find themselves enslaved by the giant and ghostly Tekelians from Poe's *Nantucket*, he argues that the act of return in effect has been "ruined" by repeated interpellations: "I am bored with the topic of Atlantic slavery. I have come to be bored because so many boring people have talked about it. So many artists and writers and thinkers, mediocre and genius, have used it because it's a big, easy target. They appropriate it, adding no new insight or profound understanding, instead degrading it with their nothingness. They take the stink of the slave hold and make it a pungent cliché, take the blood-soaked chains of bondage and pervert them into Afrocentric bling."[36] Rather than embrace the Middle Passage epistemology as the site and inspiration for being African American, Jaynes complains that he cannot participate because other members of the Black collective have, in his contemporary moment, degraded it. Jaynes, however, is an unreliable narrator, and his narrative is prone to explicit rejections of certain attitudes or traditions that are then followed by an implicit and uncritical embrace of those same behaviors and performances. As his self-serving account of his firing has already revealed, Jaynes avoids reality when it promises to threaten his fantasy life lived partially through Poe's works. His own failure to achieve academic success renders him sensitive to and negative about the achievements of others, whom he assumes must be "sell-outs." He expresses a deep, devoted love to his ex-wife (who left him because of his already lackluster career), yet his descriptions of her seem suspiciously (and hilariously) more attuned to an exoticist African fantasy than a soul mate ("the woman I used to call the Ashanti Doll, her skin a wealth of rich melanin above the white vinyl of her snowsuit").[37]

Most overwhelmingly, *Pym* is the story of return through encounters with Blackness and whiteness in their most extreme forms. Jaynes discovers that Poe's tale is in fact true—and the odd little novella is in fact an actual account by a contemporary of Poe, one Arthur Gordon Pym. Even better, he stumbles across the diary of none other than Dirk Peters, Arthur Pym's inexplicable villain-turned-loyal sidekick—and, as it turns out, a distant relation of Jaynes himself.

Perhaps the key to understanding Jaynes's desire for a specifically linear return lies in the character of Peters (in Poe's *Nantucket*) and its intertextual dialogue with Jaynes's own racial undecidability. In Poe, Peters is first described as a fearsome-looking creature of ambiguous white European and (American) Indian descent. Unlike his other compelling interpretations of Poe, Jaynes unconvincingly asserts that giving this character a mixed-race status is Poe's racist code for Black—but scholars of nineteenth-century white American literature know that racist white literature also has a tradition of explicitly mixed-race individuals. Instead, we might read Jaynes's insistence that Peters must be Black as quite personal in nature. Jaynes discovers Peters is Black through a fellow member of the family tree, one who insists she is mostly American Indian—which would cohere with Arthur Gordon Pym's description of Peters in Poe. Yet as this chapter later details, Jaynes mocks this claim, firmly asserting that Miss Mahalia Mathis is nothing if not Black.

Given that many African Americans are aware of American Indian ancestry, we know that Jaynes can still be Black *and* American Indian, so his insistence on categorizing Miss Mathis away from a mixed ancestry is confusing. However, a sad possibility comes to light: Jaynes is light-skinned, he can "pass for white," and in asserting his Black identity, he demonstrates his refusal to "pass," his loyalty to Middle Passage Blackness.[38] To also claim American Indian ancestry would confuse that assertion—as if he wants to claim he is many things, Blackness among them rather than his primary and most important identity. Because he can "pass," it is implied that part of his ancestry is clearly white, perhaps the majority of it, and it is this implication he must always put firmly to the side.

This possible need for Jaynes to insist on his Blackness to the exclusion of all other identities could be partially met (i.e., only at first glance) by claiming a strictly linear ancestry—one that coheres with the space-time of the Middle Passage epistemology. Even though he is clearly of mixed-race ancestry, Jaynes finds a way to take intersecting lines and render them one: "I am a mulatto in a long line of mulattoes, so visibly lacking in African heritage that I often appear to some uneducated eyes as a random, garden-variety white guy. But I'm not. . . . Let me be more clear, since some people can't get their heads around it even when I stand before them: I am a black man who looks white."[39] It is hard to imagine a "line" of mulattos through the ages, as mulattos are, by their racist definition, typically biracial offspring of one Black parent and one white parent.

Johnson's status as biracial (mulatto) also confuses one's reading of "line," something one is less likely to do when the ancestral line is described as (mostly) racially homogeneous.[40] In spite of the logical odds, Jaynes is quite clear that we are meant to understand him as the result of a linear cause-and-effect sequence. Each mixed-race father in Jaynes's family tree is understood to have reproduced himself, another mulatto, regardless of whom he marries.

Black women are among the more prominent casualties of this fantastic journey. As the previous quote warns, Jaynes's interpellation of himself through a single line appears to privilege one parent over another, because the intersecting strands of each ancestry cannot be represented. By naming his father as the "mulatto," we now know that this linearity will be marked only as men begetting men. His exoticizing objectification of his ex-wife, Angela, also indicates that it is men, not women, who will be agents in this narrative of return.

Intriguingly, the first female character we encounter is also a newly discovered distant relation of Jaynes and provides the essential link between Dirk Peters and his discovery that Poe's tale is true (i.e., that one of Poe's fictional characters did in fact exist). Mahalia, as Jaynes describes her, is a woman whose physiognomy clearly indicates that she is Black, yet her unstoppable mouth is always asserting the contrary. Mahalia's undisguised denial of her Blackness allows Jaynes to perform his racial solidarity—and tellingly rely on a bit of stereotypical sexism—to make the case for his race pride and her shameful rejection of Blackness. Mahalia is an obese hypochondriac hoarder who first greets him with "Niggers!" thus figuratively and literally chasing away her denigrated view of Blackness while ridiculously clad in a "muumuu of green paisley silk and a sparkled turban to match." Mahalia's aversion to Blackness is soon punished when she takes Jaynes to her acronymic mouthful of an association of Middle Passage Blacks who share her aversion to Blackness as well as her fantasy that she is mostly of American Indian descent. At the abrupt end of the Native American Ancestry Collective of Gary (NAACG) meeting, the association's members, with one exception, all discover that they are without question "Negro" and collapse into agonized hysterics.

When interpellating gender in *Pym*, only two types of female roles manifest, and as binaries to boot. In Jaynes's manifestations, a Black woman is either an Angel(a)—an ebony goddess with whom one should marry and mate—or a Mahalia—a traitor who seeks to pass. Their stereotypically described comparative attractiveness also indicates the narrow sexist lens through which Jaynes reads them—as mating material. Angela's Blackness *is* her beauty, whereas Mahalia's denials of Blackness, it is so often noted, emanate from an obese and outrageously clad body.

In Poe's tale, the savage Black Tslalians claim the greater portion of the adventure, while the solemn, white, perhaps divine Tekelians enjoy exactly one vague paragraph of description. In *Pym*, the adventure is almost wholly in Tekelia and, with ironic intertextual comment, the Tslalians receive exactly one paragraph. These two texts are also qualitatively reversed, even though, as noted before, they stumble into explicit and implicit narrative contradictions (Johnson's consciously, Poe's unknown). Johnson's (white) Tekelians are smelly, slimy, greedy, and conniving, and visually they have almost become part of their frozen ice landscape, while the Tslalians, albeit briefly glanced, are a gorgeous and welcoming island/paradise people. Johnson makes clear the role of whiteness for the Black imagination seeking return, because the greater part of the tale of encounter is spent in the "other" race's, rather than the narrator's own, collective—that is, it is easier to imagine a utopian return through what one does *not* want, rather than through what one does.

In Poe's *Nantucket*, the events leading up to the discovery of Tsal are marked by strange animals and events. Pym and his crew spot what appears to be, except for its curly hair, a polar bear (and this while on the way to a tropical clime), and a boat of grinning corpses floats by, foretelling the savagery of the Tslalians but also possibly presaging the cannibalism in which the starving white crew, Pym included, engages. The impossibility of such a polar bear indicates that the tale is fueled more by the imagination than by Arthur Pym's true experiences. Because cannibalism is most often attributed to "primitive" races, such as Blacks, Central American Indians, South American Indians, and Pacific Islanders, to have it performed by whites also upsets the binary on which the traditional racist adventure narrative relies. Finally, unlike most other racist tales that feature white adventurers and Black savages, Poe's Arthur Pym relates to the reader his intention to exploit Tslalian labor and create a factory on the island that processes the sea cucumbers the "savages" will retrieve from the abundant ocean.

In Johnson's intertextual satire, Jaynes's story is equally "unbalanced." The encounter with whiteness is interpellated, as in *Kindred*, through the experience of enslavement. When Jaynes and his crew reach Tekelia, one of their first encounters with the Tekelians is also with Arthur Pym—who, after ensuring that his narrative reached his good friend Edgar Allan Poe, remained in Tekelia. Pym has aged, but only slowly, and of course his racial politics are firmly antebellum: he mistakes Jaynes for a slave merchant and the Black crew for his cargo. Worse, once Jaynes emphatically reveals that he is also Black, Pym and the Tekelians enslave all of them.[41]

Then, also as in *Kindred* but in greater detail and more provocatively, the plot reverses itself as a Black agency is imagined and used to literally kill the white oppressor—as Dana does when she kills Rufus before her final return to the present. While in *Pym*, as in *Heremakhonon*, return can become a "tragic mistake" when imagined as a linear retracing (Jaynes literally retraces the route left by one of Poe's characters-cum-actual-ancestor, Dirk Peters), the murderer in *Pym* is the traveler, not the "native."

Like Poe's Tslalians, Johnson's Jaynes also seeks to trap and eradicate those who want to control his labor (loosely speaking, as Jaynes admits he was a lazy slave with an even lazier Tekelian master). In Johnson's novel, Jaynes and the crew plot to commit nothing less than cold-blooded (pun intended by Johnson) genocide against their former masters, liquidating men, women, and children because the Tekelians (rather reasonably) seek to destroy the human ecoshelter whose exhaust is melting their habitat. Similar to the attack of the Tslalians on Pym and his crew in Poe's *Nantucket*, the Tekelians' acts of aggression against the Black crew in Johnson can be understood as a fight for their own survival and sovereignty— Johnson's protagonist argues as much himself in his racial exegesis of Poe's unfinished novel.

Jaynes, now residing in the shelter after having escaped the Tekelians, agrees to serve the hundreds of them—men, women, and children—rat poison to avoid the certain massacre of his five colleagues and the couple who own the dome. Giving the reader yet more pause, the murder plot is effected by pretending to break bread with the enraged Tekelians in the name of peace, to which they readily agree and proceed to laugh, sing, and eat. Hundreds, in short, are to be poisoned to benefit a pitiful few whose chances for survival (the eco-dome actually runs on oil) are questionable to begin with. The plot is discovered and the rest of Jaynes's crew, with the exception of himself, Garth (Jayne's aptly named hapless sidekick), and Pym are killed in battle before the Tekelians all die. In the last few pages, the three set sail and eventually discover the now real island of Tslal. Yet before sighting the island paradise, Pym mysteriously dies and so, conveniently, it is only the two thirtysomething single Black heterosexual men (Garth and Jaynes) who make landfall. Like any utopian vision, this one most particularly suits young and single Black men who lack socioeconomic status in their own spacetime of the contemporary United States:

> l(ösing up in our pathway was a man. He was naked except for the cloth that covered his loins. He was of normal proportions, and he was shaking his hand in the air, waving it, and we, relieved, waved ours back at him. Past him, minutes later, we saw that he was joined in welcoming us by others, women, more men, and the offspring both had managed. Whether this was Tslal or not, however, Garth and I could make no judgments. On the shore all I could discern was a collection of brown people, and this, of course, is a planet on which such are the majority.[42]

Pym concludes with the destruction of whiteness; it also tellingly ends with the destruction of Black identities whose existence is also an annoyance to Jaynes: Angela (after it becomes clear she does not love Jaynes); Jeff-Free, the gay Black activist couple; and, tellingly, the only other Black male, whose convenient demise may have much to do with his withering view of Jaynes and Garth as rather questionable specimens of Black manhood. Garth, of course, an impractical dreamer like Jaynes but also a chronic overeater who is also unemployed, explicitly fails on these two counts (most importantly in Jaynes's narrow self-regard) to play anything other than the role of Chris Jaynes's comic (and therefore unthreatening) sidekick.

Pym stages its encounter with the past by literally having it encounter the present—Pym and the Tekelians, in their frozen climate, have remained at a low entropy (not so miraculous when one considers that, yes, for many elements, entropy remains at a lowered state when cold, as cold inhibits movement). Considered in the light of popular discourses on theoretical particle physics cited here in *Physics of Blackness*, *Pym* offers us an encounter between a low-entropy, ordered society and a high-entropy, chaotic society (whose members are literally melting Antarctica) and does not really come down on either side. *Pym*'s narrator relates tales of suffering under the cruel Tekelians, but some of his descriptions of his encounters with these creatures leave nagging questions. He claims that, despite hundreds of years with Pym, the first Tekelian to learn how to speak is Augustus, because of his affinity for Chris Jaynes. Jaynes also recounts an episode in which the pre-English-speaking Augustus nods in response to a question but narrates this gesture as if it were natural to Augustus, not learned. That a nod is not even a shared sign of assent on the settled continents of the earth begs belief that the Tekelians, whose difference from humans is endlessly underscored by Jaynes, nonetheless use the same gesture to stand in for the same signifier as we do. In short, *Pym* chides us on embarking on our unmediated returns through a strictly Middle Passage epistemology—not many in the collective will survive, and to do so, those survivors must both suffer and commit outrageously shameful acts while embracing an increasingly illogical set of spacetimes that must be invented to maintain the linear flow of events.

Even the experience of being enslaved loses its potential to grant authenticity. Upon being enslaved (importantly, as a twenty-first-century Middle Passage Black, not as a Black slave from the Atlantic world) Jaynes comments—in line with *Kindred's* view and Dubey's analysis of African American speculative fiction featuring time travel to the past— that knowing about slavery cannot prepare one for *being* a slave: ontology is held up over epistemology.[43] Yet Jaynes's narration of being enslaved deconstructs the slave experience itself. He is the slave of the Tekelian Augustus, whose name recalls the ancient Greek and Roman names many white U.S. slave owners liked to mockingly bestow on what they viewed as their profoundly benighted human livestock. Augustus also signifies poorly as a Middle Passage slave master because he is a sad sack: a disempowered and disliked member of the Tekelian clan from whom Jaynes escapes easily after several months of slumping around Augustus's foul hut feeling hungry.

Pym's deconstruction of Poe's novella and the monopoly of the Middle Passage epistemology in some narratives of return bear a useful resemblance to what is known in philosophy as "Münchhausen's Trilemma."[44] This "trilemma" (a deliberately humorous neologism for a di-lemma "plus one," named after Baron Münchhausen, who according to legend pulled himself and his horse out of a quagmire by his own hair) argues that justifying any question about causality means choosing one of three inadequate methods. One must either reason in a circle (citing premises to confirm a conclusion that must be cited to confirm one of the premises—as in pulling oneself off the ground by one's own hair); argue forever (because every cause is based on some prior cause, which in turn is based on a prior cause, ad infinitum); or cite putatively self-evident principles (the self-evidence of which is open to doubt). Whichever method you choose requires you to accomplish the impossible. Applied to the Middle Passage epistemology, it is tempting to give up and accept that causality cannot be determined through a linear retracing because in tracing back the cause of an event one immediately faces difficulties, either running in circles, never coming to the end, or arguing without proof. I find Münchhausen's Trilemma applicable to the futility of interpellating Blackness exclusively through the Middle Passage epistemology because Blackness is always so much richer, connecting, and varying from moment to moment, as searches for interpellations of Blackness that preserve linearity seem to lead one along endless branches rather than a single line.

Jaynes's attempt to experience slavery, therefore, fails, although we do not know exactly where and when because we become unsure as to what exactly does and does not count as authentic Middle Passage slavery. Some slaves, albeit very few, enjoyed masters who liberated them when young and perhaps educated them in a trade or for a profession—can we claim they had the authentic slave experience? In the present, the horrors of Middle Passage slavery are clear—yet in attempting to trace it back and specifically define it for a contemporary Black subject, endless questions abound, informed by what we know and what we do not know about Middle Passage slavery. We encounter Munchhausen's Trilemma and our theoretical line confusingly blossoms into a complex skein of connections.

The Middle Passage past, as James Baldwin once famously described it in "Encounter on the Seine: Black Meets Brown" in his essay collection *Notes of a Native Son*, is daunting and ambiguous to the postwar Middle Passage Black subject. Thinking back, Baldwin reflects that "it was much worse than that" and yet at the same time "not that bad"[45]—this, *Physics of Blackness* argues, is what happens when one stages return through Epiphenomenal time. Ambiguity springs up because so many pasts have occurred and are possible—most Middle Passage Blacks possess not simply one or two but many slave ancestors, hence a plethora of Black Middle Passage pasts.

Given Jaynes's deep desire for linear interpellation, this might explain one of the most puzzling anecdotes in *Pym*. Tellingly, in the moment at which he is relating his descent from a "line of mulattoes" and his rejection by his Black classmates for "looking white," "James Baldwin" improbably appears as the worst of those classmates: "In sixth grade a little effete frog named James Baldwin whupped my ass. He was a foot shorter than me, but he hung with hulking eighth-grade girls, who towered over both of us the entire time, taunting. . . . I had never even met James Baldwin, but it didn't matter, he attacked me anyway. I was different. He was puny, weak, but I was weaker."[46] On reporting the assault to his mother, she is as confused and as disbelieving as the reader in this intertextual moment. How is it that a child who matches the negative description Baldwin gave of himself, albeit having heard it first from his abusive stepfather ("ugly," with a small body, and "frog eyes"[47]), can be so violent and hateful? Read intertextually, we become more confused, because Baldwin's work is celebrated for its emphasis on love and inclusivity—on horizontal relationships between human beings, both within and across "races." As Little Jaynes's bully, however, Baldwin is now brutally vertical. Little Jaynes's mother and the librarian Mrs. Alexander respond to his tale with laughter, with the latter recommending to him, "Gets your little yellow butt down to the library. You gots to learn who you is."[48] Having lost his way in terms of his Black identity, he is encouraged to go to the library, read, and thus successfully (re)interpellate himself through a Middle Passage epistemology. Jaynes, we now know, dutifully did so, with horrific results—and perhaps because he felt disallowed from, or didn't know the existence of, other spacetimes. In order for Jaynes to be wholly Black, he must encounter and eradicate whiteness, and that entails encountering and eradicating all the forms of Blackness that threatened his own illusory linear interpellations.

Perhaps in "whupped his ass" Jaynes means to communicate that he had read Baldwin and found his worldview profoundly challenged. We will never know if this is so, but the following chapter in this book, "Quantum Baldwin and the Multidimensionality of Blackness," shows how Blackness need not limit itself to linear interpellations. More specifically, chapter 3 shows how Black Diasporic encounters can be framed to allow for a broader range of intersections than are permitted in Jaynes's fantastical epistemology, in which he is born from a "long line of mulattoes," eradicates whiteness, and achieves the "end of progress" by reaching an island whose collective offers roles that appear to favor his gender and sexuality.

3

Quantum Baldwin and the Multidimensionality of Blackness

What do James Baldwin and the quantum—a discrete quantity of energy whose non-Newtonian behavior has made it one of the foci of theoretical particle physics—have in common? Notably, in the introduction to their volume *James Baldwin: America and Beyond*, Cora Kaplan and Bill Schwarz produce Baldwin as a puzzle, difficult to categorize based on his quantum-like, peripatetic movement: "In no department of his life was Baldwin ever won by the concept of 'a straight line.' We can see evidence of this in his prose . . . adding subclause to subclause and detour to detour. Even so, when Baldwin was alive many critics were keen to describe the trajectory of his writing life as if it had traveled along a straight line, from A to B."[1] In other words, scholars have mistakenly used a wholly Newtonian spacetime to interpellate a quantum Baldwin, a misreading that may be limited to (mis)understanding not simply the spacetimes of Baldwin's travel and written expression but the multidimensionality of his Blackness: "For too long one Baldwin has been pitted against another Baldwin, producing a series of polarities that has skewed our understanding: his art against his politics; his fiction against his nonfiction; his early writings against late writings; American Baldwin against European Baldwin; Black Baldwin against queer Baldwin."[2] Kaplan and Schwarz pose both an argument and a challenge here that *Physics of Blackness* and this chapter specifically embrace: James Baldwin is an exemplar of a multidimensional Blackness that defies any attempt to make it follow a "straight line." In addition to arguing that reading Baldwin's career as a straight line produces a distorted and inaccurate portrayal, the editors assert that attempting to (mis)interpellate Baldwin through a linear spacetime can in effect "split" him into several single-dimensional selves. This chapter argues that using both linear spacetime and Epiphenomenal spacetime can help to reveal the intersections of those selves—the multidimensionality of his Blackness.

These valences of Baldwin are not in conflict with but instead intersect with the Black identities he explores in the essays in *Notes of a Native Son*. As this chapter will show, *Notes* provides a model for interpellating Blackness as multidimensional, which, in this context, means that "Black Baldwin" is not distinct from but intersects with "American" and "European" and (among other collective identities) "queer Baldwin." According to Kaplan and Schwarz, approaching Baldwin as a set of intersections is not only productively insightful and more accurate than a strictly linear interpellation; it may also be the best way to honor his own self-interpellation: "[Baldwin's] eye was always on the potential for establishing connections between contrary phenomena—even as their contrariness remained in place—rather than forcing disconnections and retreating to encampments. If we wish to make sense of Baldwin, we must do the same." We *can* do the same by beginning, as the reader might have already anticipated, with theoretical particle physics and more specifically with Lisa Randall's theory of multidimensionality.

As noted before, Baldwin's "quantum" movement defies accurate graphing through a Newtonian spacetime. Baldwin does not always follow the Middle Passage epistemology's trajectory but instead pursues other dimensions of his identity. Conceiving of collective identities as dimensions helps us, as they multiply, better understand the endless valences of Blackness in the Diaspora and intersects us with current theorizations in particle physics. In other words, interpellating identities free of linearity not only matters to Kaplan, Schwarz, myself, and a few others but in fact somewhat surprisingly connects us with attempts to understand nonlinearity as the true nature of our physical universe. Apparently, however, the physicist Lisa Randall does not find this surprising at all, as she explores and explains this multidimensionality in theoretical physics in part through the metaphor of human identities, my principal concern in this chapter.

Just as Baldwin belies any attempt to impose an "A to B" interpellation on him, so the behavior of subatomic particles as explained by quantum theory defies Newtonian laws of motion and gravity so thoroughly that physicists such as Randall have pursued the possibility of there being another spacetime that would unite and explain these dimensions. As I noted in the introduction, physicists have long sought a Grand Unified Theory: a set of common denominators that would capture, for example, the radically different behavior of subatomic particles and larger material bodies within the same theoretical framework. *Physics of Blackness* argues that, in discursive interpellations of Blackness, such a unification is achieved by understanding the individual in the "now" as the site of intersection (rather than as a common denominator by which all Blackness can be subsumed).

In chapters 1 and 2, I showed how the dominant assumption that collective identity in constituted through historically based linear progress narratives creates a cognitive dissonance between these collective epistemologies and most Black individuals at various moments of interpellation. In Randall's *Warped Passages: Unraveling the Mysteries of the Universe's Hidden Dimensions*, our inability to imagine other dimensions might be explained by our having been falsely informed about the dimensions of our universe since birth:

> The disinformation campaign began back in the crib, which first introduced you to three spatial dimensions. . . . Since that time, physical laws—not to mention common sense—have bolstered the belief in three dimensions, quelling any suspicion that there might be more.
>
> But spacetime could be dramatically different from anything you've ever imagined. No physical theory we know of dictates that there should only be three dimensions of space. Dismissing the possibility of extra dimensions before even considering their existence might be very premature. Just as "up-down" is a different direction from "left-right" or "forward-backward" other completely new dimensions could exist in our cosmos. Although we can't see them with our eyes or feel them with our fingertips, additional dimensions of space are a logical possibility.[3]

One can find a rough parallel here between Randall's theory of "crib disinformation" and the claim of this project that discourses on collective identity, in this case specifically Blackness, also misinform our interpellations. While Randall focuses on how "common sense" blinds us to the possibilities of other dimensions, this project argues that it is the way in which we imagine and deploy linear spacetime in our dominant discourses that can "blind" us to interpellating discourses on collective identities that defy this linearity, such as James Baldwin's *Notes*. As Kaplan and Schwarz point out, Baldwin has been split off into many "Baldwins" who possess only two to three dimensions each. The goal of their anthology, *James*

Baldwin: America and Beyond, is the goal of this chapter: to interpellate Baldwin through as many dimensions of Blackness as his postwar discourse manifests.

This is the only proper way to interpellate James Baldwin, a celebrated writer whose work spans African Diaspora literature and history as well as U.S., European, and postcolonial histories, literatures, and philosophies, thereby extending his interpellation far beyond the dimensions of Middle Passage Blackness, even as he connects to it. Randall admits that it is difficult to discuss the possibility of multiple extrasensory dimensions without first defining what a dimension is. To explain how dimensions correspond to qualities to be described or quantities to be measured, Randall cites human identities: "When you peg someone as one-dimensional, you actually have something rather specific in mind: you mean that the person has only a single interest. For example, Sam, who does nothing but sit at home watching sports, can be described with just one piece of information."[4] Randall then provides a simple timeline (an x graph, or simply a horizontal line) to "map" Sam through the hours he spends watching television. She then contrasts "Sam" to "Icarus Rushmore III," whom she plots through an "xyz graph" (resembling a cube with three "dimensions": age, residence, and number of times Icarus drives his car). What should we do, however, to map the dimensions of "Athena," Ike's sister?

> An eleven-year-old who reads avidly, excels at math, keeps abreast of current events, and raises pet owls. You might want to plot this too. In that case, Athena would have to be plotted as a point in a five-dimensional space with axes corresponding to age, number of books read per week, average math test score, number of minutes spent reading the newspaper per days, and number of owls she owns. However, I'm having trouble drawing such a graph. It would require five-dimensional space, which is very hard to draw.
>
> Nonetheless, in an abstract sense, there exists a five-dimensional space with a collection of five numbers, such as (11, 3, 100, 45, 4), which tells us that Athena is eleven, that she reads three books on the average each week, that she never gets a math question wrong, that she reads the newspaper for forty-five minutes each day, and that she has four owls at the moment. With these five numbers, I've described Athena. If you knew her, you could recognize her from this point in five dimensions.[5]

If one applies Randall's argument to Blackness, the case for more than three dimensions becomes quite clear, especially when we consider the broad and diverse panoply of extant discourses. It also reflects the complaint of discourses on "post-Blackness," which, I would argue, is most often expressed not as a *denial* of some dimensions (such as the Middle Passage) but as the desire to add more.⁶ This chapter works with Baldwin's critically acclaimed *Notes* because it offers an opportunity to consider the meaning of being a U.S. Black in the postwar world from multiple points in spacetime and finds him intersecting with other explicitly postwar discourses from the African and Black Diaspora that interpellate themselves through a postwar lens: Ivoirian folklorist and administrator Bernard Dadié's *Un Nègre à Paris*; playwright and novelist Ama Ata Aidoo's *Our Sister Killjoy*; and *Unsere Opfer's* (*Our Victim's*) oral histories of World War II in the words of Black African and Black Diaspora veterans from Mali, Senegal, Brazil, and Surinam.

This chapter shows how these writers interpellate themselves and thus their Blackness multidimensionally through a combined use of linear progress narratives and a postwar epistemology that reflects on the "now." They specifically do so in a way that invokes the first of the aforementioned Randall quotes that uses the concept of "directions" to explain our universe, whereby each direction corresponds to a distinct dimension. Linear spacetime, I argue, is largely limited to exploring only one direction mentioned in Randall, "up-down"; when interpellating Blackness as a collective identity, "up-down" denotes a vertical, hierarchical, and specifically heteropatriarchal frame. As this chapter will show, Baldwin himself sometimes invokes this direction alone: his exclusion of women from the vast majority of his essays in *Notes* and his tendency to use the Black male body to denote Blackness aligns with the most traditional uses of the Middle Passage epistemology.

At the same time, especially in *Notes*, Baldwin uses the moment of the postwar era to reinterpellate Blackness. In his first two chapters, largely a denunciation of Richard Wright's *Native Son* and protest novels more generally, Baldwin condemns any interpellation of Blackness that *reduces* it to *only* a series of struggles and defeats against a white racism that once again successfully denies Blackness its "humanity." In other words, Blackness must be read outside of the wholly vertical, in which it can be interpellated only as the object of and, at best, a reactor against white racist agency.

In the last four chapters of *Notes*, but most specifically in "Encounter on the Seine: Black Meets Brown," Baldwin uses what I identify as a horizontal interpellation of Blackness; that is, the African American encounters white men and Black men not as his superiors or inferiors but rather as peers who are equally disoriented by the postwar moment and who wonder to what degree the old hierarchies are still or will continue to be in play. This uncertainty between peers produces distinct dimensions—both horizontal *and* vertical—of Blackness in the postwar moment.

While I explore this topic more thoroughly later, a multidimensional interpellation of Blackness is also predicated on the assumption that Blackness possesses agency and involves choices. This does not mean that the Black subject is omnipotent; somehow to blame for his, her, or their social, political, and cultural marginalizations; or implicitly capable of ultimately overcoming any and all obstacles. It is instead to argue—as many textured and nuanced scholarly studies that interpellate Blackness through a Middle Passage epistemology have shown—that, above all else, Black subjects perform the full range of human emotions and actions and suffer from no genetic or biological proscription from any aspect of humanity due to the "impediment" of their racial designation. Rather than compose a laundry list of questionable behaviors, the goal of *Physics of Blackness* is to underscore the astonishing globality of Blackness, its location in so many spacetimes across the world and historical eras.

Notes of a Native Son collects published and previously unpublished essays that are nonetheless grouped into three coherent categories. Section I introduces the collection with three essays that focus on cultural tropes and creative works—Richard Wright's *Native Son* and its purported conflation with Harriet Beecher Stowe's *Uncle Tom's Cabin*; racist tropes and their life and death in the contemporary moment of the mid-1950s; and Otto Preminger's *Carmen Jones*, starring Dorothy Dandridge. Section II "returns" us to Baldwin's New York childhood and experiences with a vicious, pervasive, and, he argues, potentially fatal racism.

The last section of *Notes* offers the greatest number of dimensions for interpellating Blackness given its emphasis on the postwar moment and horizontal interpellations. At the same time, Baldwin's failure to interpellate women conceals a highly relevant dimension of Blackness in that moment. Yet because these chapters, especially "Encounter," stress horizontal intersections with other postwar Blacks who might be traveling through Paris/Europe in those discursive moments, I use this frame to connect "Encounter" to Black discourses that could in fact have intersected with *Notes*'s thoughtfully peregrinating narrator.

Notes begins with a withering critique of Richard Wright and his masterpiece *Native Son* in "Everybody's Protest Novel," in which Baldwin excoriates Wright for having created a world-famous postwar characterization of Blackness that, to Baldwin, is little better than the nightmare figurations of white liberals and conservatives alike:

> Bigger is Uncle Tom's descendant, flesh of his flesh, so exactly opposite a portrait that, when the books are placed together, it seems that the contemporary Negro novelist and the dead New England woman are locked together in a deadly, timeless battle. . . . Bigger's tragedy is not that he is cold or Black or hungry, not even that he is American, Black; but that he has accepted a theology that denies him life, that he admits the possibility of his being sub-human and feels constrained, therefore, to battle for his humanity. . . . The failure of the protest novel lies in its rejection of life, the human being [whose] categorization alone is real and cannot be transcended.[7]

Baldwin's use of time is informative here: bigger is *not* the product of another time, but he is nevertheless a direct, linear descendant of Uncle Tom, thus emphasizing linear descent as the flaw. This linear descent is then linked to a "rejection of life" whereby the human is disallowed from transcending its category even as *time* is transcended by "deadly, timeless battle." By understanding himself solely as a fixed effect created by a long series of causes and effects (as well as the same simple one: vicious racism creates the Black Other), according to Baldwin, Bigger restricts his own interpellation of Blackness to such a degree that he places himself outside of the category of human altogether. Whether slave or nominally free, the rebellious Black male is fated for death at the hands of a racist, white, capitalist structure.

Baldwin especially dislikes Bigger's peaceful resignation to his impending electrocution because it is a choice that is no choice at all—falling into line with the grand history of oppressor against oppressed rather than, as Wright's Bigger opines in the final chapters, the first time in which he feels he is "free." Because Bigger's "choice" is a fixed telos within his narrow self-interpellation, Baldwin rejects the possibility that this choice is anything more than a hollow signifier, empty of a true human being's intention.

When a linear spacetime epistemology begins, as many Black diasporic epistemologies do, with object status—being enslaved, colonized, relocated, and so on—the laws of cause and effect make it difficult to reverse the binary that is set in place, because oppression is asserted as the cause of all historical events (effects) in the timeline, excepting those events that are caused by a Black (resistant) reaction to an oppressor's action. Yet because it is a reaction to an action, we are again returned to a weird and dismally fixed race-ing of this Black physics, in which whiteness always retains the originary agency and, because origins dominate a linear narrative, white racism is always the central actor in Black lives now condemned to the status of reactors.

If, however, we add Epiphenomenal time to our interpellation here, the "now" is *foregrounded* by agency because Blackness begins as its own interpellation in the moment. At the same time, this moment is nuanced because it involves a potentially endless set of negotiations. Instead of the Black Subject being moved down a line through cause and effect as in a strictly linear interpellation, the Subject in the moment is variously informed by a variety of external and internal stimuli (what is witnessed and what happens; what is thought and felt) that also can intersect with one another. For example, I might watch an episode of a television show in one moment and laugh uproariously at what I find to be a daring but insightful joke about racism; in another moment, watching the same show and hearing the same joke, I might well have forgotten my previous reaction (or remember it, in whatever valence) and find myself ambivalent about or offended by the joke. In other words, I do not move through the world reacting in the same way to the same stimuli all the time—and perhaps this is because the stimuli are never the same because if not the space then the time has shifted (even if I am watching from my same place on the couch, I am doing so on different days).

This is both liberating and problematic to our lives, in which intellectual and behavioral consistency is more highly valued than its less predictable performances. It means that one does not always behave as one wishes, and for the Black Subject who seeks to adhere to a Middle Passage interpellation, the clarity of this linear timeline is often belied by the familiar complexity of lived moments. Similarly, the last paragraph of "Everybody's Protest Novel" asserts agency as an ambivalent possession, but a possession nonetheless: "Our humanity is our burden, our life; we need not battle for it; we need only to do what is infinitely more difficult—that is, accept it."[8]

While the "good news" here is that agency is intrinsic to interpellations effected through Epiphenomenal spacetimes, it comes with a series

of caveats that are less welcome. Agency here is not tied to concrete out-
comes (born of concrete goals) but to the choice to notice and wonder
at differences that the linear progress narrative struggles to wholly interpellate on its own, as these differences would encourage the exploration
of other collective identities that at times split Blacks from one another.
Unlike the moral and ethical dimension that tends to accompany such
claims of the self-realized individual in Western philosophy—whether in
Plato, Descartes, Hegel, or Nietzsche—the World War II/postwar epistemology does not understand "agency" or self-interpellation as a necessary
good or an ethical triumph over humanity's more "animal" or reactive
nature. Rather, it understands the act of interpellation as simply beginning
in the self (barring traumatic interpellation), and because interpellation
begins with the self, it is not a reactive action but one of "choice."

I tread on the concept of choice very carefully, especially given the
long train of connotations and denotations it brings to Western histories
of oppression. Individual choice is often understood as the cornerstone of
Western democracy, with free will as its *sine qua non*. Here I separate choice
from free will because in Western philosophy free will often assumes a
"neutral" spacetime in which one can identify one's truest, purest desire and
act on it, unencumbered by "outside" influences. *Physics of Blackness* understands choice as the fulcrum of agency and denotes choice as the moment
of interpellation that is not "free" of, but in fact intensely informed by, whatever in the physical and mental environment one notices in that moment.
Given this multiplicity of ever-changing factors and the presence of choice
in every moment (even when the choice is rather dismal or likely to lead
to the same damaging result), choice—like the concept of free will—holds
that human beings are ultimately unpredictable (one cannot be sure what
someone will do in every single moment) rather than rationally predictable
through the logic of cause and effect.

Lisa Randall's *Warped Passages* discusses how quantum mechanics
(a series of formulas that have influenced a range of scientific disciplines,
including, of course, particle physics) breaks from "classical" physics by relying on probability formulas to predict the path of an individual subatomic
particle. She notes that "quantum mechanics tells us that a particle can take
any possible path from its starting point to endpoint. . . . Unlike classical
physics, quantum mechanics does not assign a particle a definite trajectory."[9]

While *Physics of Blackness* focuses mainly on interpellating the multidimensional manifestation of Blackness within influential creative, scholarly,

and media-borne discourses, this argument admittedly spills over into theorizing the subject's performance within the quotidian. As in Randall's description, the moment of Epiphenomenal interpellation for an individual, even when juxtaposed with the linear, bears similarities to the behavior of a subatomic particle. One makes an educated guess but cannot absolutely predict how, when, and why that individual will interpellate in that moment. To make matters yet more confusing, the individual is not a cohesive, coherent unit but a multidimensional accretion of attitudes and feelings, some of which might contradict others. "Choice," therefore, is not the ability of a discretely bounded mind or body but rather the inevitable unpredictability of "the one" who is also "the many." This is a scene of neither defeat nor triumph but simply a moment of endless possibilities, not all of which are positive or desirable.

Yet unlike Louis Althusser's famous example of being hailed by the police, according to which interpellation verges on the involuntary (the response is wholly reactive), here the act of interpellation is unpredictable. Because the postwar epistemology holds that the individual is *not* merely an accumulation of a series of linear events in the past, there is only the "now," and there are endless possibilities in any given moment. To be sure, some reactions would attract more bettors than others, but this *choice*, this possibility of reading oneself or not reading oneself into any number of collective identities that occur in the moment, is what distinguishes the postwar epistemology from the Middle Passage epistemology and, I would argue, is specifically what Baldwin's *Notes* asserts so strikingly and defends repeatedly.

The rejection of Blackness in "Many Thousands Gone" opens with an interpellation of the Black (male) subject in the United States as mistaking himself for a "series of shadows, self-created, intertwining, which we now helplessly battle," and one that may "not really exist." Then however, Baldwin frames this moment not as a specifically "Black" problem but as a human problem that imperils all subjectivities in this postwar moment: "Our dehumanization of the Negro then is indivisible from our dehumanization of ourselves; our loss of our own identity is the price we pay for our annulment of his."[10] "Many Thousands Gone" then asserts that the true obstacle in the forward path of this bright young generation is mistaking themselves for objects of a history of white racism rather than as subjects in the "now":

Aunt Jemima and Uncle Tom are dead, their places taken by a group of amazingly well-adjusted young men and women, almost as dark, but ferociously literate, well-dressed and scrubbed, who are never laughed at, who are not likely ever to set foot in a cotton or tobacco field. . . . Some are bitter and these come to grief; some are unhappy, but, continually presented with the evidence of a better day to come soon, are speedily becoming less so. Most of them care nothing whatever about race, they want only their proper place in the sun and the right to be left alone, like any other citizen of the republic.[11]

Baldwin establishes that the self-determination of the individual can produce a Blackness that effectively breaks from its history of objecthood (figures of ridicule; slaves and sharecroppers), a move that, he notes, is very "American" in its self-generated agency: "The making of an American begins at that point where he himself rejects all other ties, any other history, and himself adopts the vesture of his adopted land."[12] Rather than switch to another linear history, the rhetoric here implies that the switch originates in the adoption, a taking on, or interpellation, of the "vesture," literally and metaphorically clothing, a costume that indicates performance. Given the conjugation in the present tense ("adopts"), Blackness is interpellated through the "now" rather than through a cause-and-effect history. It is also, I would argue, produced as a choice.

Like my own argument about choice, which differentiates it from the concept of free will, the ability to choose does not preclude the oppressive intrusions of psychic, emotional, and intellectual violence faced by Blacks. The intimate details of the potential and pitfalls of such a moment of interpellation achieve all the more poignancy when the essays of Section II reveal the highly personal parallels between the national portrait of "Many Thousands" and the harrowing narratives of Baldwin's life before Paris in "The Harlem Ghetto," "Journey to Atlanta," and "Notes of a Native Son." Here, his reaction to the virulent and unrelenting racism of whites threatens to deprive him of his humanity altogether, and small wonder: if one always interpellates one's Blackness in moments of anti-Black racism, the resulting identity is fraught with tension, anxiety, and hatred.

In the last essay of this section, Baldwin recounts a year in New Jersey in which the unbearable limits placed on his spacetime—where he is allowed to be and when, and for how long—lead to the famous encounter that shows him that his very life is at stake if he does not escape these environs. Walking in and sitting down at a "whites only" diner, he waits for the inevitable rejection from the waitress. When she does indeed tell him that they "don't serve Negroes here," he hurls a glass at her and runs out in front of the angry white patrons and staff: "I could not get over two facts, both equally difficult for the imagination to grasp, and one was that I could have been murdered. But the other was that I had been ready to commit murder. I saw nothing very clearly but I did see this: that my life, my *real* life, was in danger, and not from anything other people might do but from the hatred I carried in my own heart."[13] While it is unrelenting racism that leads to his explosion in the diner, what is most instructive here is Baldwin's recognition that it was not so much the whites' deadly hatred that threatened him; *his own* hatred was the deadliest. In effect, rather than interpellating this moment as one in which he has been rendered wholly Other, the moment is foregrounded by choice—that is, how he *chooses* to react to the waitress's refusal to serve him. It is only within a strict linear interpellation that a reaction is always already subsidiary to an action; within the "now," when one chooses how to react, how to perform and interpret that moment, the range of possibilities produces reaction as both action and reaction. In other words, Baldwin's trajectory, like Randall's explanation of the subatomic particle, isn't wholly predictable. Yet the linear progress narrative must also be used here because it tracks the collective, and the individual interpellation in the "now" thus achieves much of its validity through its dialogue and interaction with the Middle Passage epistemology.

"Encounter on the Seine: Black Meets Brown" strikingly incorporates a dialogic and diasporic metaphor, the Eiffel Tower, which triangulates the positionalities of Baldwin as a Negro *American*—that is, with nationality emphasized—and a "French African." The analysis is flawed insofar as Baldwin tends to imagine the latter as a sounding board for the former, suggesting he would rather imagine than actually engage with another during this imagined encounter. Yet in a tradition starved for discourses that fruitfully explore differences between Black diasporic identities, this essay offers the opportunity to view U.S. Blackness through more than one prism, capturing distinguishable moments of interpellation, all of which are grounded in the postwar experience yet take in both pasts and futures. The essay begins by seeking to separate myth from fact: gone are the glory days of Paris between the wars that so many Middle Passage epistemologies notate. Here is a Paris still a bit hungry and ragged after a brutal occupation and a reluctant retreat by the Nazis. Baldwin walks us through the streets at eye level, horizontally, past the old haunts of Chez Inez and its adjacent neighborhoods in this postwar spacetime, and reflects on his compatriots. The "Negro American colony" is less a coherent collective than a set of individuals who interact profoundly through "Negro entertainers," because they are the only ones "able to maintain a useful and unquestioning comradeship with the others." The explanation of this situation startles: "It is altogether inevitable that past humiliations should become associated not only with one's traditional oppressors but also with one's traditional kinfolk."[14] The Middle Passage epistemology does not disappear when engaging with Black peers, but instead the vertical relations that define Blackness as subaltern are recalled by encounters with other U.S. Blacks; stunningly, white oppression is imagined when not present. Baldwin's language invokes not only the presence but also the *dominance* of this epistemology in this moment. The manifestation of a phantom white oppressor is "inevitable," clearly the effect of a cause over which the Black subject has no control. Most painfully, it is not witnessing a racist incident, nor hearing of one, that manifests a humiliated Blackness but the encounter with peer members, or "Middle Passage Blacks" from the United States, that does so.

Disquietingly, this vertical interpellation does not manifest when Baldwin's "American Negro" encounters white American or Black African peers in Paris. This shift from U.S. Black encounters to encounters with white Frenchmen, white Americans, and Black French Africans is signaled when Baldwin's narrator encounters the Eiffel Tower, which, he muses, "has naturally long since ceased to divert the French," who also possess a tendency to view Blacks through a simplistic and overdramatically romantic lens: "All Negroes arrive from America, trumpet-laden and twinkle-toed, bearing scars so unutterably painful that all the glories of the French Republic may not suffice to heal them."[15] In this way, "Encounter" links the inability to reflect on the Eiffel Tower to the inability to interpellate Blackness through anything other an intensely simplified version of the Middle Passage epistemology created for white French consumption. These conversations are distorting because "the Negro is forced to say 'Yes' to many a difficult question, and yet to deny the conclusion to which his answers point."[16]

At this moment Baldwin's essay switches to Epiphenomenal time, because the African American sees ambiguities in the multidimensionality of the "now," not Middle Passage certainties provided by a fixed notion of linear time: "His past, he now realizes, has not simply been a series of ropes and bonfires and humiliations, but something vastly more complex, which, as he thinks painfully, 'It was much worse than that,' was also, he irrationally feels, something much better. As it is useless to excoriate his countrymen, it is galling now to be pitied as a victim, to accept this ready sympathy which is limited only by its failure to accept him as an American."[17] Unlike *Physics of Blackness*, which asserts the need to use both epistemologies together, Baldwin switches between these spacetimes. Suddenly, interpellating himself through the Epiphenomenal spacetime of the postwar epistemology serves as a *corrective* to his previous experience. By conversing with both white Americans and white Frenchmen in Paris, the Black American realizes (as the last lines of the quote spell out) that he need not manifest vertical interpellations in encounters with his countrymen and that the effect of assuming victim status through this interpellation is undesirable. This does not mean, however, that this will change how others see him; choice over one's own interpellations does not extend to the ability to control how one is interpellated by others.

The story of the final encounter in this essay, occurring just two paragraphs away from that of his encounters at the Eiffel Tower, is that of the "Negro students from France's colonies," in which the Black American finds "the ambivalence of his [own] status thrown into relief."[18] There are many possibilities when one reflects on the meaning of the past in a moment. Baldwin writes that the African American is confused not by ignorance, a lack, but rather by a complexity that *exceeds* easy characterization.

The moment of encounter between the "Negro and the African" reflects the ambivalence and ambiguity Epiphenomenal time can produce. In language that is both illuminating and uncritically essentialist, "Encounter on the Seine" reveals the complexity behind what seems so simple a title:

> They face each other, the Negro and the African, over a gulf of
> three hundred years—an alienation too vast to be conquered in
> an evening's good will, too heavy and too double-edged ever to be
> trapped in speech. This alienation causes the Negro to recognize
> that he is a hybrid. Not a physical hybrid merely: in every aspect
> of his living he betrays the memory of the auction block and the
> impact of the happy ending.
>   The American Negro cannot explain to the African what surely
> seems in himself to be want of manliness, of racial pride, a maudlin

ability to forgive. It is difficult to make clear that he is not seeking to forfeit his birthright as a black man, but that, on the contrary, it is precisely this birthright which he is struggling to recognize and make articulate. Perhaps it now occurs to him that in this need to establish himself in relation to his past he is most American, that thin depthless alienation from oneself and one's people is, in sum, the American experience.[19]

This passage first establishes horizontality, or some semblance of it, by positioning the two as facing each other yet divided by a fixed gulf of time that also connects them. This mutual alienation is no small obstacle, Baldwin notes, before moving to focus wholly on the interpellation of the "American Negro" through the "African" interlocutor, who nonetheless remains a cipher. This, one supposes, is the result of an encounter in which at least one party is unfamiliar with the collective identity of the other on an intimate, multidimensional level—perhaps the result of two linear progress narratives (i.e., fixed dimensions) intersecting with one another.

This interpellation is, of course, wholly masculine, which further increases the possibility that we have two mostly or wholly linear manifestations of spacetime in these moments. In such moments of writing, Baldwin may not have possessed very much information about Black Africans, which might explain why, despite the title, most of this essay focuses on U.S. Blackness. Yet by engaging here with Ivoirian writer Bernard Dadié's own anthro-travelogue through Paris, *Un Nègre à Paris* (*A Negro in Paris*), we can put these two texts into dialogue through this shared spacetime.

Both Dadié and Baldwin would have tales of departure and arrival to tell one another (perhaps in that night of goodwill and drinking mentioned by Baldwin). Through *Notes*, Baldwin relates an "emigratory" trajectory (more a matter of leaving New York than of moving to Paris) based on racist encounters that threatened to rob him of his multidimensional humanity. Dadié, by contrast, is leaving his countrymen for a trip of edification—to see the colonizer and colonial capital up close, as it were.

The travelogue begins, almost tongue in cheek, with the narrator excitedly announcing to his friends the "good news" that he finally has his ticket for Paris. Given his high expectations, the narrative foreshadows their collapse in grimmer moments of reality: "I'm going to see Paris, me, with my [own] eyes. However, I'll be a little like everyone else, I'll carry a halo, a perfume, the halo and perfume of Paris. I'm going to touch the

walls, the trees, cross paths with the men."[20] The imagery here is a mixture of the vertical and horizontal: although encountering men and seeing
(straight ahead) are experiences he will have in common with other visi-
tors, he also admits that he won't be encountering Paris as its peer but
rather as one enchanted with its verticalities, boundaries, and influences.

Our narrator's time in Paris is produced through a powerful divide
between the ideal and the real, beginning with his frustrated attempts to
secure a ticket for the flight. Unlike Veronica Mercier of *Heremakhonon*,
Dadié's interpellation on the plane is wholly vertical and thoroughly reminiscent of the moment of being Othered that is described by Fanon in
Black Skin, White Masks: "I am the only Negro among many white travelers. I take a window seat; no-one wants to sit next to me."[21] Bizarrely, upon
arriving to the city, he makes a similar observation: "I look around: whites
everywhere; white employees. Nowhere is there the head of a Negro; it's
really a white country."[22] This particular whiteness, as he also learns, bears
little resemblance to that of its vaunted ancestry, often recalled in *Un
Nègre à Paris* (e.g., Marat, Mirabeau, Tallyrand, Fouché)—allowing Dadié
to perform his knowledge alongside those contemporary Parisians who
fall so woefully short. In this moment, *A Negro in Paris* first appears to
interpellate Blackness as isolated and likely subaltern, but as his journey
unfolds, he sees a whiteness that is progressive only in its own eyes.

One of Dadié's first visits in Paris—and a principal signifier for a theme
to which he returns again and again—is to the Bastille and its capture by an
antimonarchist crowd on July 14, 1789, signaling the downfall of absolute
Bourbon rule in France. While "Encounter on the Seine" uses the Eiffel
Tower to manifest a series of postwar comparisons between Middle Passage Blackness and colonized Black Africans, *Un Nègre à Paris* uses the
Bastille to reflect on the heart of the French Empire and its own succumb-
ing to a new capitalist climate of acquisition: "And for masters [the Parisian
man] has Tallyrand and Fouché.[23] Understanding nothing, or perhaps I
understand it very well, that which matters most to him is to build his fortune on the shoulders of time. And to do this he runs to get ahead of the
time that he awaits at the sidewalk café. . . . Don't worry, time will not find
him there, he will already be en route, having decided to slow the advance
that was gained by not living."[24] Beginning with "masters" (and two historical figures who are viewed as moneygrubbing and amoral to boot), Dadié's
observed Parisian is not free, instead seeking to enrich himself. Interestingly, Dadié posits that this man seeks to gain wealth by outpacing time

itself. This competitive asynchronic state provides material gains, but it does not allow for living "in the moment" as it were, suggesting that to interpellate oneself as in competition with linear time is no life at all.

With few kind words for this new modern lifestyle, which treats time as the tortoise to its fortune-seeking hare, Dadié also has little to say of the Eiffel Tower that "Encounter on the Seine" finds so useful for triangulating a postwar Blackness. Perhaps with a truer glimpse into the future than Baldwin's in *Notes*, he dismisses the opportunity to admire this impressive industrial verticality to explore the Paris metro—which, as he notes with some satisfaction, is truly a "Negro" predisposition: "I have to laugh at those hordes of tourists climbing the Eiffel Tower or the Arc de Triomphe, these opulent clients of the rich hotels. . . . And what matters to me? The metro. One really has to be pure Negro to admire nothing in Paris but the metro."[25] Dadié's account adds another dimensionality here: not all Blacks will flock to the Eiffel Tower to wonder both at it and at their differentiated relationships to it. Some will be speeding underground, far more fascinated by "this gigantic underground spider" that connects all Paris. While the tourists doggedly climb upward to understand, Dadié's desire to laugh suggests that he expects their efforts will not be nearly as rewarding as his own, given the ease of travel, not to mention its interconnecting reach (the Eiffel Tower, after all, extends in only one direction).

This emphasis on the horizontal, and on connection, extends to the second fascination of Dadié's narrative—Parisian women. Indeed, the narrator's focus on (white) Parisian woman is so varied and multifaceted, from the famous to the mundane, the glamorous to the repulsive, that he betrays his own claim of finding no Blacks in Paris—the encounter for *Un Nègre à Paris* features a Black African woman, "*une ravissante Africaines des territories Anglaises*" (a delightful African woman from the British colonies) who is limited to English among Western languages, just as Dadié admits he can speak only French. This is a brief encounter in the extreme: "We smile at each other constantly. Same color in this country of whites and no means of connecting. If our color brings us together, everything else separates us. A gap that a multitude of smiles could not fill. What do you think?"[26] Rather than conflation, Dadié highlights intersection: they are both Black, but not alike; they meet rather than merge. As in "Encounter on the Seine," here the narrator soberly notes that no amount of goodwill can overcome the gulf that separates them, and both men are quite serious about this. Baldwin's "gulf" comprises three centuries of time; Dadié is more absolute: this gulf is "everything" ("*tout*"). Most pro-vocatively, Dadié sturdily rejects a central tenet of so many Pan-African, Afrocentric, Middle Passage, and Black nationalist ideologies by claiming that color may be a commonality shared among Blacks, but it is a poor foundation for connection when it is the *only* one.

Despite the depressing silence of the French African male in Baldwin's "Encounter," one can intersect it nonetheless with Dadié's discourse on postwar Blackness in the West through the shared spacetime of Paris in the mid- to late 1950s. In a similar way, although *Un Nègre à Paris* also grants us a rather limited interlocutor (an African woman who cannot speak French), we can see the intersection of Dadié's discourse in this moment with that of Ama Ata Aidoo's *Our Sister Killjoy* because it is an extended, almost wholly internal monologue of the thoughts and views Dadié's narrator seeks—that is, the postwar viewpoint of an Anglophone African woman from the (former) British colony of Ghana.

Like Dadié's pilgrim (and lover of metros), Aidoo's protagonist also feels quite alone in Europe—but she is traveling with a group of fellow Ghanaian students. Dadié finds a mixture of the atavistic and modern in Paris (for the most part, however, only in the metro), but Sissie encounters rural Germany and London and her interpellation through the modern, and her return flight home at the end of *Killjoy* creates a sensation of isolation rather than connection to Blackness.

Sissie, or Our Sister / Our Sister Killjoy, first greets us, Burma Shave sign fashion,[27] with "'Things are working out" in the center of the first page, then "towards their dazzling conclusions . . ." on the next, and on the third,

... so it is neither here nor there,
what ticky-tackies we have
saddled and surrounded ourselves with,
blocked our views,
cluttered our brains.[28]

Our Sister Killjoy is playing a game with us from the start, because read-ing the first page alone suggests optimism, but when added to the second page, especially with "dazzling," this optimism becomes ambivalent because those "things" that were said to be in the *process* of being worked out in the first phrase are now *actually* in process, and therefore a bit more vulnerable to change. Nonetheless, these first two pages are used to gently convince the reader that what we carry with us from earlier moments ("saddled and surrounded ourselves with") possesses, literally, no spatial/directional relevance ("ticky-tackies"). Put together, one can read the first three pages as encouraging people to relinquish their worries to the fates—rendered, it should be noted, through a combination of Epiphenomenal time and the linear progress narrative, as multiple "things" work themselves through toward conclusions.

Killjoy consists largely of reflections on the dispossession and disempowerment of Black African women who find themselves encouraged to return to their "traditional" roles after the successful eradication of colonial regimes. In the first half, a triptych of parallels are drawn between the fascist orientation of Germany under Hitler, the almost equally constrained way in which a young German wife and mother must live in her village under watchful eyes, and the freedom Our Sister Killjoy, or Sissie, possesses in the now to wonder at this dismal cage rendered no more meaningful by a resentful but equally hemmed in and disempowered German husband (usefully named "Big Adolf").

Killjoy is a prose-poem-cum-epistolary short story of a Black Ghanaian woman encountering a series of old and revised verticalities, opening with Sissie at a cocktail party hosted by the German ambassador to celebrate the unnamed travel fellowship she has been awarded. The chumminess of the primarily European dignitaries with their host—their horizontality—prevents her from learning exactly with whom she is dining: their emphasis on informality and first names renders them unknowable to Sissie, who could only recognize them through their positions in the Nigerian state—their verticalities. "It is fairly clear" she reflects, that she is the "only insignificant guest."[29]

In an explicit foreshadowing, the one "African . . . her fellow countryman," known only to her as "Sammy," fits right in with this elite and is eager to impress on her the honor of her award. "Time was to bring her many many Sammys," she thinks—that is, "fellow countrymen" who interpellate themselves as successful postcolonial Subjects through the postwar European progress narrative and in turn attempt to interpellate her as their subaltern within this epistemology, a mentee ("He was very anxious to get her to realize one big fact. That she was unbelievably lucky to have been chosen for the trip").[30]

Aidoo, like Condé and Dadié, also uses the trope of flight to interpellate her transatlantic traveler. While *Heremakhonon* uses an airplane to interpellate Veronica as both an empowered and disempowered Black diasporic cultural tourist, and Dadié highlights jet-age travel as almost the exclusive preserve of whites, *Killjoy*'s Sissie is effectively segregated. The flight attendant assumes she must be accompanying the two "handsome Nigerian men" at the *back* of the plane and ushers her to their row, ignoring the seat assignment on Sissie's ticket. While Condé emphasizes the horizontality of the plane and its movement between times and spaces, Dadié and Sissie experience a distillation of European colonial hierarchies—while on the passenger list, they are ontologically separated Others among white European Subjects. Yet Aidoo adds one complication: these passengers, explicitly located "in the back" by the text, also turn out to be among the Fellows who were awarded this trip. Multidimensionality creates ambivalence in the moment: was the flight attendant racist by herding Sissie to the back of the plane to be with the other Blacks, or had she either guessed or known that Sissie was traveling as a scholar on the same junket as the two Nigerian men? In any event, Sissie relates that she had a lovely time.

Killjoy offers neither a progress narrative nor an antiprogress narrative. Like *Un Nègre à Paris*, it provides a series of moments in which the false promises of progress are pointed out and analyzed. Progress, both texts argue, produces yet more verticalities, more hierarchies, rather than the egalitarian set of peer relations Ghana and France respectively claim in the two texts. In what he asserts to be a natural predilection on the part of Black (male) subjects to embrace modern technology that enhances living—such as the metro's ability to connect people across vast distances in short amounts of time—Dadié holds out hope for his African countrymen if not the white West. Aidoo adds more dimensions to this equation by seeing the former colonies and the former colonizers as much more deeply intertwined—damningly so, because it is their shared hierarchies, their heteropatriarchies, that impede what Sissie so desperately seeks from her countrymen: recognition and understanding.

Sissie intersects with Marija, both women in their early twenties whose relationship to one another cannot be fully understood by the dimensions of race or gender, nationality, sexuality, or class. The particular moment in which they are meeting is of key significance, but there is no "where" or "when." Although this will be the focus of chapter 4, it is useful to note here that framing the "where" and "when" through the postwar era is especially amenable to the interpellation of these two women's relationship because Nigeria's changing status as a postcolonial power rich with oil wealth is emerging just as Germany is seeking to accommodate its past into a Marshall Plan postwar present. Within this frame, one need not assume that these women's race and gender automatically lock them into a postcolonial heteropatriarchy—that is, a vertical interpellation in which their status as women places them at the bottom of both nations' social hierarchies, and Sissie's Blackness places her "below" Marija. Instead, the postwar epistemology interpellates Sissie's Blackness as multidimensional, a Nigerian woman and scholar who, with her nation's blessing, has traveled to Germany and encountered Marija, a perfect *Hausfrau* who appears almost suspended in a spatiotemporal stasis. Indeed, that Marija must worry over the villagers' assessment of her in this role every time she steps outside, and that she is married to "Big Adolf" and has given birth to "Little Adolf," reinforces the notion of a Subject almost wholly interpellated through heteropatriarchal forces. As the naming indicates and reinforces, Marija's identity is no more than the medium through which yet another oppressive German(ic) Adolf begets his eponymous son and heir.[31]

In *Killjoy*, Sissie and Marija's encounters produce both implicit and explicit queerness; in queer theory, the failure of their relationship to conform to the heteropatriarchal logics explained before means that they are "queering" those logics, or subverting them. When Marija plans to get Sissie alone (Big Adolf at work, Little Adolf alone upstairs) and kisses her, Sissie pushes away and slaps her in surprise. At first, Sissie attempts using spacetime to understand the moment: "And now where was she? How did she get there? What strings, pulled by whom, drew her into those pinelands where not too long ago human beings stocked their own funeral pyres with other human beings, where now a young Aryan housewife kisses a young black woman with such desperation right in the middle of her nuptial chamber?"[32] Although Sissie attempts to understand her spacetime, she assumes (although *she* is the one asking the question) that the interpellation is in fact due to "strings pulled" by someone else. She locates Germany on a linear timeline, just one step out of the savage irrationality of barbarian culture (humans using other humans as firewood), and where Marija is "Aryan," which this quote denotes as primitive. Marija's attempted seduction is one of desperation, also hierarchically interpellated, because as a "housewife" who kisses another woman in the space of the "nuptial chamber," she is violating that order by seeking a queer sexual alignment.

This emphasis on hierarchical interpellation is foreshadowed in the moments when Sissie and Marija first meet up for this evening and Sissie first silently interprets Marija's confession that she wishes just to get away from Little Adolf to spend time with her as a "Heresy / In / Africa / Europe, / Everywhere."[33] Two pages later, Marija's statement that she is happy that Little Adolf is a boy because she cannot have any more children is reflected on by Sissie as, unlike the previous statement, quite within this (global) heteropatriarchal order: "Any good woman / In her senses / With her choices / Would say the / Same."[34] Yet this kiss between her and Marija, which was followed by an almost involuntary slap from the former, like an outraged woman protecting her honor, confuses Sissie. It is, after all, a suddenly horizontal moment in which Marija is neither wife nor mother but potential lover, to which Our Sister responds through a displaced verticality: "Sissie looked at the other woman and wished again that at least, she was a boy. A man."[35]

When she interpellates herself as a Nigerian woman, Sissie sees the impossibility of relating what has just happened to her family and friends back home within a heteropatriarchal logic: "What do you say even from the beginning of your story that you met a married woman? No, it would not be easy to talk of this white woman to just anyone at home," pointing to the lack of an epistemological framework through which she could interpellate this moment for people at home—and with a married white German woman to boot. Yet *Killjoy* does not restrict itself to the vertical here either—or rather, it reveals how queerness for Sissie is always deeply imbricated within the vertical: her recollection of erotic play with her fellow boarding school girls is recalled through the hailing of the outraged schoolmistress: "Good Heavens, girl! / Is your mother bush? / is your father bush? / Then / Why / Are / You / Bush?"[36]

In this recollection, same-sex desire between schoolgirls is interpellated as "bush," recalling the behaviors of Nigerians before British colonialism that linger still outside the civilized urban centers. Here queerness isn't the dastardly and humiliating legacy of the colonizers but rather operates wholly outside of their spacetime. In her recollection, Sissie adds a sad postwar twist in which she imagines telling the "Miss" that this behavior is no longer "bush," "But a / C-r-i-m-e / A Sin / S-o-d-o-m-y"—in other words, now condemned in her society, viewed as criminal in Christian and English legal terms. Here, *Killjoy* suggests, the hierarchy of British colonialism has left its legacy by refashioning the Nigerian past to reflect the bigotries of the former, now rendering Sissie unable to do more than wish that the desire between her and Marija could be legitimated by one of them being male. Strikingly, it is neither Marija's married status nor their racial difference that is named here as the obstacle, but heterosexism, suggesting that in this moment of interpellation, the heteropatriarchal logics of colonizer and colonized now coalesce in the postcolonial and postwar era. This coalition of Black West African and Western European heteropatriarchies informs not only the rest of *Killjoy* but also other works by Aidoo, such as her short story collection *No Sweetness Here*. This coalition marginalizes the Black African woman, but it also troubles the postcolonial African state as a whole: in the second half of *Killjoy*, Sissie fights a losing argument against her expatriate countrymen in London who reject her call to serve their fledgling and needful nation. By interpellating themselves through a heteropatriarchal Western definition of progress and cosmopolitanism rather than Sissie's strict (and rather punitive, as it seems, based on little more than the need to serve through sacrifice) postcolonial heteropatriarchal spacetime, *Killjoy* shows how vertical structures such as heteropatriarchies inevitably simplify into purely phallic ones. Promised privilege by virtue of their gender (and sexuality), some male bodies, such as those Sissie encounters, will seek ever more power, bypassing the Black hierarchy should another heteropatriarchy promise yet greater privilege. Sissie writes, albeit without hope of a favorable reply, against what she sees as an emerging interracial heteropatriarchal alignment between Black African and white European men: "My Brother, if we are not careful, we would burn out our brawn and brains trying to prove what you describe as 'our worth' and we won't get a flicker of recognition from those cold blue eyes."[37]

In response to Dadié's "What do you think?" Sissie might ecstatically embrace the opportunity to interpellate herself through this hailing, not unlike her final recollection to her old lover: "Sitting yourself down in a chair, right opposite me and with the smile around your eyes, you saying, 'I know everyone calls you Sissie, but what is your real name?'"[38] In other words, Aidoo suggests that Dadié's Black Anglophone African woman might actually prefer to be engaged not as a "Black sister" but as an individual who, in this "now" of encounter, seeks a peer rather than (hetero)patriarchal relationship. Dadié's comment that their Blackness is not enough to join them might be an indication that he would be quite happy to converse with his Anglophone acquaintance as two individuals rather than as Subjects who achieve identity only through a Pan-African or Afrocentric progress narrative.

In Baldwin's "Encounter," the "Negro American" seeks to explain his want of manliness to his French African acquaintance; Dadié's narrator looks for no such explanation, but he does wish he could engage with an Anglophone sister he encounters in Paris. As an Anglophone sister, Sissie has much she wishes to say and, unlike in these other postwar texts, ends with the desire to be asked questions rather than have answers provided. One cannot pretend that these exchanges would be idealized diasporic moments in which Blacks from different parts of the globe find communion, however brief: after all, Sissie has made clear she is tired and frustrated with the preponderance of male voices talking about freedom yet doing nothing. Instead, as my reading of Dadié's and Aidoo's construction of encounters suggests, Sissie and the protagonist of *Un Nègre à Paris* might actually seek an exchange that is *not* grounded in their diasporic identities created by a Pan-African progress narrative rooted in white European colonialism and racism (i.e., as Black African Subjects with a precolonial past now emerging from the colonial into the postcolonial) but instead one that is grounded in the identities they find most useful in the "now." In other words, they might, exactly as the French, bypass Baldwin's Eiffel Tower and its signification of those complex histories of racist oppression, leaving his Black American *seeking* an interlocutor rather than facing one.

"Encounter on the Seine" imagines the intersection of two Black men from separate parts of the Diaspora, but it limits itself in its imaginings, as Black veterans from World War II belong to almost every continent. In this moment the largely oral but also narrative history *Unsere Opfer Zählen Nicht: Die Dritte Welt im Zweiten Weltkrieg* (*Our Victims Do Not Count: The Third World in the Second World War*) offers a much broader variety of narratives. The largest category is of course that of soldiers, Black men who were forcibly recruited across the European and Japanese colonies, including the British-held Solomon Islands and their commonwealth of Australia, which brought aboriginal men into training, as well as the French protectorate over the greater part of the Polynesian islands.

Yet it was not just European powers conscripting the men in their colonies through which Blackness and the World War II/postwar moment intersect. By foregoing a linear narrative to reach all these men and women who served in World War II, *Unsere Opfer* instead uses geography and thus becomes one of the few narratives of the Second World War that comes so close to fully denoting that world and all its relevant geographies. As a result, horizontal relationships are revealed within the vertical, such as Brazil's decision to send Black troops to (now Allied-friendly) Italy, revealing a Brazil–Italy connection that most dominant narratives, focused as they are on the most powerful nations of the Allies and the Axis, will bypass, thus foreclosing or delaying the manifestation and recognition of those Black identities. As veteran Danilo de Andrade recounts it, his experience liberating Italy bears little difference to that of white troops: "Simple. With a block of chocolate one could score the most beautiful Italian women"; this is in contrast to Astrogildo Sacramento's experience of having Italian villagers rub the soldiers' skin to see "if the color came off."[39]

While only briefly rendered, Sacramento's story manifests the same interesting nuance as the final essay in *Notes*, "Stranger in the Village." "Encounter on the Seine" ends with the encounter between the Black American and the Black French African soldier in a moment of ambiguity. The essays sandwiched between "Encounter" and "Stranger in the Village," "A Question of Identity" and "Equal in Paris," focus on interpellating the U.S. Black male through the U.S. postwar experience in Paris and through the Parisian male collective, respectively. In the first essay, Baldwin expands on the ambiguity of encounter between Black Americans and their white countrymen who, no longer bound by the social mores of the United States, are unsure about how to engage with one another but also seek to avoid performing the racist hierarchy that is a hallmark of the U.S. nation-state in the immediate postwar era. In the second essay, a series of misunderstandings lands Baldwin in jail, which, he argues, did not lead to an interpellation of his Blackness as subaltern but as horizontally intersecting with Parisian habits and customs, including a justice system that treats everyone with equal and often confusing doses of insouciance, indifference, and heavy-handedness. He is "equal in Paris," Baldwin opines, because his Blackness does not place him either above or below the law, which treats all Parisians equally (badly).

The grandest statement *Notes* makes on Blackness in the postwar moment, however, is interpellated through his experiences in a small and isolated Swiss village in "Stranger in the Village." Not unlike the way in which Dadié embraces his metro and sadly notes some of the strange habits of the Parisians, and not unlike the way in which Sissie, when confused by sexual desire, imagines Marija as the latest descendant of murderous barbarians, Baldwin frames modernity as closer to Blackness than whiteness.

Baldwin plays a rhetorical trick in "Stranger," one common to precolonial narratives, in which the capacities and abilities of Europe are displaced from the cosmopolitan metropolis of Paris to a less populated and more rural hamlet in Switzerland. When he writes that no American, Black or white, can return to this village, he implies that this tiny hamlet *is* Europe because Americans, by virtue of not being able to go "back," have once been there. Because this place is small, we cannot take Baldwin literally here—we cannot imagine that very many Americans, in seeking Europe, think first of this tiny village or its equivalent, as we might should he have used Paris as his example. One might instead see the metaphor of a progress narrative here, in which civilization is marked by the move from rural, isolated villages to large, thriving metropolises or, more significantly, by the ability of a place's denizens to interpellate Blackness as part of the modern world:

> The time has come to realize that the interracial drama acted on the American continent has not only created a new black man, it has created a new white man, too. No road whatever will lead Americans back to the simplicity of this European village where the white men still have the luxury of looking on me as a stranger. I am not, really, a stranger any longer for any Americans alive. One of the things that distinguishes Americans from other people is that no other people have ever been so deeply involved in the lives of black men, and vice versa. This fact faced, with all of its implications, it can be seen that the history of the American Negro problem is not merely shameful, it is also something of an achievement. . . . This world is white no longer, and it will never be white again.[40]

Just as W. E. B. Du Bois's *Souls* successfully linked antiracism to progress, creating an image of the racist as rural and backward, so Baldwin's "Stranger" successfully links Blackness in the West with the entrance of Western modernity. America, the quote suggests, is ahead on this progress narrative, Europe behind, because the former recognizes the Black American, however reluctantly, as part of the modern Western nation-state. This essay does not condemn all Europe to the backwaters of this timeline; *Notes*'s emphasis on the freedoms to be found in Paris for the Black American suggest that it is "European villages" that are located in the past, while modern cities where Black men can travel with ease are sites of progress and civilization. This meaning of Blackness is then extended to the world:

if modernity is changing the world, and Blackness signifies the entrance to modernity, then logically the "world is white no longer."

The Eiffel Tower was created to celebrate France's indisputable entry into the ensemble of "first world" nations whose economic might could be symbolized through this architectural marvel of mass and industrial technology. Yet as Baldwin, Paul Gilroy, Lerone Bennett Jr., and many others remind us, the history of the Middle Passage is deeply intertwined with the Modern Era of industry and science in Europe—with the latter deeply dependent on the *intelligent* labor of millions of African Americans who worked both on agricultural plantations *and* in corporate industries, first as slaves, then as exploited (but not technically owned) workers. The relationship of both Baldwin and Dadié to the Eiffel Tower is ambivalent: as both Hegel and Marx would assert, while both share in its triumphant creation and the freedom of the French to display it, they are disallowed from owning their labor in the public sphere.

There is an interesting difference here, too: it is likely that the French African soldier at this time finds his and his father's generations forcibly interpellated through the vertical power of French national-colonial agendas, while the U.S. Black would likely read his nation's history as a step forward toward sociopolitical equality for Black men. If we imagine the Eiffel Tower and interpret its steel girders as timelines, we can see them reflecting these intersecting histories and realize that one can read those timelines as soaring upward, crashing downward, or zigzagging, creating an image of intersection without homogeneousness. When we read Baldwin's, Dadié's, and Aidoo's discourses on postwar Blackness through this image, we can see all this. These three discourses on postwar Blackness, like the girders of the Eiffel Tower, intersect yet retain important differences.

They intersect where all three assert that Blackness best understands this postwar moment and all the relevant spacetimes that intersect. Baldwin notes the complexity of Blackness—the ease with which it significantly intersects with a range of postwar identities. Dadié argues that Blackness embraces and uses modernity to seek diverse and broad connections while whiteness seeks no life, only an endless pursuit of material wealth. Aidoo's is the most complicated because it rejects the simplified view provided by the first two authors, in which the postwar world is one of encounters between Black men and white men in their struggles for supremacy and self-determination. Instead, to return again to the Eiffel Tower as a trope for postwar Blackness, *Killjoy* shows the preponderance of verticalities in the structure, despite (or perhaps because of) all the intersections. In Aidoo's text, Black African women face a daunting series of challenges and erasures in the postcolonial African spacetime. Whereas we might read Baldwin's "Encounter on the Seine" as encouragement to ponder how it was Black male labor that built the Eiffel Tower and white male ownership that allows them to use it as a signifier of white Western national might, *Killjoy* bluntly points out that in this battle between men for control of the postwar world, it is women, Black and white, who will always be the casualties. Read through our trope, Aidoo is simply stating that, regardless of its color, the Eiffel Tower will always be a phallic-shaped paean to power.

Unsere Opfer's oral histories show us that as long as the concept of power remains vertical, or hierarchical (like phallic towers, obelisks, and the Washington Monument), it is not just women who will always be interpellated as subaltern but the vast majority of men as well. This is because *most* texts that protest asymmetries of power nonetheless wish to retain some of these hierarchies and simply switch their position (or that of their collective) from the bottom to the top. Writ large, World War II also reflects this paradox, as those nations that dubbed themselves the Allies, fighting for the right of all people to self-determination, were all brutal colonizing regimes, whether in South America, the Caribbean, Africa, Asia, Oceania, or South Asia.

Even "Encounter," which seeks connection between postwar African Americans and Francophone Black Africans, uses troubling hierarchies in its sweeping statements on the collective mind-set of the latter: "This bitter ambition is shared by his fellow colonials, with whom he has a common language, and whom he has no wish whatever to avoid; without whose sustenance, indeed, he would be almost altogether lost in Paris. They live in groups together, in the same neighborhoods, in student hotels and under conditions which cannot fail to impress the American as almost unendurable."[41] By reading them so disparagingly as "colonials," Baldwin invokes a vertical interpellation, their dimensionality collapsed into one of a subaltern Other, suggesting that he is attempting to retain multidimensionality for his African American *flâneur*. After all, what is most striking about *Notes* is its refusal to interpellate the African American in Paris vertically. Upon encountering white American men, the two are more tongue-tied, confused as to their relation to one another in this postwar spacetime, raising an interesting comparison with Sissie and Marija, in which Black Subjects wonder at how to interpellate the whiteness they encounter and their own relationship to it. However, in *Notes*, as in *Killjoy*, Black African men are overwhelmingly interpellated through a colonialist spacetime in which, whether colonized or recently postcolonial, they remain "in-between": above Black women but below white men. Through these considerations, the metaphor of the Eiffel Tower now suggests a hierarchy of Blackness, a structure that supports horizontality but, at the end, is vertical: Baldwin's "Negro American" is a far more complex, reflective human being than the vague collective of the French African in *Notes*.

These hierarchies are not limited to "Encounter on the Seine": even as *Notes* provides these spaces for Blackness to intersect, it closes down others, not simply through being unaware or unreflective, but through explicit foreclosure. That is, Baldwin's interpellations sometimes reveal highly vertical logics that act against his ultimate ideals. This, I would argue, is the threat of the Eiffel Tower metaphor: that it is easy to collapse back into hierarchical thinking.

The last part of Geraldine Murphy's essay "Subversive Anti-Stalinism: Race and Sexuality in the Early Essays of James Baldwin" engages with this problem: it goes where many Baldwin scholars fear to tread—his implicit and sometimes explicit hierarchization of bodies and his very human bigotries and phobias that we recognize in our now and can thus see existing unrealized in the personal experiences he narrates. Murphy locates these failed moments through rhetoric: where it turns from respectful, sympathetic, careful, and considered—as when considering a peer—to denigration and insult. In other words, it is when the interpellative rhetoric shifts its interpellative viewpoint from the horizontal to the vertical, either looking up in wondrous awe or, in this case, looking down with contempt.

Murphy begins with Baldwin's problematic rhetoric in "Everybody's Protest Novel," pointing out that his is not an intellectual critique of Wright's work but rather a critique based on the suggestion that Wright and Beecher Stowe are "locked together" in battle, "this web of lust and fury" where "Black and white can only thrust and counter-thrust, long for each other's slow, exquisite death."[42] This section adds nothing to the argument and at best is juvenile, at worst phobic, as if the two authors' creative claims are as grotesque and amoral as the idea of the two of them having sex.

"Subversive Anti-Stalinism" ties its critique to Baldwin's discussion and defense of homosexuality through "Cold War liberalism," asserting that "Baldwin staked the male homosexual's claim for the same kind of complex subjectivity he had demanded for the African American." Murphy writes that "the title of his most explicit postwar statement, 'Preservation of Innocence' (1949), suggests his strategy for reconciling homosexuality and Cold War liberalism."[43] Yet as William A. Cohen notes in his review of *Another Country*, gender is "rigidly fixed" for Baldwin. Murphy concurs, pointing to *Giovanni's Room* and the "models of essentialist feminine masochism and passivity" that characterize his female characters in his novels. While I would argue that the misogyny Murphy finds expressed by David and Giovanni is ambiguous, possibly descriptive rather than prescriptive, Giovanni is often a painful stereotype of the sexually ambiguous and effete Mediterranean male, one who falls victim to floods of tears and crimes of passion over his virtue, while David, described as "blonde and gleaming," is the stereotypical white American butch—perhaps in turmoil within but outside always projecting a stony masculine strength. In other words, it is not coincidental that "Encounter on the Seine" chooses such a phallic structure to interpellate only male Subjects.

Equally if not more important is Baldwin's almost exclusive use of "he" in *Notes* as well as the majority of his essays, late or early, when discussing the "Negro." Murphy never comments on this, but in her critique of Baldwin she does remark that "Baldwin was essentially a critic of heterosexism rather than sexism" and "he wasn't above deploying gender categories to his own advantage. Suspect as a gay man, politically and psychologically, Baldwin was more eager to appropriate masculinity than revise it."[44] In other words, whether consciously or not, Baldwin is not seeking to upend gender hierarchies but to manifest equal, or horizontal, relations between men across racial and sexual boundaries. In "What Does It Mean to Be an American? The Dialectics of Self-Discovery in Baldwin's Paris Essays," Kingston University scholar James Miller has shown how Baldwin's "On the Discovery of What It Means to Be an American"[45] describes an all-male world in which the only Black female to emerge is Bessie Smith, who brings out the "nigger" in him.[46] Smith is hailed as an icon for strong Black womanhood in Black feminist discourses, but Baldwin's reference is at best ambivalent: "[Smith] helped me to dig back to the way I myself must have spoken when I was a pickaninny."[47]

This blindness—the marginalization of women, sometimes even of queerness—is of course quite common to many discourses from the postwar era, underscoring that, while the World War II and the postwar epistemology offer multiplicity, they are far from delivering it in every moment. If nothing else, this highlights the difference between the dominant way in which these eras are narrated—through linear spacetimes—and the ways in which they are thus distorted.

Chapter 4 of this book, "Axes of Asymmetry," explores the material effects of that distortion—that is, when World War II is narrated through linear spacetime and how Epiphenomenal time proves a useful remediating agent. More specifically, after noting the way in which discourses on the African Diaspora in World War II starkly reveal the asymmetrical socioeconomic and political clout of distinct Diaspora collectives, the chapter then points to a stunning erasure—that is, the histories of hundreds of millions of Black African women in the war.

It is hard to find these women, I show, when histories of Africa from both Africa and the West coalesce in their verticalities to produce a spacetime narrative that effectively bars the majority of women from acknowledgment. By dividing African histories into, roughly, three periods, all of which signify one period of specifically white domination from the late nineteenth to the mid- to late twentieth century, the history of Africa is reduced to a simple notation depending on whether white men or Black men were in power. All the other people, events, histories, changes, and so forth are erased because they fail to be recognized, ironically, as meaningfully intersecting with the ramifications of European colonialism. In other words, while it is women who are most obviously erased, most Black African men are erased from this as well—or else reduced to statistics.

Aidoo's *Killjoy* focuses on this problem of coalescing hierarchies—specifically Black African and white Western heteropatriarchal logics of interpellation. It is also *Killjoy* that provides the first solution to this problem of a linear history that marginalizes if not erases female agency—a solution that will be explored and further expanded on in "Axes of Asymmetry" but is briefly outlined here.

By beginning with Epiphenomenal time, the fact of her existence, her movement, *Our Sister Killjoy* effectively inserts Sissie into an otherwise forbiddingly patriarchal spacetime—not unlike the way in which Condé manifests Veronica through the fact of her present existence. This incursion is most subversive in Sissie's queer encounter with Marija. Although "nothing really happens," the text upends a patriarchal linearity by creating same-sex desire as "bush" and "bush" as that which lies outside the colonial spacetime, both temporally and spatially—that is, performances that used to predate, but now defy, colonial laws and mores.

"Bush" literally refers to a space, but now it also enjoys a complex time of being precolonial (because it is "bush"), colonial (we know the colonial rulers frowned on it as illegal and immoral behavior), and postcolonial in that Sissie recollects it through the frame of the colonial past. "Bush" now signifies practices and performances, like same-sex desire, that not only manifest as anticolonial but also link to interracial encounters outside of Africa. "Bush" becomes a signifier of the multivalent Epiphenomenal moment that is subsumed by no one linear spacetime but intersects with all of them. In a moment of queer desire, one that she notes bars her from interpellating herself as queerly desiring on the linear spacetime that marks precolonial, colonial, and now postcolonial Ghana, Sissie uses her "bush" memory to reflect on how and where this queerness does manifest in her "now." It does so in the romantic admiration of a postwar German housewife toward a Black African woman;[48] it does so in that African woman's displaced expression of wishing she were a Black man so that she might have a sexual affair; and it does so in the scandalized tones of a colonizing white female teacher in Ghana, in the unspoken reference to erotic play in the school between the girls and the also vaguely referenced practice of same-sex desire that precedes colonial rule. Queerness, then, *Killjoy* shows us, is not nonexistent in linear timelines but is manifested at the intersection of those timelines (postwar Germany and postcolonial Ghana). Far from being marginal and therefore isolated, Aidoo shows us how queer desire actually links and connects, producing richly layered, textured moments.

Our Sister Killjoy's "bush" strategy is a useful and necessary corrective to the "Eiffel Tower Effect"[49]—when hierarchies like heteropatriarchy coalesce to produce a grand vertical structure that easily incorporates horizontal relationships and is not challenged by them but perhaps made even stronger. Despite its multiplicities and erratic movement, its defiance of linear graphing, both white and Black discourses on World War II often resemble the Eiffel Tower in that they are composed of many intersecting strands but generally move vertically rather than horizontally—that is, linear spacetimes and their hierarchical arrangements create a mostly vertical structure. Yet as "Axes of Asymmetry" shows, once Epiphenomenal time is added to this interpellation, World War II and the postwar era offer astonishing possibilities for manifesting Blackness as it intersects across the globe and reflects back profound nuances on the human condition.

4

Axes of Asymmetry

The discipline known as Black Atlantic studies has, arguably, long escaped the confines of its explicit spatial and temporal parameters—at least informally. Scholars such as Ivan Van Sertima, Stefan Goodwin, Jeremy Lawrance, and John K. Brackett have uncovered Atlantic histories of Black Africans and Black Europeans who lived before "Blackness" was invented as a racial category—indeed, before "Europe" was conceived as an organizing identity for the Western part of the Eurasian continent.[1] The historians Edward Alpers ("The African Diaspora in the Indian Ocean")[2] and Cassandra Pybus (*Black Founders*)[3] have complicated our understanding of Middle Passage trajectories, showing us Black slaves shipped to India, U.S. Blacks who owned Black slaves (slaves who were not loved ones purchased because they could not be freed under law), U.S. Black slaves who were taken with the British "First Fleet" to England's new Australian penal colony, and an African slave trade that was not limited to West Africa but was active in East Africa, the Indian Ocean, and beyond.

Discourses that lean toward or even advocate a vertical or hierarchical organization for Blackness (wherein one body represents the many) typically exclude these Blacks from their purview, but they can be excluded even when the goal is quite the opposite—that is, to simply seek and recapture *all* the histories of the "Black Atlantic." In "The Legacy of the Atlantic Program," the famed anthropologist and former head of the Johns Hopkins University Atlantic Program, Sidney Mintz, reflects on the effects of these strictures on the program's scholarly mission:

> The limitations of [Johns Hopkins University's] Atlantic Program, I suppose, had to do principally with a kind of conceptual problem that is difficult to explain concisely. One could say—and this has been my view of it all along—that the Program represented a particular epoch in the history of the world economy; and because it did, it had to do with a particular relationship among societies

and states, a relationship that over time has continued changing. Since, let's say, the zenith of this Atlantic system or this Atlantic economy . . . there has been a continuing rearrangement, renego-tiation, reordering of relationships among regions and continents, and among states. In a sense, then, the Program had committed the participants to a particular history and geographical frame which is not always easy to leave behind.[4]

Here Mintz identifies "a particular history and geographical frame" as the cause of this "conceptual problem"—in other words, the arrangement of time and space as a theoretical analytic. He goes on to argue that "this Atlantic system" has experienced a "continuing rearrangement, renego-tiation, reordering of relationships" that is reminiscent of Epiphenomenal spacetime in its emphasis on interpellations through horizontal, or peer, relations and its differing manifestations from moment to moment. This is contrasted against the "particular history and geographical frame" through which researchers were expected to create their projects, suggesting a stric-ture based on borders that interfere with this "continual rearrangement."[5] Without meaning to, Mintz and his colleagues in the Atlantic Program found themselves restricted by borders of their own making.

I call this phenomenon "qualitative collapse"—that is, the collapse of meaningful, layered, rich, and nuanced interpellations (in this case, of Blackness) that occurs when seeking to interpellate the diversity of Blackness through the parameters of linear spacetime. I would argue that qualitative collapse happens far more frequently than we realize: as Mintz notes, he and other well-meaning, highly accomplished, and intelligent scholars realize that the seemingly neutral parameters they have chosen, such as the "Black Atlantic," preclude the undertaking of research proj-ects that I believe are vital to a more comprehensive understanding of Blackness. As *Physics of Blackness* has demonstrated already, it is often the implicit linearity we attribute to space and time that inhibits our research and causes a qualitative collapse of Blackness, in effect collapsing multiple dimensions of interpellation and generating paradoxes within the dis-course, as the complexity of the construct runs up against the simplicity of strictly linear spacetime parameters.

This limitation against inclusive, diverse interpellations, or interpreta-tions of Blackness that are rich, nuanced, and varied in their meaning, is hardly limited to scholars who engage with the Black Atlantic. This frustrating failure to create cogent narratives that interpellate a collective's identity as diverse and complex (and therefore usefully applicable to understanding the complicated nature of that collective) has been noted as a problem for left-wing progressives by social scientist, feminist theorist, and geographer Doreen Massey. In her 1992 article "Politics and Space/Time" published by *The New Left Review*, Massey, in a section titled "An Alternative View of Space," writes,

> A first requirement of developing an alternative view of space is that we should try to get away from a notion of society as a kind of 3-D (and indeed more usually 2-D) slice which moves through time. . . . Second, we need to conceptualize space as constructed out of interrelations and interactions at all spatial scales, from the most local level to the most global. . . . Third, this in turn means that the spatial has *both* an element of order and an element of chaos (or maybe it is that we should question that dichotomy also).[6]

Massey constructs these "requirements" in order to overcome dichotomous interpellations in which a Subject must be split one way or the other. This can also be understood as the collapse of dimensions, or ways of seeing and understanding (interpellating) the collective in all its diverse intersections with other collectives. Massey also argues that the interpellative space should incorporate "interrelations and interactions," or what *Physics of Blackness* reads as horizontality and, as I explain later, what Evan Mwangi terms "internal heteroglossia," or the need to focus on how members of a peer collective speak to one another rather than pose questions through an inhibiting analytical frame: linear spacetime. Massey usefully critiques ostensibly leftist poststructuralist theorists such as Fredric Jameson and Michel Foucault for divorcing the complications of space in their theorization of time. While Massey reads Jameson as initially calling for a corrective to this separation, her book *For Space* asserts that it has been used to negative effect in the process of interpellation, or "invention."[7] Yet, later in *For Space*, Massey almost wistfully acknowledges that the dream of realizing the potential of horizontality remains worth pursuing, even if it seems tantalizingly out of reach: "We know then that the 'presentness' of the horizontality of space is a product of the multitude of histories whose resonances are still there, if we would but see them, and which sometimes catch us with full force unawares."[8] Massey's use of "presentness" recalls

Epiphenomenal spacetime's emphasis on the "now," although here Massey has space alone in mind. Like *For Space*, *Physics of Blackness* also asserts that horizontal interpellations render a "multitude of histories whose resonances are still there" and can in fact be seen by us if we understand that moment of horizontal interpellation as the intersection of two spacetimes rather than of a separate time and space, as Massey seems to imply.

The solution I embrace in this chapter can also be inferred from Massey's third "requirement" quoted before: that there be both chaos and order. As shown throughout this book, by combining the fixity of linear spacetime with the chaos of unpredictable and immeasurable dimensions of interpellations, we can use the orientation provided by the fixed frame to then interpellate the diversity of that moment in all its manifestations in that spacetime.

Here I translate Massey's critique of limited 2-D/3-D interpellation as the moment of qualitative collapse when linear strictures erase or marginalize the interpellation of multidimensional Blackness—and may then "cast off" that part of its collective that is thereby deemed irrelevant or inauthentic. The first half of the chapter focuses largely on the World War II/postwar era, seeking to illustrate how it imposes limits even as it offers greater opportunities for interpellating multidimensional Blackness than are available when focusing only on the four centuries of the Middle Passage as a time frame, because it directly involves all collectives in the Black and African Diasporas: the Americas; Europe; North, West, East, Central, and South Africa; Australia and New Zealand; South Asia; Asia; the Middle East; and the islands of Oceania. At the same time, the very linear, vertical, and hierarchical way in which the Second World War is narrated in almost all dominant discourses creates exclusions that operate on a scale that equals if not surpasses that of the linear spacetime of the Middle Passage epistemology. The second half of this chapter therefore specifically examines how addressing this collapse in the now and reorienting one's question about these absences from the vertical to the horizontal can in fact help retrieve these lost collectives. Moving through my own research as well as studies conducted by others who are far more qualified than I am, the chapter shows how one can begin to secure answers to the question "What happened to the tens of millions of Black African women during World War II?" by reorienting the question from one based on vertical, hierarchical presumptions to one that seeks what Mwangi calls an "internal heteroglossia," or horizontal orientation.

One can see how space and time can become divorced from one another in theorization: it was Einstein who added space to Newton's concept of time, and Massey laments that the former somehow has once again become foreign to left-wing progressive theorizations. Yet Epiphenomenal time relies on an intersection of space and time, or spacetime, and in fact stresses this combination by using both space and time coordinates from the linear progress narrative in the production of the now.

Epiphenomenal time bears affinities with a phenomenological interpretation of time, because it insists that the time and place in which one uses one's senses to perceive and reflect always mediate one's interpellation through the "now." In philosophy, phenomenology holds that because our world can be observed and analyzed only through our senses, we can never claim to have unmediated access to it, to truly understand it independently of how our senses first present it to us. Consider how we experience time. We experience time in moments: moments of thought, observation, conversation, action, listening, daydreaming, fright, love—sometimes all at once. Some moments seem very long to us as we pursue a thought or activity; others incredibly brief. Some moments are wholly conscious and seemingly self-controlled (when we are clear as to where we are and what we are doing); others are almost unconscious, reluctant, or wholly involuntary; most fall somewhere in between. However, if one consciously interpellates a given moment in order to understand the multiple dimensions of Blackness that manifest then, the more resistant interpellations (that can happen in any moment) can be understood as representing an ambiguous set of productive possibilities rather than a limitation.

Whereas linear time understands the past, present, and future as chronological, Epiphenomenal time understands one spacetime: the moment of the now, through which we imagine the past and also move into future possibilities (walking, thinking, talking). *Physics of Blackness* argues that one cannot use Epiphenomenal time without first locating oneself where and when one is in that now, then locating where and when one's space and one's time are fixed by the construct of linear spacetime. Yet once located in the now on that linear timeline, the moment is freed for exploring a broad variety of intersecting spacetimes for Blackness, some of which may contradict interpellations that make sense in other moments. Linear progress narratives are, as it were, "allergic" to contradictory interpellations, almost forcefully expelling them from discourse, especially when they fail to cohere to the cause-and-effect dynamic that drives their spacetime. Because they cannot interpellate dimensions of Blackness that offer nonlinear or nonprogressive interpretations (e.g., Equiano's possibly lying about his life), forcing nonprogressive narratives into linear narrative frameworks will cause a qualitative collapse of Blackness. Rather than capturing the full multidimensionality of Blackness, linear spacetime generates paradoxes that manifest through failed interpellation, or qualitative collapse, which can create an either/or Blackness according to which one must choose one interpretation over the other to reposition Blackness in that linear spacetime.

A common example of such a qualitative collapse can happen in moments of Black counterdiscourse if one attempts to interpellate a Blackness that predates its "invention" as a racist category in the eighteenth and nineteenth centuries.[9] When racist discourse falsely asserts that African peoples and their descendants have contributed nothing to world civilizations, firmly shoving them off the plane of "world" (or Western) "civilization," Afrocentrists respond by citing the empires of Egypt and its predecessor Kush, the former being one of the few African cultures acknowledged by Eurocentric historians as worthy of recognition. Without question, the continent of Africa boasts a number of civilizations (to explicitly meet the white European definition of the term: societies with permanent buildings, organized systems of government, and flourishing trade, as well as cultural or religious practices) that predate ancient Greece/Rome and should be included in dominant timelines of world civilizations. Most certainly the majority of peoples who ruled and contributed to these societies would meet our stereotypical notions of "Black" physiognomy. Yet were the Egyptians and Kushites "Black," at least within the qualitative dimension established by the linear progress narrative of the Middle Passage epistemology?

To historicize an identity within a linear progress narrative provides "order," as Massey puts it, or as this chapter specifies, origin, direction, and stability—but linear spacetime also complicates or even limits the historical fluidity of such an identity. One must pause at the Afrocentrists' counterracialization of Ramses (in response to Eurocentric attempts to read the ancient Egyptians as almost anything *but* African) and question the logic of what is being asserted here. As noted before, Ramses meets a stereotypical physiognomy, but he would not be called "Black," much less understand himself as matching *our* meaning of the term: a proud symbol of Black progress and its struggle for equal rights in a largely racist world.

The interpellation of Ramses is now paradoxical: he is either an oppressive African pharaoh or, as a "strong Black man," a symbol of resistance to oppression. (Ramses of course owned bodies that one would recognize as Black slaves.) In order to determine what Ramses is, then, once again through the linear progress narrative (whether based on the Middle Passage, Afrocentric, postcolonial, or Pan-African epistemology), Blackness is split into "authentic" and "inauthentic," "relevant" and "irrelevant." Each individual considering this question then places Ramses in one category or another. ("Ramses, then, is relevant to our discussion of Blackness" or "Ramses, then, is not really Black.")

When interpellated through the Middle Passage epistemology, Blackness has a limited set of *qualitative* values or denotations that link it to the events in that epistemology such as the commitment to collective and individual struggle, "racial uplift," and the maintenance of strong communities through "traditional" or heteropatriarchal family structures. More generally, the Middle Passage epistemology (like other established Black linear progress or antiprogress narratives—e.g., Afrocentrism, Pan-Africanism, Negritude, Afropessimism)[10] also links all Black collectives across the Diaspora to the experience of racism and the need to overcome it—so how can Ramses II be "Black"? Even further, what does it mean for us to claim him as "Black"? It is hard to interpellate Ramses (or any of the other African kings, queens, leaders, intellectuals, politicians, scientists, etc., whose physiognomy we would acknowledge as stereotypically "Black") within the qualitative definition of Middle Passage Blackness as making common cause with African Americans—or any other "Black" community fighting racism and seeking socioeconomic and political equality in the African Diaspora. In attempting to interpellate Ramses within this definition, we must produce Blackness as a fixed identity that transcends time and space; through this, Ramses no longer belongs to his own spacetime but retroactively becomes a denigrated "Negro" who must combat his oppression. A paradox or—as Massey terms it, "a dichotomous result"—now confronts us: was Ramses II a Black freedom fighter or a ruler of extraordinary and largely unquestioned power, one of the greatest and most oppressive in the history of Egyptian pharaohs?

It is the qualitative definition of Black progress that creates this dichotomy, a paradox that then "empties out" all meaning in qualitative collapse. The attempt to interpellate Ramses II through a Black progress narrative exposes the continuing attempt and subsequent failure of the progress narrative to interpellate Ramses. He is Black because he is a Black African, but he is not Black, because neither "Black" nor "African" operated as identities in Ramses's spacetime. Ramses II's life speaks to the greatness of African empires, but his unapologetic use of massive slave labor should "expel" him from Black progressive membership, the same way in which some discourses attempt to expel Blacks whose actions deliberately harmed other Blacks.

While we should perhaps not lose sleep over the "odd individual" whose terrible behaviors bar him, her, or them from full or perhaps even partial mention in a Black progress narrative, there are other Black individuals who are barred from mention who have not acted against the principle of striving for collective progress. This dichotomy also threatens to create interpellative problems for Blacks who, unlike the Egyptian pharaoh, move across the Atlantic at the same time as millions of Black Africans are being sailed to and sold into the Americas, but not in the same directions, veering away from our progress narrative.

Black slaves transported outside of the Americas to Europe, India, and elsewhere do not retain a collective identity. They are sold individually and disappear into households, perhaps factories, fields, or country roads and city streets, intersecting with populations at large. From the point of view of Black linear progress narratives, progress has not been achieved because the collective has evanesced (and is therefore unable to achieve its goal of overcoming racism), or read another way, their histories have become irrelevant to the collective historical theme of overcoming racism. Qualitatively speaking, it appears difficult if not impossible to interpellate Blackness using a Black Atlantic linear progress narrative in a significant and lasting way. In "The World Is All of One Piece: The African Diaspora and Transportation to Australia," which is included in Ruth Simms Hamilton's book *Routes of Passage*, Cassandra Pybus reprises a version of Sidney Mintz's question about the qualitative limits of Black Atlantic studies:

> A transnational historical consciousness and a capacity to encompass experience in disparate time and space are great strengths of African diaspora studies. In so far as there is a weakness, it is that the Atlantic world remains the locus of discussion. While some attention has begun to drift toward the Indian Ocean, less scholarship has been directed toward the distant Pacific. . . . In the diaspora at the detailed penal transportation records we can find

information about the African end of the eighteenth century that is very hard to come by elsewhere and that points in directions in which historians may not otherwise look.[11]

Pybus understands that her topic is framed by African Diaspora studies yet constrained by its "Atlantic focus", she then observes that despite this swirl of scholarly activity in the Atlantic, there is a "drift" and "direction" toward the Indian Ocean and the "distant Pacific." This passage draws a connecting line moving horizontally (well, south by southeast) from the moment of the American Revolution in the Middle Passage timeline to other moments in those kingdoms and empires that border the Indian Ocean and, more specifically, to the moment of the British penal colony of Australia.

By moving us horizontally into the Pacific, Pybus traces the journey of those (primarily) U.S. Blacks who allied with the defeated British and accompanied them on their return to England. Once there, the promised support from the Crown never materialized, and many of these former soldiers, spies, and support staff found themselves on the London streets. These (primarily) men would have been in competition with an already burgeoning class of the dispossessed filling the streets of London and other industrial centers. As Robert Hughes argues in his monumental history of the settling of white Australia, *The Fatal Shore*, land grabs by the aristocracy and the replacement of cottage industries with large industrialized factories deprived farmers, laborers, and urban workers of their former careers as well as prospects for new ones (many machines, such as looms, required fewer adult workers). Theft, especially with the poor now rubbing shoulders with the wealthy in crowded urban centers, skyrocketed, and Parliament responded with deeply punitive measures; to steal a bit of ribbon or bread could send you to prison or heavy labor or, most fearful of all, condemn you to "transport" (to a British penal colony). With the American colonies no longer available for convicts, Britain turned to its recently neglected "discovery" of Australia as a convenient replacement, and so white and Black Britons, along with a few U.S. and Caribbean Blacks, found themselves transported as part of the First Fleet settlers.

Pybus's second horizontal reading comes, counterintuitively, mostly through records created by hierarchies such as court, maritime, colonial, and penal records, due to the paucity of "horizontal" archives (correspondence between peers, diaries, etc.). Pybus, not unlike Hughes in *The Fatal*

Shore, constructs a *horizontal* narrative of these Black convicts and settlers through (unavoidably) mostly *vertical* archival sources: state, judicial, colonial, and penal records that read these human beings as mere numbers filling ships, accepting punishment, and perhaps enriching the Crown through forced labor. To an even greater extent than Hughes, Pybus works to retrieve the very multivalent human experiences behind these records of discipline and punishment, to see the interactions denoted, denounced, and pronounced through their eyes, so to speak, looking out horizontally rather than down from the (at least figurative) heights of the judge's bench and foreman's lash.

Yet despite these two horizontal readings, qualitative collapse looms here because Pybus has framed this history as a horizontal connection to what is ultimately a vertical framework that finds meaning in the struggle against racism. Pybus's *Black Founders* offers us a notable exception to our assumptions about Blackness, but in her work, as in other histories she mentions, Blackness evanesces as the convicts and settlers perhaps married, procreated, and most certainly died without moving a coherent Black Atlantic collective forward in its quest for equality in a majority white society. Or, rather more complicatedly, in *Black Founders* Blackness evanesces into either the white Australian population or the Australian Aboriginal population, in the latter case an indigenous Blackness. Most likely reflecting on this, Pybus herself does not think that this discovery of Australia's "Black founders" radically changes the history of the African Diaspora or Australia: "My point is not that this cohort of convicts is especially significant to the history of Australia—though it certainly challenges the conventional reading of the colonial experience—but to examine what it can tell us about the wider world."[12]

If we add Epiphenomenal time to our Black Atlantic frame, however, we can avoid the qualitative collapse that (re)produces these histories as interesting in their own right but marginal to our understanding of Black Atlantic history. Interpellated through Epiphenomenal time, the Blackness in *Black Founders* first changes a person's relationship to Blackness and indigeneity. Rather than simply "losing" indigenous status once captured and then sold, Blackness intersects twice more with indigeneity, and on two continents: North America and Australia. In both cases, indigenous peoples sometimes helped Black slaves escape, the latter often marrying into specific American Indian nations. Middle Passage U.S. Blackness now shares a spacetime through indigeneity and raises questions about

Central and South American intersections (such as the Garifunas of Nicaragua).[13] One might also see a third, more controversial intersection, between U.S. Blacks who "returned" to establish the free state of Liberia and the indigenous populations who found themselves oppressed in the resulting socioeconomic and political hierarchy. The qualitative value of Pybus's Blackness now meaningfully intersects with the Americas but is not swallowed by it, because the frame is horizontally comparative rather than vertically subordinating.

The intersection of Blackness with indigeneity in the Americas, Australia, and Africa also subverts the notion of a "purely" diasporic Blackness, even within the progress narrative itself, because the latter honors indigeneity as the "origin" to which the collective must eventually return. In this moment of interpellation, origin/home is achieved not necessarily through return but through intersections with other "first nations" in the Atlantic and Pacific. Even further, we can see how Blackness, in intersecting with indigeneity when (formally) seeking "return," as in Liberia, might produce not egalitarian unity but instead oppressive hierarchy.

Black Founders also provides us with perhaps unheard of dimensions of Blackness that, once recognized, might usefully connect to other possible spacetimes that share this dimension. As noted before, the "Atlantic Blacks" who arrived with the First Fleet and on subsequent convict ships experienced a range of lives or careers that cannot be summed up through one collective trajectory, especially that of the progress narrative. Pybus shows that in our present moment of reading, Blackness becomes ambiguous in its meaning in these early colonies. On the one hand, racial designations are clearly marked in the official records, but unlike in the Americas, socioeconomic and political castes are not created to wholly segregate them. There are many marriages one would designate as "interracial," but even if one could access some understanding of how "interracial marriage" would translate in this spacetime, marriage is rarely an ideal that denotes the cessation of difficulties over differences. As more than one wag has pointed out, the dominance of heterosexual marriage certainly does not reflect an egalitarian harmony of relations between the sexes. The marriages in question are thus racialized outside of social racializations, meaning that to be Black in these colonies does not automatically designate a subaltern status below that of whites. In cases where Black convicts were executed or subjected to physical punishment (whipping was the most common), we might see racially motivated causes, but in the brutal tide of regular executions and torturous punishment, it is difficult to extrapolate consistently a narrative in which this Blackness can be separated from the brutal imperial and capitalist caste system that ruled all British subjects, including the white working poor.

Blacks intermixing with the white working poor populations in England and Australia intersect with similar interactions during the earlier spacetime of indentured servitude in the United States and the later one of late nineteenth-century Irish immigration to northeastern urban centers of the United States. If we step back from Pybus's initial frame, which connects the history of the Black Atlantic in Australia horizontally, and instead honor the horizontality of her interpellations of Black individuals and their intersections (through marriage, penal life, executions, manumission, etc.), one can read this history as a series of moments that intersect not only with Black Atlantic histories in the Americas but also with histories in Europe, Africa, and perhaps India. It should be noted that, while we are discovering intersections of collectives, we do so wholly within idealist frameworks that can be further interpellated only through individuals who make up those collectives; beneficially, however, the collective identities that intersect with these individuals produce yet more collectives in more spacetimes—more dimensions of Blackness across the Atlantic, Pacific, and Indian Oceans.

While the era of the Middle Passage produces many and varied kinds of Blackness through the intersection of linear and Epiphenomenal time, the conflated eras of World War II and the postwar era offer yet more. I understand World War II and the postwar period as a conflation of eras because it is impossible to pinpoint where one ends and the other begins; however, when we are operating with Epiphenomenal time, this ambiguity is productive rather than restrictive. Indeed, breadth, depth, ambiguity, ambivalence, and dominance are the strengths contributed by these overlapping eras: breadth because World War II involved almost the majority of Black Africans and Black Diasporans across the globe, whereas slavery—which forms the cornerstone of the Middle Passage epistemology—did not; depth because the various narratives, such as that of Black African men attempting to resist forcible conscription by French and British colonial forces, or that of African American men and women who fought for the right to be drafted, require explanation and further research; ambiguity because we find Blackness where we do not expect it and struggle to interpret it, such as Black German individuals who served in Hitler's army and Black Brazilian troops tasked with defending Italy; ambivalence because it is a war and its equally destructive aftermath ironically connects the African Diaspora many times over with ease and diversity; and finally, dominance because World War II and the postwar era constructed an interpellative frame that has been used by so many across the globe, a frame that highlights the contemporary and global importance of Blackness far more frequently than themes of the Middle Passage ever do. While the rise of the BRIC nations (Brazil, Russia, India, and China), the Arab Spring, and other sociopolitical and economic events seem to signal the framing of a new era, journalists, pundits, and politicians alike still interpret many of these events as effects of the World War II/postwar era.

Even the most rigid histories cannot sustain a completely linear Second World War narrative. For example, the invasion of Poland in 1939 must be explained by the rise of Nazism, which perhaps requires a notation about the Versailles Treaty. Likewise, the bombing of Pearl Harbor is necessary to explain the entrance of the United States into the war as a direct combatant. The Second World War, therefore, has at least two beginnings and, even by conservative estimates, at least two endings: the surrender of the Nazis in Berlin and the signed surrender by the Japanese on the USS *Missouri* in Tokyo Bay.

This gives us a war with at least two timelines to which there correspond two themes, two notions of progress, and many ways in which occupied nations must be understood: as collaborators, as wholly oppressed, as underground resisters, and so on. This nonlinear set of peoples, places, and events forces anyone seeking interpellations through World War II to accept all the exceptions to its linear progress narrative—that is, it forces researchers to incorporate great nuance into their interpellations (in asking when the Second World War ended, for example, we have to amend the question to reflect all the surrenders and dates that dominant discourses on World War II cite in response because, whether there were multiple wars or one great war may be a matter of definition, but there is no question that there were multiple narratives that intersected). This means that qualitative collapse will occur less frequently in interpellations made through a wholly linear progress narrative on the war (because dominant discourses do not offer, really, any wholly linear narratives of it), but when it does, the effect is almost always "deafening," as if it were drowning out alternative interpellations.[14]

Blackness can manifest through this multidimensionality, in most cases quite easily. In contrast to the difficulty involved in explaining how Blacks from the Atlantic found themselves in Australia, the global reach of the Second World War makes it easy to explain how Blackness has spread almost everywhere. When using both Epiphenomenal and linear space-times to interpellate Blackness in these eras, no long, creative narratives are needed to explain the presence of West Africans under British rule, East Africans under Italian Fascist rule, or the fight for equality both at home and abroad that was the self-appointed task of many an African American man or woman in uniform; moreover, using both spacetimes enables Black European studies to explain without much difficulty how Blacks of African descent came to fight under Hitler. We can arrive at these explanations by starting with the individual, rather than the collective, as a point of interpellation. We can then link such an individual to his, her, or their variously realized collective identities (understanding that we should never claim that an individual is fully realized, as we can work within distinct spacetimes only as they are imagined in the now, not in both the present and the past).

Unfortunately, many of these dimensions as interpellated through the postwar epistemology are easily achieved through vertical structures: we need only locate (in ascending order) a military battalion, a regiment, or a division that would contain Black soldiers and its encampments and headquarters. Vertical readings alone can often interpellate an agential and diverse Blackness: Black soldiers and field nurses with agency, Black civilians with choices, and a whole roster of intersections with a broad variety of peers (soldiers and civilians) across vast geographies. At first glance, performing vertical interpellations through linear narratives appears to bear the same fruit as a horizontal reading: Blackness with agency and diversity.

This might explain why so many Black collective progress narratives of World War II use this multidimensionality to produce hierarchical, or vertical, interpellations for the collective. The "Windrush narrative" of Black Britain, for example, readily narrates the contributions of Black British Caribbeans in the Second World War, yet uses a progress narrative to interpellate this Blackness. Like the histories of African American men who fought for the United States during World War I, the "Windrush" narrative underscores the painful hypocrisy of serving the British Crown only to be treated as an undesirable emigrant in the postwar era.[15] Drawing on oral histories of service in the war and archival records from the British War Office, *Windrush: The Irresistible Rise of Multi-Racial Britain* (1999) interpellates Black Britishness as agential and diverse, a proud component of the history of World War II but of official British histories of the war more particularly.[16]

To be sure, even when operating within World War II/postwar frameworks, we encounter obstacles. Hierarchies of power are not (unfortunately) wholly erased, and they can be complicated by the complexities of global alliances and rivalries (no matter how easily they are manifested in the postwar epistemology). The postwar epistemology's emphasis on the "now," in the absence of a geographical center (a component of even the most traditional narratives of the Second World War/postwar era),[17] allows, say, Samoan warriors aiding the Allies to be interpellated through collective identities that certainly include hierarchal structures (e.g., the military command structure) but also relationships whereby power must constantly be negotiated (e.g., in relationships between soldiers or between soldiers and civilians). The "now" complicates power, meaning that while an Epiphenomenal interpellation enables agency, it will also reflect those vertical hierarchies that inevitably accompany so many moments of interpellation in every individual life across the globe.[18]

Dominant discourses on World War II reflect these hierarchies and suffer from both spatial and temporal "narrowness."[19] Spatial narrowness is a consequence of the way in which the spacetime of "the world" is denoted. The Second World War was a global war that claimed tens of millions of civilian lives both directly and thousands of miles from the frontline battlefields, in locations including South America, South Asia, Australia, and of course sub-Saharan Africa. Yet narrative manifestations of this war rarely stray beyond pitting Germany and Japan against Britain and the United States (with Italy switching sides again). This bifurcates a considerably more unwieldy geography into what has become known as the European and Pacific theaters.[20] There is also a temporal constriction: those who seek to study the Second World War beginning with 1939 will not understand why both the Allies and the Axis powers became anxious over their colonial holdings, why Russia-cum-the-Soviet Union and Italy switched sides, or, for that matter, why this supposedly grand and perhaps "ultimate" moral conflict between the forces of democracy and the forces of fascism appears to have benefitted Germany and Japan far more than those who suffered under their yoke.

These spatiotemporal constrictions and their painfully ironic postwar ramifications are not lost on Black African scholars and leaders seeking to interpellate their nations through the postwar era through their roles in World War II. In Birgit Morgenrath and Karl Rössel's anthology of oral histories, *Unsere Opfer Zählen Nicht: Die Dritte Welt im Zweiten Weltkrieg* (*Our Victims Do Not Count: The Third World in the Second World War*), the scholar and activist Kum'a Ndumbe III notes in the foreword,

> The history of the Second World War has proven, like every history, to be that of the victors, but also that of the wealthy and propertied. In spite of their military defeats Germany and Japan are still counted among the victors in the writing of this story: Even though the historiography produced by both countries has had to submit to critical scrutiny and corrections, they are still accorded an equal ranking on the scale of humanity. However, those who were forgotten after the War—as if they had never even existed during the war—who, with their children, must (re)learn this history without ever finding their own deeds in the historical narrative, they belong in fact to the defeated. Defeated and without a voice, this is how hundreds of millions of people and their descendants still live even today in Africa, Asia, Latin America and the Pacific region.[21]

What *Unsere Opfer* underscores, above all else, is that the Second World War looks very different when interpellated from the viewpoint of the formerly or still colonized, and it is this set of ever-shifting minority viewpoints (the diversity of which will be discussed later in the chapter) that the postwar epistemology incorporates as the template for the collective identities of the African Diaspora.[22] *Unsere Opfer* does not distinguish between the colonial rulers who were part of the (supposedly prodemocratic) Allies and those who were part of the Axis. From the postcolonial viewpoint, they were all colonizers. Yet in interpellating in the "now" and assembling peer groups for its oral histories of collective identities (laborers, prisoners, soldiers), this collection of horizontal or peer histories interpellates the "Third World in World War II"[23] in a way that belies traditional frames of a battle between good (Allies) and evil (Axis):

> Great Britain was the largest colonial power when the Second World War began, presiding over an empire that encompassed a quarter of the earth as well as a quarter of the world's population,

and stretched from Jamaica and Latin America over East Africa
and India almost to Southeast Asia and the [Central Pacific]. Taken
altogether, the French colonies in the Caribbean, North and West
Africa, Vietnam, Melanesia and Polynesia were twenty times larger
than France itself and had more than one hundred million inhabitants. With Libya, Eritrea and Somaliland, the fascist government
of Italy also ruled over a conglomerate of colonies four times larger
than its own country, and the colonial Netherland-Indies, for
example Indonesia, was owned by greater Western Europe.

Germany had to abandon its colonies after the First World War,
so their reconquest became one of the war aims of the National
Socialist regime. For the Allies the colonies were indispensable.
They provided the essential raw materials for war at bargain rates,
had millions of soldiers to be placed into the armed forces as well
as millions more men and women to be put to work, often through
forced labor.[24]

Despite *Unsere Opfer*'s exciting range of discourses—in addition to
Black African combatants from Mali, Ethiopia, Senegal, Cameroon, and
Burkina Faso and Black Diasporan combatants from Brazil and Suri-
nam, it incorporates the voices of nonwhite official combatants, guerillas,
and civilians pressed into service or who volunteered, such as Austra-
lian Aboriginal/Torres Strait Islanders, Black and indigenous Brazilians,
Palestinians, Egyptians, Filipinos, Vietnamese, Chinese, Thai, Burmese,
East Timorese, Maori, Solomon Islanders, and more—the largest group it
does not capture is enormously sobering: hundreds of millions of Black
African women.

This omission, we should be quick to acknowledge, is not unique to
Unsere Opfer: while most qualitative collapses are avoided through the
ambiguity of these conflated eras, the ease with which vertical interpellations offer pathways forward for Blackness means horizontal interpellations
occur far less often. The majority of books, articles, films, and television
programs devoted to Blacks in World War II focus on African American
men, with African American women a distant second, but still outnum-
bering Black African men, Black Anglophone Caribbeans / Black Britons,
Black Europeans, and Black Central and South Americans and Hispano-
phone/Lusophone Caribbeans, in that order. Black African women are
almost wholly absent.

As elaborated in chapter 2, the impossibility of firmly establishing a linear and direct causality from its origins to the occurrence of a complex event (which can prompt the feeling of being caught in Münchhausen's Trilemma) can make it difficult to establish one single cause of this absence, but hierarchies abound in both Black and white histories that intersect with the Black and African Diaspora. Such causes may include the relative wealth of the United States and the ability of a few hundred African American scholars to access its publishing houses but also the way in which Black U.S. participation in World War II neatly dovetails with the U.S. progress narrative that seeks to highlight its antiracist practices against those of fascist Germany, Italy, and Japan. In other words, the ease with which predominantly heteropatriarchal white and Black male narratives can provide a broad overview of antiracist progress that supposedly benefits all subaltern collectives has been taken to mean that women (and queers, and other Black collectives) need not be explicitly named, much less narrated.

At the same time, there is also socioeconomic clout that many African Americanists can access and deploy to continue the research and dissemination of African American progress narratives, and World War II offers a wealth of exemplary heroes, from the Black GIs dealing with racist white officers to the activism of A. Philip Randolph in seeking the desegregation of the armed forces. Through this valence—the U.S. Black struggle to progressively integrate into the armed forces and thus the nation-state more effectively—the narratives of Black women who served in the armed forces nicely combines patriotism with "race pride," and Black women can be interpellated as part of this grander narrative of World War II as "America's Battle for World Democracy" without the heterosexist and homophobic logics that prevent those hierarchical, vertical militaries and nation-states from ever being examined or questioned. In this frame, we see how African American men and women can interpellate their own histories through the themes established by the U.S. nation-state regarding its goals in fighting this war.

Yet not all Black minorities under domination by one of the Allies can interpellate themselves through patriotic nation-state narratives. While white national narratives that can accommodate Black progress during World War II allow for wholly or almost wholly vertical interpellations of this Blackness, the same is not true, of course, for those combatant nations that seek to minimize or hide their colonial histories, especially in narratives of national defense. In the case of France, the central role of its conscripted colonial forces challenges its own narrative of liberation at the hands of white Americans and the Free French forces. As Myron Eschenberg notes in his work "'Morts Pour La France': The African Soldier in France during the Second World War," "until recently many Frenchmen have preferred to avoid the painful story of France's defeat and later re-entry into the war as a minor player."[25] Eschenberg estimates that "Africans in 1940 constituted almost 9 percent of the French army in France, whereas for the entire First World War they may have approximated only 3 percent," but after the fall of Paris, the number increased dramatically: "At a conservative estimate, then, the French recruited in excess of 200,000 Black Africans during the Second World War."[26] Indeed, that so many prominent Black men of the Francophone Diaspora served in World War II—Léopold Senghor, Aimé Césaire, Frantz Fanon, and Léon Damas—attests to the extensive reach of the French military and later the Free French Army.[27]

In order to prevent the enormous qualitative collapse that is threatened by applying a vertical, linear progress narrative to the World War II/postwar era, in which Blackness is reduced to male combatants and Black women from Allied nations who served in the military, one must shift quite firmly to the horizontal, beginning with one's interpellative frame. Not unlike the historian who understands state historical documents as partial and subjective histories that lean heavily on vertical interpellations, applying a horizontal approach to research means reorienting the research question. The next part of this chapter explains this process first through a theorization by Evan Mwangi for Black African texts, then in reference to its application in the production of a history of Black Anglophone Caribbean women during World War II, before showing how it might be applied to retrieving and interpellating Black African women in the World War II/postwar and postcolonial eras.

Like this book and Massey's *For Space*, Evan Mwangi's *Africa Writes Back to Self: Metafiction, Gender and Sexuality* also circumvents vertical structures by arguing that we should understand African literary traditions as (horizontal) conversations between members of that tradition rather than as responses to Western interpellations through the postcolonial frame (which reflect a hierarchical, and thus vertical, status):

Since the mid-1980s, African novels have become markedly self-reflexive in the way they rewrite one another and draw attention to their own fictionality. They mark stylistic and thematic departures that deliberately undermine the nationalist and realist impulse that governed earlier writing. The novels further depart from the tradition of "writing back" to the European colonial center by focusing their gaze on local forms of oppression that are seen to parallel classical colonialism. . . . Examined here are contemporary African novels that demonstrate perceptible shifts in focus from issues of external colonialism to a more self-reflexive treatment of gender and sexual relations.[28]

By conflating self-reflexivity and fictionality, Mwangi's analysis in effect allows readers to overhear a conversation that does not posit Massey's unloved three-dimensional reality or fix the meaning to particular space-times. This emphasis on fiction points to many possibilities. Because these possibilities are self-reflexive, produced by the individual text in conversation or intersecting with other "interlocutory" texts, one can understand this as a model of Epiphenomenal time: "In the novels I examine here, resistance to the West may be seen to reside more potently in the texts' disregard or demotion of the West as the categorical and ineluctable point of reference in the representation and self-fashioning of the Global South; the texts resist the West by erasing it from local discourses on postcolonial cultures, aesthetics, and politics of identity."[29] Similar to Massey's call for a horizontal application of space that would enable interpellation and analysis to posit a multiplicity of dimensions, Mwangi understands horizontal resistance to verticality through the specific and explicit use of space as place, or an individual's locale. He adds that "individual texts are more preoccupied in writing back to themselves and other local texts to address emerging realities and to express the growing diversity of identities in Africa."[30] These moments *resist* vertical structures of interpellation in their "internal heteroglossia," suggesting that they cannot be read as answers that presciently respond to the questions we formulate about their status as "womanist" or "postcolonial" or "queer"—Western terms that frame the text as an informant rather than as an interlocutor.

In asking how any Black African novel published in the 1980s reads itself through the "postcolonial moment" with no regard for its actual content, the reader has already begun a distorted process of interpellation, even if the intent behind the question is to achieve a sympathetic understanding. Mwangi spells out the politics of this vertical interpellation in the negotiation between African author, text, and Western literary scholar:

Given the predominant notion that African literature is about "writing back" to the European canon, my proposal that African arts are primarily writing back to themselves might give the impression that this book is a subversion or parody of . . . *The Empire Writes Back*. . . . It is not. Rather, I am extending the idea in Ashcroft and colleagues' authoritative and seminal analysis in a direction they have indicated, especially in their discussion of how we can rethink postcolonial studies to pay more attention to local texts and contexts. I am particularly attracted to their prognosis toward the end of their book to the effect that the future of postcolonial studies resides in the consideration of local conditions and the influence of global moments on particular instances and spaces.[31]

As Mwangi reveals, the implied horizontal exchange of "writing back" belies its implicit verticality in postcolonial studies as we understand them today. Scholars of the postcolonial tradition might understand themselves as sympathetic readers of these African texts of "internal heteroglossia," because they are intent on making horizontal, or peer, interpellations as allies, but this passage shows how verticality remains in these moments. It is present through the question itself, which presumes that the African text interpellates itself as a subaltern expression in a postcolonial history rather than as an African text engaging likeminded interlocutors in the interpellation of its "now" through many possible distinct spacetimes. Returning briefly to our question about Ramses II ("Was he Black or not?"), we can see the hierarchical, or vertical, logic that girds our question: in one valence, we subordinate Ramses's spacetime to ours by assuming our category of Blackness is transcendental—figuratively above any of the identity categories he might have used (and the latter are likely quite lofty!).

Western readers are not the only ones to pose vertical questions to contemporary Black African discourses; the desire on the part of Black Atlantic scholars to retrieve a marginalized history through what they *know* to be vertical sources and restrictions can also lead them to pose a question that appears to be "horizontal" but is in fact irretrievably vertical. We find this phenomenon in a work by Ben Bousquet and Colin Douglass, *West Indian Women at War: British Racism in World War II*, in which they take up such a historical task as a corrective to the paucity of extant histories on their chosen topic. Yet as the title itself indicates, the text does not understand itself as wholly "free" of the vertical as Mwangi stresses that horizontality should be. The introduction makes more explicit the central role of hierarchical state structures and colonial regimes in the interpellation of Black Anglophone Caribbean women through World War II:

> To fully appreciate the position of West Indian servicewomen, we have to look at a range of wider questions, which touch on fundamental issues of war policy and colonialism. These wider questions address the role of women in the war, the position of Black people in Britain and the Caribbean, the political climate in the Caribbean, the different faces of wartime racism and the relationship between Britain and America. These are all major issues, which are integral to this book. It is only once we get a clearer picture of these issues that we can ask the all important question: why did they join?[32]

This passage appears to stress multidimensional interpellations, but the categories chosen are overwhelmingly vertical ones: collective identities located in military and state hierarchies. Unlike *Black Founders*, which uses state documents to explore individual lives, *West Indian Woman at War* at first attempts a collective interpellation, which, combined with these hierarchical identities, precipitates a qualitative collapse, and the paradox produces these women as subalterns, either objects or duped supporters of the British military-industrial complex. As chapter headings such as "From Plantocracy to Third Reich," "A Woman's Place," and "Forgotten Heroines" attest, Bousquet and Douglas choose to read these women as objects whose heroic struggle is a testament both to their courage and to the obstacles that lie ahead for the Black Atlantic collective as a whole.

In the interviews that follow, we catch a glimpse into these women's lives, but primarily we read their reactions to being negatively interpellated by these various hierarchical and deeply bigoted powers—politicians, military brass, and so forth. We do not learn how Black Caribbean women relate to West Indian men, to Black African women, to white working-class women, or to many of the other collective identities with which they would have come into contact and that no doubt would have produced rather rich insights and interpellations. As Mwangi warns, this is what happens even when we attempt a sympathetic reading with the intention of recognizing and blunting the impact of vertical interpellation.

Yet when interpellating Black African women's identities out of World War II, attempting to draw a "Pybusian" horizontal line to connect Black African women to a Black African or Black Diasporic progress narrative will not work. Pybus can point to a "new" spacetime (Australia during the era of the Middle Passage), but Black African women are still in Africa and thus folded into and erased by the linearity of Black African progress narratives that divide the history of Africa into "precolonial," "colonial," and "postcolonial" eras. Because these eras are wholly hierarchical, denoting only which race of men controlled the widest swathes of Africa, the Black African women of the World War II era cannot interpellate themselves through this epistemology's linear spacetime. Because the conscription of African men by the colonial powers radically altered the agricultural, commercial, and industrial landscapes of the colonies, the histories of Black African women would be quite prominent in the histories of Africa during World War II.

As Mwangi emphasizes, it is the *question* that must be changed and reoriented, no longer driven by the expectation that the text is the informant or even the interlocutor. Because no one has yet written a text that answers the question, "What were Black African women doing during World War II?" we must assume that the texts that contain our "answer" are not in conversation with us. In this moment of "now," we are unlikely to find a text that will answer that, because the "internal heteroglossia" of these texts will not interpellate Black women as an absence. Even further, they may not even interpellate Black African women as Black African women but rather through some other collective that actually foregrounds their agency—that is, the collective that defines what they were *doing* during these years. Finally, as I promised in the introduction, I can now explain why the use of "World War II" is also hierarchical, because it presumes that Black African women experienced these years primarily through the Second World War and thus would be located somewhere in its far-flung and relatively vast if mostly underfunded archives.

In struggling with this question-that-must-change over the past few years, I simply could not imagine what sorts of collectives and what sorts of texts possibly could produce this Blackness—one in which Black African women between 1936 and 1945 could interpellate their own Blackness.[33] My research assistant at that time, Bernard Forjwuor, also hit a wall. A few weeks later Bernard came to me with a solution, one that can be best explained by reference to Epiphenomenal time. He told me that Black West African women have historically been known as producers and sellers of food for the family, village, or community.[34] These roles, he reasoned, would expand further under the colonial and wartime eras with the evacuation of able-bodied men into the army or prisons, work gangs, or through their own agency—either by joining resistance movements or by training for and securing positions within local or colonial administrations that promised some form of socioeconomic agency. Thus these women would be denoted as agricultural and urban workers (not Black African women) in economic reports from 1939 to 1945 (but not necessarily labeled as "agents in World War II").[35]

As might (albeit unhelpfully) be anticipated, the "answer" to my question lay in texts that did not interpellate Black West African women as an absence and did not interpellate them as Black women but instead interpellated them as a *presence* as agricultural laborers, merchants, and urban workers. Because such an interpellation remains vertical, although we begin to learn who these women really were, we do so in a frame that still reads them quite narrowly and often inhumanely. Admittedly, we glimpse their existence, but only through a colonial lens—meaning the interpellative frame requires yet more revision.

The majority of the records that answer this question on the history of Black African women during World War II verge on the illegible for a poor humanities scholar: data tables and acronyms abound, with rarely an (intelligible) word in sight. There were no qualitative narratives, of course, under our original search terms, but by focusing on what these women *did* during the war, Bernard was able to provide me with a handful of articles that allowed us to see where Black African women intersected through the postwar epistemology with Pan-African or postcolonial progress narratives.

Within a horizontal framework, we can answer our question about Black African women's agency from 1939 to 1945 by using a term provided by political scientist and sociologist Janet M. Bujra: *entrepreneur*. Bujra studied an early part of the era of Kenyan women's entrepreneurship as they moved from rural areas to the urban center of (in this case) Nairobi, interpellating this collective through other largely unanticipated collectives, all of which are agential. In "Women 'Entrepreneurs' of Early Nairobi,"[36] Bujra begins what she terms her "social" history by carefully subverting the analytical categories that are typically dispensed by a vertical, heteropatriarchal interpellation of East African women. Bujra must first explain that the occupations held by these women were indeed *occupations* and not states of moral decay:

> It is not easy to find models for an objective sociological analysis
> of prostitution. Much of the literature on the subject, if not merely
> descriptive, is charged with a moralistic tone or with psychological
> insinuations—it sees prostitution as a "social problem," as "deviant behavior," or as an indication of psychological immaturity.
> From my point of view there are two basic inadequacies in such
> formulations. The first is that they fail to locate prostitution as a
> social phenomenon with social implications. Only rarely do they
> shift focus from the prostitute herself to her social context. The
> second problem is that they assume a cultural universalism in relation to prostitution. Most of these analyses stem from the study
> of prostitution in Europe or America. When transposed to other
> contexts they are often misleading since prostitution assumes a
> different social character and is differently regarded in different
> social contexts.

Bujra provides us with a reorienting frame here, noting that the category of analysis, prostitution, is far from an objective category in the West, much less one that carries universal significance. In other words, an "internal heteroglossia" is needed. Bujra also underscores the need to focus on the individual in her environment or, as I would term it here, the need to interpellate individuals through Epiphenomenal time. Bujra also uses a linear progress narrative, but it is not the precolonial-colonial-postcolonial timeline we would expect. Instead, she tracks the progress of individual women from dependency to self-sufficiency as they move from rural areas to Nairobi:

> The underlying assumption here, as in most other writings on the
> subject, is that prostitution "degrades" and that those who practise
> it are its "victims." My interpretation will be somewhat different. Whilst accepting that the women I describe were, in a sense,
> "forced" into prostitution by economic necessity, I shall argue that
> they turned the situation into one of economic advantage. Far from
> being degraded by the transformation of sexual relations into a sale
> of services, they held their own in "respectable society" with men.

From being passive sexual objects, they became actors in a social drama of their own making. And in a very real sense prostitution allowed them an independence and freedom from exploitation that would not have been possible had they chosen any of the other socioeconomic roles open to them—as wives, or as workers in the formal economy of Kenya.[37]

Bujra highlights both agency and intersections using an Epiphenomenal spacetime that manifests not qualitative collapse but a multidimensional Blackness that intersects with a number of collectives outside of "female prostitutes." She achieves this analysis, as advocated by Evan Mwangi, by rejecting vertical time frames that cohere with our questions and instead seeking internal heteroglossia. By interpellating these women as "entrepreneurs of Nairobi" rather than as "Black African women during World War II," she successfully resists the hierarchical structures that *African Writes Back to Self* criticizes, choosing instead a category that describes how these women would understand one another rather than how the reader might first interpellate them. If we were to use only a (sympathetic) vertical interpellative frame, we would see its dichotomous result: these women are either prostitutes made good or good women gone bad.

Entrepreneur is a gender-neutral term that foregrounds agency and diversity (whereby the individuality of one's chosen role in commerce matters more than the specific business or industry chosen). By understanding prostitution as entrepreneurship, Bujra changes these women from objects moved by other forces into agents who choose their own paths and transformations through interactions with the people and socioeconomic and political forces of Nairobi (most especially with one another).

In this way, the manifestation of Black African women's collective agential identities as reactive to white European colonization (and its effect on Black African men, which in turn affected the women) aligns Bujra's article with works such as Stephanie Urdang's "Fighting Two Colonialisms," Susan Abbott's "Full-Time Farmers and Week-End Wives," and Barbara Bush's sections on Black African women in the colonial era in *Imperialism, Race and Resistance*.[38] Bujra's interpellation goes yet further than these other texts, however, because she stresses (like Pybus) the individuality of each woman, foregrounding how she intersects with alternative collective identities rather than interpellating her through a Black female African collective alone. By intervening through their agency, as a group of entrepreneurs (rather than pitiable prostitutes) these women both affirm and diverge from each other's accounts, producing more dimensions of Blackness, both in the contemporary choices of the interlocutors and in their related recollections of oral histories about earlier generations.

Because these women are not interpellated as resistant to a particular ται ist or ming point movement, their histories need not be subsumed by vertical spacetimes that trace subalterns through their resistance to dominant powers and therefore are always defined through those dominant powers and as subaltern to boot. If we took Bujra's spacetime of Nairobian entrepreneurship and reached out to find other women entrepreneurs across African nations, we might produce a Black African women's epistemology that provides whole new dimensions of Blackness that, while perhaps never thought of before, nonetheless intersect across the globe as we discover yet more collectives through which Blackness interpellates itself in multiple spacetimes.

The collective identities that manifest are not predictable, to say the least. In the case of Nairobi during the colonial era, startlingly, it was through prostitution, beer brewing,[39] and the conversion to Islam that these women found agency and moments through which they could manifest the full range of collective identities to which they individually belonged. According to "Women 'Entrepreneurs' of Nairobi," this is due to the *spacetime* Islam occupied in Nairobi:

> In East Africa Islam had largely been an urban religion. In Nairobi it offered a complete social system owing nothing to rural modes of life and taking no account of ethnic differences. This urban religion provided a framework within which people could interrelate on a new basis, it provided an authority structure, it ordered life crises, it offered literacy and formal education, and it even structured the passing of time with communal celebrations of one form or another. To convert to Islam involved at one and the same time the rejection of a person's tribal origins and his or her acceptance into a new set of urban relationships. Since women had often cut themselves off more critically from their rural origins than had most men (due to the circumstances in which they left home and to the occupation they had adopted in town) they had more need of an urban substitute for rural securities than had men. Indeed, some women spoke as if coming to live in town was synonymous

with conversion. "Why," said one, "*everyone* who came to Nairobi changed and became a Swahili Muslim."

Bujra underscores that Islam in Nairobi, although it represented an "authority structure," also recognized the multidimensionality of Blackness in the city and found ways to attract members by providing institutions and practices that intersected with their own cherished moments of performance that they used to interpellate themselves as members of local collectives, such as communal celebration or simply the need for sustained communal interaction: "The Islamic community was conceived of in the idiom of kinship. Once having become a Muslim, all other Muslims became one's 'relatives' or *jamaa*. This word may have many shades of meaning, but it is usually used to mean kindred, plus perhaps neighbours and friends—fellow members of a cohesive community . . . [that] replaced that of their tribe and relatives at home. One woman, when asked why she became a Muslim, replied simply: 'I wanted *jamaa*. They will bury me.'"[40] What Bujra finds, in effect, is women cast out and marginalized under one vertical interpellation and finding another means of collective identity that is also largely horizontal, multidimensional, and rooted in the individual intersection with collective identities. Islam enhances these dimensions rather than demanding a qualitative collapse back to traditional heteropatriarchal roles: it does not require them to marry or bear children in order to retain their role in the community. Perhaps most valuably, Bujra's interpellation reveals how a shift in spatiotemporal coordinates (here from rural to urban) can make an interpellation possible through an epistemology we imagine to be structured as vertical (Islam, which grants men agency as closer to God and gives women protected status) but that, in the "now," makes a horizontal interpellation through peer relationships possible as well.

Bujra's determination to "change the question" produces a formidable network of horizontal interpellations that intersect with a variety of Black identities, but the multidimensionality of her work and its intersection with a broad variety of disciplines too often produces qualitative collapse in the world of poststructuralist theory in the humanities and the social sciences that Massey analyzes. I could not find Bujra through my own rather large vertical search parameters of Blackness and World War II, and my research as a theorist into alternative models for spacetime brought me no closer. Without Bernard Forjwuor, I wonder what this chapter would look like.

These are the "axes of asymmetry" that attend the postwar epistemology. The qualitative parameters that accompany all research are always swinging, shifting, and suddenly collapsing when in their last iteration they might have been richly multidimensional, reminding us that *all* collective identities are contingent on the specific spacetimes through which we interpellate them. To be even harsher (perhaps just to myself), staying "true" to an Epiphenomenal interpellation of Blackness (alongside the vertical) means we must face our own moments of hypocrisy, wherein even those of us who champion gender and sexual equity in our research parameters sometimes provide a foothold for certain hierarchies to function. I would argue that this occurs through our desire to retrieve the histories of a specific collective (such as Black women across the Diaspora), but moving across distinct spacetimes erroneously categorizes these identities as transcendent. The result of our error is asymmetry: while some Black women can be found, others—tens of millions—go missing, because not all Black women are the same across all spacetimes. This is why the postwar epistemology begins with the individual, then moves horizontally, developing peer groups within this spacetime. Importantly, "peer" in the postwar epistemology is defined as sharing the same qualitative and quantitative parameters. If one mistakes collective identities as not constructed but essentialist (i.e., they transcend space and time), one ends up either measuring Beethoven's skull and facial features to prove he wasn't "Black" or facing puzzling disappearances that cannot be retrieved through the same spatiotemporal parameters one initially deployed.

There is a final verticality that needs to be reconciled to finish this book, and that is the relationship among the humanities, the methodological domain of *Physics of Blackness*, and discourses on spacetime written by physicists and science journalists. By turning to lay discourses in physics to seek out nonlinear models of spacetime, this book is always, in some ways, *reacting* to these physics discourses rather than acting on its own. A larger, more troubling symbolism emerges in which physics, that stereotypical exemplar of white Western male achievement, must intervene in and inform a wayward theorization of Blackness by Blacks and Black Africans across the Diaspora. In short, this is a vertical interpellation that threatens to produce a horrific qualitative collapse.

One can also, however, change *this* question, as one audience member did for me after a talk I gave on the book at Mills College in November 2011. "Where did Newton get his idea of linearity?" she asked, and I had to admit that the question had never occurred to me because I had unconsciously located physics as the origin of these theorizations. Put another way, I had read Newton only vertically through a linear progress narrative in which he was a physicist rather than an individual who intersected with many other collectives. In this specific case, I had never thought of Newton as anything other than a scientist even though it would have made sense to ask what, as an intellectual at that time, his *religious* beliefs were. In other words, did he communicate with a peer group of fellow religious practitioners or did he individually interpellate himself through personally selected readings?

The answer invokes, for the final time, the impossibility of establishing a direct, linear causality in that there are many possible causes that point to other causes for Newton's idea of linearity. We know for sure that Newton did not hold with all Anglican beliefs, but the degree to which he did and did not cohere is debatable. In "Isaac Newton, Heretic: The Strategies of a Nicodemite,"[41] religious studies professor Stephen Snobelen observes that, while we know for sure that Newton was both deeply religious and "what the orthodox would have deemed extremely radical," "scholars are still unraveling his personal beliefs."[42]

By stressing a horizontal approach in which Newton's work cannot be read as harboring an answer to our question about his beliefs, Snobelen instead informs us that we can understand Newton's orthodoxy as specifically anti-Trinitarian[43] but that we also must interpellate Newton's discourses on religion as most likely seeking to obscure rather than render clear the question of his religious beliefs. This ambiguity, interpellated through Epiphenomenal time, provides a wealth of possibilities, all of which indicate that Newton's specific religious identities are numerous because so many could intersect with his scientific work. Snobelen suggests that Newton was heavily influenced by the work of Socinus (a mid-sixteenth- to early seventeenth-century Italian theologian) and might therefore intersect with the anti-Trinitarianism of Socinian beliefs, but we cannot be sure.[44]

Physics of Blackness is less interested in Newton, however, than in the circulation of ideas about space and time, or spacetime, and within this moment we can locate one of the earliest influential discourses on linear time in Western civilization. This much earlier manifestation of anti-Trinitarianism, known as Arianism, holds that the Son of God was preceded by and thus created by God, an assertion of divine vertical interpellation if ever there was one. Preceding Socinus, a.k.a. Sozzini, by several centuries, in its heyday of influence in the third and fourth centuries CE, Arianism attracted two Byzantine emperors as followers before fading from influence in Christianity.

Arius, the founder of Arianism, was a Black African theologian, taking us outside of Europe before there was a Europe to a Black African who would not have identified with the term *Black*. In this "now" of the conclusion, pausing at Newton's intersecting with Socinus and Arius on our progress narrative of spacetime concepts, *Physics of Blackness* underscores what it hopes to bring to the interpellation of Blackness: that the latter is simply too complex and broad, too catholic and global, to be confined by any parameters, including those set by itself.

In 2011, Sharon Bertsch McGrayne introduced lay audiences to Bayes's Theorem in her book *The Theory That Would Not Die*. Rather than seek to uncover and deploy fixed absolutes in our exploration of the universe, Bayes's Theorem, a mathematical equation, argues that we must routinely "update" our epistemologies if we hope to achieve consistently accurate results. In Bertsch McGrayne's narrative, human ego and other forms of self-interest have marginalized the impact of Bayes's equation across the sciences and social sciences. In her introduction to *The Theory That Would Not Die*, Bertsch McGrayne argues that despite the successful application of Bayes's Theorem (which was actually further developed by a French researcher, Pierre Simon LaPlace, returning us to the impossibility of origins) to many "real world" problems—not unlike physics—the theorem was rendered *verboten* by "researchers and academics." She notes, "In a celebrated example of science gone awry, geologists accumulated the evidence for Continental Drift in 1912 and then spent 50 years arguing that continents cannot move."[45]

Arius argued that the Son of God was subordinate to "his Father" because Jesus follows God chronologically, asserting a vertical hierarchy whereby that which precedes is superior to that which follows. This is the implicit if not explicit value applied to origins in the linear progress narrative, why all events that follow on a linear timeline (as an effect of the original cause) must subordinate themselves to the meaning of the origin. Yet the concept of progress complicates this understanding of origin: if the "story" of the time is to move away from the origin toward a better state of affairs (e.g., from enslavement to freedom), then the origin operates against itself; it urges us to end its dominant resonance in our lives. The origin of the Middle Passage epistemology effectively asks us to achieve total freedom and thus obliterate the need for more struggle—to reach a spacetime coordinate where and when no more progress is needed because all is perfect.

Bayes's Theorem, with its emphasis on updating as an essential component of progress, effectively adds a layer of Epiphenomenal time to the progress narrative. One can update only in the "now," of course, meaning that it makes sense to update one's understanding of the origin in a moment of reflection in order to accurately deploy that origin. This means that the "origin" is lifted from its place at the beginning of our timeline and remanifested in the present moment. Visually, it is as if, while we stand on a timeline, we reach back and pick up the glowing orb that symbolizes our collective's origin. Then, standing in place and holding that orb, we reflect on multiple pasts, multiple presents (either of our contemporaries or of other things we may have been doing in that moment under different circumstances), and multiple futures, with each reflection radiating out from that orb so that we appear to be at the intersection of all those radiating lines of light.

That is as far as the purple prose will go before it reaches the limits of imagination: after all, those radiating timelines all express possibilities imagined in the moment, not a broad choice of actions we can take. Yet in the act of interpreting our lives and (re)determining our actions—as well as those of others—this ability to imagine is crucial, guiding both the linear progress narrative and Epiphenomenal time. When it comes to scholarly, mass media, and quotidian analysis and interpretation of identities like Blackness, Thomas Bayes and Arius, Sir Isaac Newton and Ama Ata Aidoo, when brought into conversation, emphasize that Blackness must continually update itself in the moment at the level of the individual in order to accurately reflect and honor its trajectory "forward." The physics of Blackness is this mechanism in a nutshell, radiating outward from the individual and achieving meaning through the continual updating of intersecting interpellations in the "now."

Acknowledgments

So much of this project took place in auditoriums and lecture halls where I was invited to speak—that is, in both preparing these talks and fielding questions afterward, I was able to develop, revise, and edit my arguments. The list is long because the process was some six years in the making. I apologize in advance for failing to name all the personnel involved; my memory fails, but my gratitude does not. I would like to thank the following people and organizations for inviting me to come speak on this project: Professor Cally Waite and the Mellon Mays/SSRC Planning and Advisory Committee; Professor Susan Rice and the Center for the Study of Race, Ethnicity and Gender (CSREG) at Bucknell University; Professor Sara Lennox, organizer of the Race and the New Europe Lecture Series hosted by the University of Massachusetts at Amherst; Professor Lann Hornscheidt, organizer of the *Zentrum für transdisziplinare Geschlechtsstudien* (*Center for Interdisciplinary Sexuality Studies*) speaker series sponsored by Linköping University and Humboldt University; the organizers for the MESEA Symposium at Joensuu, Finland; Professors Peggy Pietsche and Fatima El-Tayeb and the second annual Black European Studies (BEST) conference; Professor Lynda Ng and the Rethinking Diaspora conference at Oxford University; Professors Nandini Bhattacharya and Mikko Tukkanen and the Bodies, Inc. symposium at Texas A&M University; Professors Salah M. Hassan and Dagmawi Woubshett and the Departments of African Studies and English at Cornell University; Professors Tyler Stovall, Trica D. Keaton, and Marcus Bruce, organizers of the Black France Colloquium sponsored by Reid Hall in Paris and Columbia University; Professors Werner Krauss and Ben Carrington, organizers of the Making Europe / Making Europeans Symposium held at the University of Texas at Austin; Professors Michelle Stephens and Melina Pappademos, hosts of the MARHO, Radical Historians Reconceptualization of the African Diaspora roundtable held at ASA; Professors Gesa Mackenthun, Nora Kreuzenbeck, Jürgen Martschukat, and Patricia Wiegmann, organizers of the "Being on the Move: Transfers, Emancipation and Formations of the Black Atlantic" conference hosted by University of Erfurt; Professor Charles Rowell, editor-in-chief of *Callaloo* and host for its thirtieth anniversary held in Baltimore, Maryland; Professor Laura Doyle, sponsor of the "Where Is Aqui?" roundtable held at ASA; Professors Pilar Cuder-Dominguez, Benedicte Ledent, and Mar Gallego, hosts of the "European Perspectives on the Black Atlantic" symposium sponsored by the University of Huelva, Spain; Professor Faith Adiele and the faculty of the 2012–13 Mills Contemporary Writers Series; Professor Sandra Jackson, director of the De Paul Center for Black Diaspora Studies and organizer of the 2009–10 speaker series; Professor Badia Ahad and the Department of English at Loyola University Chicago; Professor Eva Boesenberg and the Department of English and American Studies at Humboldt University, sponsors of the annual W. E. B. Du Bois Lecture Series; Professor Maria Diedrich and the Department of English and American Studies at the University of Münster; the Fulbright Distinguished Speaker Series cohosted by the University of Leipzig and University of Jena; Professors Darlene Clark Hine and Trica Keaton, organizers of the Black Europe and the African Diaspora conference hosted by Northwestern University; Professor Daylanne English, organizer of the Afrofuturism panel at the 2011 ASA conference; Professor Jean-Paul Rocchi, organizer of the Textual Dissensions and Political Dissidence in Identity Construction symposium hosted by the University of Paris VII; and Professor Donna Gabaccia, organizer of the 2007–8 Global, Race, Ethnicity and Migration lecture series, hosted by the Immigration History Research Center (of which Professor Gabaccia was also director) at the University of Minnesota–Twin Cities.

I would also like to thank Professors Daylanne English, Rod Ferguson, E. Patrick Johnson, and Nikki Brown for their friendship and encouragement; Professor Fatima El-Tayeb for her inspirational work, most recently and exceptionally *European Others*; the late Professor Richard Iton for reading through the manuscript's introduction and providing me with such detailed and encouraging notes; Professor Daniel Stolarski, part of the CERN research team, also for reading the introduction to comment on its deployment of principles in physics—any inaccuracies in this book are of course my own; Professor Laura Doyle for taking time away from an exceptionally busy schedule to read through a truly mangled book proposal and offer such cogent and productive insights; Professor Berndt Ostendorf for inviting me to spend a year as a Fulbright scholar at LMU in Munich, which provided me with crucial time to begin my research, and to his lovely wife, Jutta, whose warmth, hospitality, insight, and wit made our stay so thoroughly memorable. Great thanks to my undergraduate research assistant, Myrtie Williams, for helping me clean up errors and clarify arguments in the first draft and to Dr. William Barnett of Wordcraft, whose ability to edit everything from the incorrect use of an intransitive verb, to the process that turns coal into diamonds, to key nuances between theories such as epiphenomenalism and Munchhausen's Trilemma and my own arguments proved invaluable to this rather demanding, broadly ranging manuscript. My deepest thanks to editorial assistant Erin Warholm-Wohlenhaus and Richard Morrison, former editorial director of the University of Minnesota Press, who picked up on this project at an extremely early date and in its most ungainly form—and supported it throughout. Finally, I must thank my partner, Virginia May Nugent, for seeing me through yet another book project, chiding me when I was discouraged, cheering me when I was despondent, and for always, no matter the circumstance, being that engaged listener.

Notes

Introduction

1. Peterson, *The Portable Thomas Jefferson*, 187.
2. Reid-Pharr, *Once You Go Black*, 10.
3. This has not, however, prevented Michaels from continuing to write and publish on Blackness.
4. *Culture* and *ethnicity* are often used to connote "race" without acknowledging as much; these terms provide the illusion that one is speaking of a clearly defined and delineated people without having to acknowledge that such delineations can be achieved only through an essentialized—and of course ahistorical—notion of race.
5. Here the "postwar" moment should be distinguished from equally important specific postwar periods in history.
6. Young and Braziel, *Race and the Foundations of Knowledge*, 5.
7. Hall, "Cultural Identity and Diaspora," 222–37.
8. Dickerson, "Colorblind."
9. I am not sure how Dickerson would feel about an increasingly large number of African Americans having one parent who is Black as per Dickerson's definition and another parent who is either African or "West Indian" or Central or South American. History is often used to divide, but its accurate application usually reveals far many more joined lives, experiences, and ancestries than segregated ones.
10. Dickerson also specifies that Blackness requires "West African" ancestry, but historians of Middle Passage slavery are increasingly finding evidence of the trade's reach into Africa's interior and East Coast, rendering her geographic border for ancestry unusable.
11. Stolberg, "Obama Has Ties to Slavery."
12. Falk, *In Search of Time*, 129–30.
13. Greene, *Fabric of the Cosmos*, 8.
14. Newton's concept actually allowed time to flow both forward and backward with equal ease, despite the lack of evidence that this happened in the physical world. This problem of what is called the "arrow of time" is explored more fully in chapter 2, on diasporic Blackness, and first explained in the chapter breakdown following in this introduction.

15. This is Einstein's "fault" (or at least, he felt guilty enough to try to realize the GUT for the rest of his career following the Miracle Year and the ensuing fame)— that is, trying to find some way in which one could reconcile the motions and behaviors of planets and icebergs and other "big things" with the very dissimilar motions and behaviors of "small things," like subatomic particles.

16. Diedrich, Gates, and Pedersen, *Black Imagination*, 8–9.

17. Randall, *Warped Passages*, 29.

18. I use the term "they" to denote those individuals who do not identify as either male or female.

19. These two spacetimes differ, however, where they need and meet each other: while the Middle Passage epistemology focuses on concrete locations, actions, and interpretations of a collective history united in struggle, the postwar epistemology focuses always on the changing and multidimensional ways in which individuals constitute Blackness in any given moment.

20. Bakhtin's distinctly un-Marxist-Leninist ideas required him to be discreet about his publications, creating a situation in which scholars are unsure whether Voloshinov and Bakhtin are at times the same author.

21. Carretta, *Equiano, the African*.

22. Frank, "Cracking the Quantum Safe."

23. See my discussion of Thomas Jefferson and Blackness in *Becoming Black*. Jefferson famously argues that Blackness is a reducible physical quality, a "veil" that has been placed on the face so that whites may recognize Black inferiority despite its human shape (under the section labeled "Property" in *Notes on the State of Virginia*).

24. I distinguish between Henry's capitalization of all three words ("Middle Passage Epistemology") and my own to at least underscore that Henry's concept comes before my own and is also embraced as a useful means of interpellation for all U.S. Blacks, in spite of its apparent problems.

1. The Middle Passage Epistemology

1. Ouellette, *Black Bodies and Quantum Cats*, 37–39.

2. Falk, *In Search of Time*, 129.

3. Ibid., 129–30.

4. Challenges to Newton's concept of linear spacetime can be found in Einstein's assertion—later proved correct through experiments—that time both speeds up and slows down. In other words, time does not always flow uniformly forward. As chapter 3 will consider, "spacetime" might also move backward (even if such occurrences are rare and assumed to occur only at the subatomic level).

5. Falk, *In Search of Time*, 134.

6. Pinkard, "Speculative Naturphilosophie," 26.

7. See Melber, "How to Come to Terms with the Past"; and English, "Kanpur Massacres in India in the Revolt of 1857."

8. See Monter, *Frontiers of Heresy.*

9. Greene, *Fabric of the Cosmos*, 190.

10. Ibid., 191.

11. Ibid., 189.

12. Ibid., 209.

13. Both Middle Passage histories of the West and those that seek to elide this ugly history often fail to mention that slavery has unfortunately always been (and remains so today) a global practice and hardly limited to the exclusive exploitation of Black bodies. Nell Irwin Painter's *The History of White People* reminds us of this sobering fact, begging the question of how appropriate, if not inaccurate, it is to always align Blackness with slavery.

14. Henry, "There's Saltwater in Our Blood," 334.

15. Ibid., 332.

16. However, the potential of reading *Souls* through Epiphenomenal time is not pursued, and the citing from Gilroy of "striving" returns us to one (or more) linear progress narratives—to the same conundrum about how to understand the relationship between Black progress and the obstacle of racism.

17. Henry, "There's Saltwater in Our Blood," 338–39.

18. Du Bois, *Souls of Black Folk*, 9.

19. Carby, *Race Men*, 10.

20. Whether or not these words were first composed by a white suffragette or the actually rather eloquent Truth herself, the message is the same.

21. Gates, *Signifying Monkey*, 3–4.

22. Ibid., 68.

23. Ibid., 256.

24. Ibid.

25. Ibid., 258.

26. Progress narratives that are deployed in mainstream literary studies at the high school and college levels also adopt this strategy: the racism of *Huckleberry Finn* is denied because, it is argued, Twain intended it to be an antiracist tale, so it must be one (or it "was" for "its time"). The racism here is not the use of *nigger* but the uneven description of Jim, whereby he lurches from wise sage to unbelievable idiot (despite a life enslaved, he must be told by Huck to lie down in the boat as they cross into a slave state) to sadistic figure of fun (his imprisonment and pending punishment for escaping are used by Twain to lampoon the romantic prison narrative in Dumas's *The Count of Monte Cristo*). Because Twain is canonical and, I would add, a formidable novelist, it is then reasoned that as part of a progressive tradition of literature—in which writers supposedly experiment with increasingly complex, diverse, and nuanced styles—he cannot symbolize a step back, say, from

Alexander Hamilton's defense of Black equality. See Hamilton's letter to John Jay dated March 14, 1779, in which he discusses the possibility of recruiting Blacks for the Revolutionary Army, writing, "The contempt we have been taught to entertain for the blacks, makes us fancy many things that are founded neither in reason nor experience." See http://press-pubs.uchicago.edu/founders/documents/v1ch15s24.html.

27. Gikandi, "Race and Cosmopolitanism"; Barnes, "Black Atlantic—Black America"; Chrisman, "Rethinking Black Atlanticism."

28. Gilroy, *Black Atlantic*, 4.

29. Adesanmi, "Nous les Colonisés."

30. Woubshet, "Tizita."

31. Gilroy, *Black Atlantic*, 4.

32. Ibid., 7.

33. See Davis, *Women, Race, and Class*; Collins, "It's All in the Family"; and Young, "Logic of Masculinist Protection."

34. Gilroy, *Black Atlantic*, 6.

35. These dimensional limits of the Middle Passage epistemology have been noticed before, perhaps most tellingly by famed anthropologist and founder of the renowned Atlantic Program at Johns Hopkins University, Sidney Mintz, himself a scholar on the Caribbean and South American Diasporas. I engage with and further elaborate on Mintz's arguments in chapter 4.

36. See Wright, *Becoming Black*; Zamir, *Dark Voices*; and English, *Each Hour Redeem* for analyses that link Du Bois and Hegel, as well as Gates, *Figures in Black*; and Gilroy, *Black Atlantic*.

37. Gates, *Signifying Monkey*, 4.

38. Dickerson, "Colorblind."

39. Walters, "Barack Obama and the Politics of Blackness," 8–9. It also underscores the degree to which an uncritical engagement with history—that is, failing to read that history as what one is constructing in the "now"—can sabotage an argument. Historians such as Starobin, *Industrial Slavery in the Old South*, and Evans, "Economies of the American Negro," remind us that there were times when family-based plantation slavery employed fewer slaves than large-scale industries and corporations.

40. Walters, "Barack Obama and the Politics of Blackness," 25.

41. Dickerson, "Colorblind," 8–9.

42. See Simons, "Brazil's Blacks Feel Bias 100 Years after Slavery." By contrast, U.S. Blacks make up about 13 percent of the U.S. population, or just over 40 million people. Yet these statistics do not make clear whether Blacks born outside the United States are included or whether the U.S. Census Bureau's 2012 estimate of 313 million for the total U.S. population also speaks to the presence of undocumented workers and those who overstay their visas. See United States Census

Bureau, "State & County QuickFacts," http://quickfacts.census.gov/qfd/states/ 00000.html.

43. By underscoring the possibility of "Africanizing America," Du Bois grants agency, but primarily through explicit examples of Black men. *Signifying* takes up the cause of Black female agency but also curtails it by turning deaf ears to sexist practices that violently read Black female bodies as objects. *Black Atlantic* underscores agency for all Blacks but does not pursue this possibility through texts that explicitly manifest female and or queer agency.

44. Biracial identity is another concept that epistemologies constructed through a linear progress narrative cannot incorporate. See my reading of Johnson, *Pym*, at the end of chapter 2.

45. Rimer and Arenson, "Top Colleges Take More Blacks, but Which Ones?"

46. Dickerson's readership seems equally bifurcated—some praising her courage in bringing uncomfortable truths to light, others arguing that her column is simply clever satire and therefore the humorless accusations and pained questions are unwarranted.

47. The latter is qualified as belonging to this second group "to a lesser extent."

48. All things come full circle. See English, *Unnatural Selections*, a fascinating study of the history of eugenics among early twentieth-century white and Black American activists, writers, and journalists—including W. E. B. Du Bois.

49. Of course, many "white" Americans proudly claim nonwhite ancestries somewhere on their family trees. Yet while American Indian ancestry is a favorite, Black or African ancestry is rarely mentioned.

50. Ironically, Gates himself has asserted this finding based on the genetic research he is conducting. See Hicks, "It's Rare."

51. While hardly true of every community and individual, many African Americans like to speak of a grandparent, usually a grandmother, who was indisputably of "pure African descent." This is a point of pride, for the purity automatically denotes successful resistance to white slave masters' desires. Yet even here we run into trouble, as "pure African" is an oxymoron given the broad and rather distinct varieties of nations and ancestries that inhabit a continent: to be of combined Ibo, Ife, and Ashanti blood is hardly "pure," and the chances that that grandmother's ancestors were able to choose mates who shared the exact same point of origin is highly unlikely. At the very least, for the thousands who claim one "pure" ancestor, the majority of them are likely to be disappointed should they submit to a DNA test.

52. In *Becoming Black* I argue along similar lines—that is, that "Blackness" as a concept is a relatively recent white European invention that was then claimed by the people who had been labeled as such and since then has enjoyed a fascinating if complex history of discourse and counterdiscourse. Yet I would distinguish my definition from that of Gates and Guinier, above all else because I reject any one

homogeneous definition of "Blackness," whereas they propose a scholarly rigidity with a similar nod toward historiography.

53. I am not sure what to make of the designation *"children* of biracial couples," as this is an exceptionally small category—significantly smaller than that of children of *interracial* couples—which is perhaps what was meant, given the tendency of many white Americans to confuse the two terms and use them interchangeably. In any event, if we follow the exact category delineated, we are still speaking of people who, while once classified as "quadroons," would now be called "biracial" regardless of their own affiliation or self-defining.

54. I drive in Chicago.

2. The Problem of Return in the African Diaspora

1. Carroll, *From Eternity to Here*, 29–30.

2. Many popular narratives on time travel do in fact play with this notion that time travel makes someone old younger, but the human time traveler either is encased in a machine that withstands the effects of reverse-entropy or in some other manner withstands that irresistible force of our molecules reacting in reverse (which might be so shocking we wouldn't want to see it recreated—to think of reverse digestion and eating, reverse growing, "dispersing" back into the womb, and Lord knows what else).

3. The impact of Spillers's essay is too vast to cogently notate, but for the latest scholarship (all award-winning), see Moten, *In the Break*; Yancy, *Black Bodies, White Gazes*; and Young, *Embodying the Black Experience*.

4. Spillers, "Mama's Baby, Papa's Maybe," 65.

5. Ibid.

6. Ibid. Here, being "at the podium" suggests a speech to be given and Spillers's own status as a famous academic who travels the world to give talks.

7. Ibid.

8. Ibid.

9. Spillers, "Mama's Baby, Papa's Maybe," 65.

10. Ibid.

11. Tellingly, the female equivalent has already been co-opted to denote marriage.

12. Spillers, "Mama's Baby, Papa's Maybe," 66.

13. Ibid.

14. Ibid.

15. Spillers, "'Watcha Gonna Do?,'" 304.

16. Indeed, most sexual iterations of African cultures stress a vibrant heteropatriarchal culture, creating a utopian or near-utopian notion of harmonious communal living that suspiciously resembles the prelapsarian era narrated in the Bible, the Torah, and the Qu'ran.

17. For example, while African American history buffs will be familiar with the "Buffalo Soldiers"—African Americans who served in the nineteenth-century U.S. cavalry—less known is their role in the attempted genocide of American Indian tribes. This means that a history book may feature the first dimensions of these soldiers but have less to say about the second, perhaps massaging it into a generic statement about Custer's Last Stand.

18. See chapter 1 for a discussion of how origins must dominate all events located on a linear progress narrative.

19. This assumption seems further borne out by the fact that each "yanking" back appears occasioned by Rufus's emergency needs and that Dana always manifests around his (and her) family's plantation.

20. Dubey, "Speculative Fictions of Slavery," 780.

21. Ibid., 786–87.

22. Ibid., 802.

23. Andrade, "Nigger of the Narcissist," 223.

24. Condé, *Heremakhonon*, 3–4.

25. In Pfaff, *Conversations with Maryse Condé*, Condé explains that she chose the title *Heremakhonon*—which means "wait for happiness" in Malinke but can also be found in Mali—because it represented a transnational context. Most important, "the name merely symbolized for me all the illusions fostered by the newly independent African nations" (39).

26. Condé, *Heremakhonon*, 166–67.

27. Perhaps Guinea, perhaps Mali, but most likely an "everywhere" and "nowhere."

28. See Harris, *Native Stranger*; Wright, *Black Power*; and Campbell, *Middle Passages*.

29. Hartman, *Lose Your Mother*, 3.

30. In childhood studies, children are also often interpellated as "whole" human beings rather than as incomplete beings in the making—the latter being the logical conclusion of interpellating the human life cycle through a linear progress narrative (in spite of all the experiences to the contrary). Interpellating children through Epiphenomenal time leads to the former manifestation, as shown in the reading of Mavis and Samaya in chapter 1—in their "now," children are whole, not incomplete, and as multidimensional as adults.

31. Hartman, *Lose Your Mother*, 3–4.

32. Ibid., 234.

33. See Peters, *Eldorado of the Ancients*.

34. See Haggard, *King Solomon's Mines*.

35. Morrison, *Playing in the Dark*, 69.

36. Johnson, *Pym*, 159.

37. Ibid., 83–84.

38. Here I should note that the "prohibition" on naming non-Black ancestries (in a nonderogatory way) is almost wholly specific to contemporary African Americans who trace their lineage through slavery on U.S. shores. Black collectives in the Caribbean, Central America, and South America do not generally view non-Black ancestries as a source of shame that, if named, must also be rejected in the same breath.

39. Johnson, *Pym*, 135.

40. Perhaps adding to the irony is the fact that the origin of the term *mulatto* is from "mule" because, like the offspring of a horse and a donkey, human beings with one Black and one white parent were often believed to be barren. The charge of being barren was a common one in eighteenth- and nineteenth-century discourses on race, and white European philosophers such as G. W. F. Hegel had no compunction about making this charge against white American men as well: their virility, he claimed, having been sapped by the intense climate. See Emmanuel Chukwudi Eze's *Race and the Enlightenment* and James W. Caesar's *Reconstructing America* for each respective claim.

41. All except Jaynes's best friend, Garth, who escapes initial capture and then barters to keep his freedom by giving the Tekelians his remaining supply of beloved Little Debbie snack cakes.

42. Johnson, *Pym*, 322.

43. In an interview with Charles H. Rowell, commenting on her inspiration for writing her novel *Kindred*, Butler notes, "I wanted to take a character, when I did *Kindred*, back in time to some of the things that our ancestors had to go through, and see if that character survived so very well with the knowledge of the present in her head" (Rowell, "An Interview with Octavia E. Butler," 51).

44. Rudolph Raspe's tale of Rabelaisian proportions is largely forgotten except through these two markers: the "trilemma" story and of course the controversial diagnosis of "Münchhausen's syndrome by proxy," in which (usually) mothers harm their children in order to receive (perhaps intensely caring and concerned) attention for themselves from medical professionals (often assumed to be male, thus confusing what might be a desire for attention with a romantic-sexual craving for masculine authority figures).

45. Baldwin, *Notes of a Native Son*, 120–21.

46. Johnson, *Pym*, 136.

47. Campbell, *Talking at the Gates*, 7.

48. This suggests that they also read his complaint of assault as a case of confusion between the literal and the figurative.

3. Quantum Baldwin and the Multidimensionality of Blackness

1. Kaplan and Schwarz, *James Baldwin*, 1.

2. Ibid., 3.

3. Randall, *Warped Passages*, 1–2.

4. Ibid., 13.

5. Ibid., 14–15.

6. In their books on post-Blackness, journalists Ytasha Womack and Touré do not seek to erase, deny, or minimize the importance of the Middle Passage epistemology but instead stress how generational, economic, sexual, gender, and political differences produce many distinct Black discourses that do not cohere with "traditional" definitions of Blackness. Both books, I would argue, denote "traditional" views of Blackness in the United States through the Middle Passage Epistemology. See Womack, *Post Black*; and Touré, *Who's Afraid of Post Blackness?*

7. Baldwin, *Notes of a Native Son*, 22–23.

8. Ibid., 23.

9. Randall, *Warped Passages*, 134–35.

10. Baldwin, *Notes of a Native Son*, 24–25.

11. Ibid., 27.

12. Ibid.

13. Ibid., 97–98.

14. Ibid., 118.

15. Ibid., 120.

16. Ibid.

17. Ibid., 120–21.

18. Ibid., 121.

19. Ibid., 122–23.

20. "*Je vais voir Paris, moi aussi, avec mes yeux. Désormais, je serai un peu comme tout le monde, je porterai une auréole, un parfum, l'auréole et le parfum de Paris. Je vais toucher les murs, les arbres, croiser les hommes.*" Dadié, *Un Nègre à Paris*, 7.

21. "*Je suis le seul Nègre parmi tant de voyageurs blancs. Je prends place près d'un hublot. Personne ne veut s'asseoir près de moi.*" Ibid., 21.

22. "*Je regarde, partout de Blancs; des employés blancs. Nulle part une tête de Nègre. C'est bien un pays de Blancs.*" Ibid., 25.

23. Two Napoleon-era politicos who, it is believed, plotted to depose Napoleon but were foiled.

24. "*Et il a pour maîtres Tallyrand et Fouché. A ne rien comprendre ou si je le comprendre bien, ce qui lui importe c'est de bâtir sa fortune sur le dos du temps. Et pour ce faire il court, devance le temps qu'il attend assis à la terrasse d'un café à boire à petits coup à la manière des oiseaux, un demi de bière. Sois tranquille, le temps ne le trouvera pas là, il sera déjà en route décidé à conserver l'avance gagnée à ne pas vivre.*" Dadié, *Un Nègre à Paris*, 60.

25. "*Je vais faire rire les nombreux tourists hissés sur la Tour Eiffel ou l'Arc de Triomphe, ces opulents clients des riches hotels. . . . Et qu-est-ce que j'emporterai moi?*

Le métro. Il faut vraiment être Nègre de pure souche pour n'admirer à Paris que le métro." Ibid., 83.

26. "*Nous nous sourions constamment. Même couleur dans ce pays de Blancs et pas moyens de se lier. Si la couleur nous rapproche, tout nous sépare. Un fossé que les multiples sourires n'ont pu combler. Qu'en penses-tu?*" Ibid., 196.

27. I am harking back to 1950s Burma Shave ads in which the "jingle" was broken up into a series of successive signs posted along the highway—one read the message bit by bit while driving forward.

28. Aidoo, *Our Sister Killjoy*, 3–5.

29. Ibid., 8.

30. Ibid., 9.

31. Adolf Hitler, of course, was born and raised in Austria but, as German-speaking, can be understood as Germanic.

32. Aidoo, *Our Sister Killjoy*, 64.

33. Ibid., 49.

34. Ibid., 51.

35. Ibid., 67.

36. Ibid., 66–67.

37. Ibid., 130.

38. Ibid., 131.

39. "*Einfach. Mit einer Tafel Schokolade kriegte man die schönste Frau Italiens*" (translated in text, by the interviewee, Andrade); "*In einer kleinre Stadt in Norditalien schrubbten die Bewonhner die Haut des Schwarzen Astrogildo Sacramento, um zu sehen, ob die Farbe abging*" (In a small town in north Italy the inhabitants rubbed at the skin of one of the Blacks, Astrogildo Sacramento, to see if the color rubbed off). Morgenrath and Rössel, *Unsere Opfer*, 166.

40. Baldwin, *Notes of a Native Son*, 178.

41. Ibid., 121–22.

42. Ibid., 22.

43. Murphy, "Subversive Anti-Stalinism," 1038–39.

44. Ibid., 1040.

45. Not to be confused with Professor James Miller of George Washington University, a prominent scholar of African American literatures.

46. Miller, "What Does It Mean to Be an American?"

47. Baldwin, *Nobody Knows My Name*, 5.

48. "Postwar" because Aidoo names Marija's husband "Big Adolf" and her son "Little Adolf" and manifests the former as a looming, oppressive presence.

49. Yes, I am aware of the unfortunate connection between the names of these two tropes. Perhaps it is a testament to my literary devotion that I did not notice the subtext of the "bush" and "Tower-phallus" tropes until almost the final round of edits.

4. Axes of Asymmetry

1. See Van Sertima, *African Presence in Early Europe*; Goodwin, *Africa in Europe, Volume One*; Lawrance, "Black Africans in Renaissance Spanish Literature"; and Brackett, "Race and Rulership."

2. Alpers, "African Diaspora in the Indian Ocean."

3. Pybus, *Black Founders*.

4. Mintz and Reed, "'The Legacy of the Atlantic Program.'"

5. Interestingly, Mintz is framing this problem very much along the lines of Bayes's Theorem: The conditions that produced the intellectual parameters of the Atlantic Program have changed, rendering those parameters now less accurate because they have not been "updated."

6. Massey, "Politics and Space/Time," 154–56.

7. Massey, *For Space*, 77. "The process of invention seems itself to be constrained by deconstruction's horizontality" (54).

8. Ibid., 118.

9. See chapters 1 and 2 on the invention of Blackness in the West in Wright, *Becoming Black*, 27–110.

10. Afrofuturism is an interesting case—is it a linear progress narrative? I think this depends on how future Blackness is imagined by each specific discourse. Sun Ra intersects his Afrofuturist visions with aspects of Afrocentrism and Pan-Africanism and imagines the future as potentially progressive, so many of his interpellations of Blackness may cohere with a linear progress narrative. Janelle Monae, by contrast, who is also identified as an Afrofuturist artist, often uses visuals (as in "Tightrope") that intersect various eras, real and imagined, with one another through costume, imagery, and sometimes music. There are at least aspects of epiphenomenalism present at these intersections, but it might also be the dominant frame of interpellation in the video.

11. Pybus, "World Is All of One Piece," 181.

12. Ibid.

13. My thanks to Paul Joseph (Pablo) López Oro for this information.

14. This is also true for the postwar era, not the least because it does not cohere with the thematic conclusions many linear progress narratives attach to the end of the war. If World War II was a victory of democracy over fascism, why did one of the Allied powers (Russia) become an enemy of the rest? And why did two and one-half (given the division of Germany into East and West) of the Axis powers then become trading partners and political collaborators with their opponents? Many films and other creative treatments of the immediate postwar era highlight this moral ambivalence, so multiple meanings of the era, or multidimensions, are easily recognized and interpellated, sometimes even in dominant texts.

15. The "Windrush" narrative is named after the *Empire Windrush*, the ship that transported the "first" postwar Black Caribbean "immigrants" to England on June 22, 1948. See Mike and Trevor Phillips's BBC documentary and book of oral histories, *Windrush*, for the most common interpellation of the "Windrush" generations. See also Barnor Hesse's essay "Diasporicity" in his edited volume, *Un/settled Multiculturalism*.

16. Similarly, Hans-Jürgen Massaquoi's autobiography, translated as a single volume in English as *Destined to Witness*, interpellates Blackness through a Middle Passage epistemology. Despite his Cameroonian and German parentage, Massaquoi explains that he was able to interpellate his Blackness (especially with an absent father) only after hearing about Joe Louis and Jesse Owens on the radio. Using these models, Massaquoi finds a way to survive living in Hitler's Germany, and after rejecting a life in Cameroon following the Allied victory, he emigrates to the United States and into its established Black collective. As a result, a life that intersects with so many experiences and peoples restricts these encounters to those grounded in a purely heteropatriarchal logic: men are encountered as either enemies to be vanquished or allies; women are either attractive sexual objects and models of demure femininity or else dear old mother. Even narratives that we might hope to be horizontal and multidimensional then, emanating as they do from a single and very agential individual, can interpellate a relatively unique life uncritically through dominant hierarchical structures. Massaquoi hates the Nazis and their fascism and loves the United States and its freedom-fighting African American men—producing a Black German narrative that sits quite comfortably next to both Black and white (U.S.) progress narratives that use the Second World War.

17. Even traditional narratives must switch between urban capitals and various battlefields, calling attention to such distortion by explaining again and again that certain events, although necessarily narrated sequentially, were in fact happening simultaneously.

18. One could read Smith's first novel as interpellating Blackness through *U.S. versions* of Afropessimism, but this is a distinction lacking meaningful difference. While it eschews the Middle Passage Epistemology's progress narrative (Blacks are destined to always be oppressed), it needs this linear progress narrative to argue *against* progress. While claiming to be static, U.S. versions of Afropessimism nonetheless doggedly track each moment of the Middle Passage Epistemology to state yet again that no progress has been made.

19. My thanks to Myrtie Williams for this contribution.

20. Before Einstein, physicists followed the shared assumption that space and time were distinct categories. In the instance cited here, I use parentheses to indicate that while in the ideal this is assumed to be a problem of time, in the material it is a problem of spacetime.

21. Morgenrath and Rössel, *Unsere Opfer*, 9. My translation.

22. In the West, we are most often taught that it was Nazi Germany's invasion of Poland in 1939—after a series of broken promises and creatively named invasions of Austria and Czechoslovakia—that precipitated the outbreak of hostilities. Yet, the previous postcolonial critique argues that, if this war was only about fighting the forces of fascism, it is fair to ask why Britain and France did not declare war when Hitler began his persecution of German Jews or when Hitler's initial inspiration for Nazism, Mussolini's homegrown and rather amorphous fascism, first began beating its chest. In fact, many historians who have worked on Mussolini's 1935–36 invasion of Ethiopia, such as Zabecki (*World War Two in Europe*, 1476) and Metaferia (*Ethiopia and the United States*, 35), have argued (respectively) that "the Italian invasion of Ethiopia . . . in 1935 and military actions in 1936 were part of the chain of events that preceded the European nations' entry into World War II" and that "the Italian attack heralded the demise of the League of Nations and the beginning of World War II."

23. Like many others, I dislike the term *Third World* because it derives from an argument in which capitalist, majority-white democracies in the West are the "First World" and Communist nations are the "Second"—an irrational ordering notable only for its blatantly superficial ideology.

24. Morgenrath and Rössel, *Unsere Opfer*, 9.

25. Eschenberg, "'Morts Pour La France,'" 363.

26. Ibid., 365.

27. I have not yet been able to find any histories of German conscription in Africa, which would have taken place during Rommel's invasion because Germany lost its few colonies in the Treaty of Versailles (although more than 100,000 German citizens remained—see Henderson, *Studies in German Colonial History*, 34). Black Germans who served in the army were few and far between, and the bulk of the Black civilian population lived in hiding and near starvation, as most were deprived of ration cards and other means of sanctioned subsistence. These histories, then, are largely found in autobiographical narratives given the intensely individual routes, some of which ended up in the death camps while others emerged to tell their tale—one of whom eventually immigrated to the United States to become editor-in-chief of *Ebony* magazine, as we learn in Massaquoi's autobiography. Likewise, Blacks from South America are also in short supply, mostly available through individual narratives of soldiers and civilian activists.

28. Mwangi, *Africa Writes Back to Self*, 1.

29. Ibid.

30. Ibid., 1–2.

31. Ibid., 3–4.

32. Bousquet and Douglas, *West Indian Women at War*, 1–2.

33. As noted earlier, some scholars believe that World War II should be marked as having begun in 1936, the year of the Italian fascists' invasion of Ethiopia, rather than 1939, the year of the Nazis' invasion of Poland.

34. As I show later in the chapter, similar logic can be applied to finding the histories of East African women, in this case in Kenya.

35. It is possible that future research will bear out military records of Black African women who served or aided the colonial militaries (or perhaps resisted the forced conscription of their male loved ones). At the moment I do not know of the colonial authorities using anyone other than Black African men as soldiers and support staff (i.e., staffing kitchens, performing clean up, etc.) in the war effort.

36. Articles such as Bujra's, which breaks with conservative readings and categorization of women, often dispensed with the pre/post/colonial altogether and used temporally vague markers, albeit often paired with spatially specific sites, such as "early Nairobi."

37. Bujra, "Women 'Entrepreneurs' of Early Nairobi," 214–15.

38. See Abbott, "Full-Time Farmers and Week-End Wives"; Urdang, "Fighting Two Colonialisms"; and Bush, *Imperialism, Race, and Resistance*.

39. Which Bujra describes as a low-profit, morally marginalized auxiliary activity that supplemented (usually retired) prostitutes' incomes.

40. Bujra, "Women 'Entrepreneurs' of Early Nairobi," 227.

41. My deepest thanks to Professor James Force (and my colleague Sanford "Sandy" Goldberg for suggesting I contact him) for guiding me to his own work and to Snobelen's, which helped me to resolve a host of confusions I encountered during my solo attempts to answer this question.

42. Snobelen, "Isaac Newton, Heretic," 1.

43. While there are many variations, Trinitarianism holds that the Holy Trinity of the Father, Son, and the Holy Spirit are epiphenomenal in their manifestation— that is, they occur not in sequence but simultaneously.

44. John Maynard Keynes, in "Newton, the Man," theorizes that Newton must have been a "Judaic monotheist of the school of Maimonides."

45. McGrayne, *Theory That Would Not Die*, ix.

Bibliography

Abbott, Susan. "Full-Time Farmers and Week-End Wives: An Analysis of Altering Conjugal Roles." *Journal of Marriage and Family* 38, no. 1 (1976): 165–74.

Adesanmi, Pius. "'Nous les Colonisés': Reflections on the Territorial Integrity of Oppression." *Social Text* 22, no. 1 (2004): 35–58.

Aidoo, Ama Ata. *No Sweetness Here and Other Stories*. New York: Feminist Press at City University of New York, 1995. First published in 1970 by Longman.

———. *Our Sister Killjoy*. London: Longman, 1997.

Alexander, Jacqui M. *Pedagogies of Crossing: Meditations on Feminism, Sexual Politics, Memory, and the Sacred*. Durham, N.C.: Duke University Press, 2005.

Alpers, Edward. "The African Diaspora in the Indian Ocean: A Comparative Perspective." In *The African Diaspora in the Indian Ocean*, edited by Shihan da Silva Jayasurya and Richard Pankhurst, 19–50. Trenton, N.J.: Africa World, 2003.

Althusser, Louis. *On Ideology*. London: Verso, 2008.

Andrade, Susan Z. "The Nigger of the Narcissist: History, Sexuality, and Intertextuality in Maryse Condé's *Heremakhonon*." *Callaloo* 16, no. 1 (1993): 213–26.

Appiah, Kwame Anthony. *In My Father's House: Africa in the Philosophy of Culture*. Oxford: Oxford University Press, 1992.

Ayim, Mai. *Grenzenlos und unverschämt*. Berlin: Orlanda Frauenverlag, 1997.

Badiou, Alain. *Being and Event*. Translated by Oliver Feltham. London: Continuum, 2005. First published as *L'être et événément* in 1988 by Editions du Seuil.

Baker, Houston A. *Blues, Ideology, and Afro-American Literature*. Chicago: University of Chicago Press, 1984.

Bakhtin, Mikhail. *The Dialogic Imagination: Four Essays*. Edited by Michael Holquist. Translated by Caryl Emerson and Michael Holquist. Austin: University of Texas Press, 1981.

Baldwin, James. *Nobody Knows My Name: More Notes of a Native Son*. London: Penguin, 1991. First published in 1964 by Michael Joseph.

———. *No Name in the Street*. New York: Vintage, 1972.

———. *Notes of a Native Son*. Boston: Beacon, 1955.

Barad, Karen. *Meeting the Universe Halfway: Quantum Physics and the Entanglement of Matter and Meaning*. Durham, N.C.: Duke University Press, 2007.

Barnes, Natasha. "Black Atlantic—Black America." *Research in African Literatures* 27, no. 4 (1996): 106–7.

Bergson, Henri. *Time & Free Will*. London: Elibron Classics, 2005. First published in 1910 by George Allen and Unwin.

Bodanis, David. *E=mc2: A Biography of the World's Most Famous Equation*. New York: Berkeley, 2000.

Bosquet, Ben, and Colin Douglas. *West Indian Women at War: British Racism in World War II*. London: Lawrence and Wishart, 1991.

Brackett, John K. "Race and Rulership: Alessandro de' Medici." In *Black Africans in Renaissance Europe*, edited by T. F. Earle and K. J. P. Lowe, 303–25. New York: Cambridge University Press, 2005.

Brown, Nikki. *Private Politics and Public Voices: Black Women's Activism from World War I to the New Deal*. Bloomington: Indiana University Press, 2007.

Bujra, Janet M. "Women 'Entrepreneurs' of Early Nairobi." *Canadian Journal of African Studies* 9, no. 2 (1975): 213–34.

Bush, Barbara. *Imperialism, Race, and Resistance: Africa and Britain, 1919–1945*. London: Routledge, 1999.

Butler, Octavia. *Kindred*. Boston: Beacon, 1979.

Caesar, James W. *Reconstructing America: The Symbol of America in Modern Thought*. New Haven, Conn.: Yale University Press, 1997.

Campbell, James T. *Middle Passages: African American Journeys to Africa, 1787–2005*. London: Penguin, 2007.

———. *Talking at the Gates: A Life of James Baldwin*. New York: Penguin, 1991.

Carby, Hazel. *Race Men*. Cambridge, Mass.: Harvard University Press, 2007.

Carretta, Vincent. *Equiano, the African: Biography of a Self-Made Man*. London: Penguin, 2007.

Carroll, Sean. *From Eternity to Here: The Quest for the Ultimate Theory of Time*. New York: Dutton, 2010.

Césaire, Aimé. *Discourse on Colonialism*. Translated by Joan Pinkham. New York: Monthly Review, 1972. First published as *Discours sur le colonialisme* in 1955 by Editions Présence Africaine.

Chakrabarty, Dipesh. *Provincializing Europe: Postcolonial Thought and Historical Difference*. Princeton, N.J.: Princeton University Press, 2000.

Chrisman, Laura. "Rethinking Black Atlanticism." *The Black Scholar* 30, nos. 3/4 (2000): 12.

Close, Frank. *Nothing: A Very Short Introduction*. Oxford: Oxford University Press, 2009.

Cohen, William A. "Liberalism, Libido, Liberation: Baldwin's *Another Country*, et al." In *Genders—Art, Literature, Film, History—12*, edited by Ann Kibbey, 1–21. Austin: University of Texas Press, 1991.

Collins, Patricia Hill. "It's All in the Family: Intersections of Gender, Race, and Nation." *Hypatia* 13, no. 3 (1998): 62–82.

Condé, Maryse. *Heremakhonon: A Novel*. Translated by Richard Philcox. Boulder, Colo.: Lynne Rienner, 1996. First published in 1982 by Three Continents.

Crummel, Alexander. *Destiny and Race: Selected Writings, 1840 1898*. Edited by Wilson Jeremiah Moses. Amherst: University of Massachusetts Press, 1992.

Dadié, Bernard. *Un Nègre à Paris*. Dakar, Senegal: Présence Africaine, 1959.

Davis, Angela Y. *Women, Race, and Class*. New York: Vintage, 1983.

Delaney, Samuel R. *Shorter Views: Queer Thoughts & the Politics of the Paraliterary*. Hanover, N.H.: Wesleyan University Press, 1999.

Delany, Martin. *The Origin of Races and Color*. Baltimore: Black Classic, 1997. First published in 1879 by Harper and Brothers.

Dickerson, Debra J. "Colorblind." *Salon*, January 22, 2007, http://www.salon.com /2007/01/22/obama_161/.

Diedrich, Maria, Henry Louis Gates Jr., and Carl Pedersen, eds. *Black Imagination and the Middle Passage*. New York: Oxford University Press, 1999.

Douglass, Frederick. *Narrative of the Life of Frederick Douglass*. Mineola, N.Y.: Dover, 1995. First published in 1845 by the Anti-Slavery Office, Boston.

Dubey, Madhu. "Speculative Fictions of Slavery." *American Literature* 82, no. 4 (2010): 779–805.

Du Bois, W. E. B. *The Souls of Black Folk*. New York: Penguin Classics, 1997. First published in 1903 by A. C. McClurg.

Earle, T. F., and K. J. P. Lowe, eds. *Black Africans in Renaissance Europe*. New York: Cambridge University Press, 2005.

Edgcomb, Gabrielle Simon. *From Swastika to Jim Crow: Refugee Scholars at Black Colleges*. Malabar, Fla.: Krieger, 1993.

Edwards, Brent Hayes. *The Practice of Diaspora: Literature, Translation, and the Rise of Black Internationalism*. Cambridge, Mass.: Harvard University Press, 2003.

Einstein, Albert. *Relativity: The Special and the General Theory*. New York: Penguin Classics, 2006. First published in 1916 in German and in 1920 in English by Henry Holt.

El-Tayeb, Fatima. *European Others: Queering Ethnicity in Postnational Europe*. Minneapolis: University of Minnesota Press, 2011.

English, Barbara. "The Kanpur Massacres in India in the Revolt of 1857." *Past and Present* 142 (1994): 169–78.

English, Daylanne. *Each Hour Redeem: Time and Justice in African American Literature*. Minneapolis: University of Minnesota Press, 2013.

———. *Unnatural Selections: Eugenics in American Modernism and the Harlem Renaissance*. Durham: University of North Carolina Press, 2004.

Equiano, Olaudah. *The Interesting Narrative and Other Writings*. Edited by Vincent Carretta. New York: Penguin Classics, 2003. First published in 1789.

Eschenburg, Myron. "'Morts Pour La France': The African Soldier in France during the Second World War." *Journal of African History* 26, no. 4 (1985): 363–80.

Evans, Robert, Jr. "The Economies of the American Negro." In *Aspects of Labor Economics*, edited by the National Bureau of Economic Research, 185–256. Princeton, N.J.: Princeton University Press, 1962.

Everett, Anna. *Digital Diaspora: A Race for Cyberspace*. Albany: State University of New York Press, 2009.

Eze, Emmanuel Chukwudi. *Race and the Enlightenment: A Reader*. London: Blackwell, 1997.

Fabian, Johannes. *Time and the Other: How Anthropology Makes Its Object*. New York: Columbia University Press, 1983.

Falk, Dan. *In Search of Time: The History, Physics, and Philosophy of Time*. New York: St. Martin's, 2008.

Fanon, Frantz. *Black Skin, White Masks*. Translated by Richard Philcox. New York: Grove, 2008. First published in 1952 by Éditions du Seuil.

Ferguson, Roderick A. *Aberrations in Black: Toward a Queer of Color Critique*. Minneapolis: University of Minnesota Press, 2004.

Feynman, Richard P. *The Pleasure of Finding Things Out: The Best Short Works of Richard P. Feynman*. Edited by Jeffrey Robbins. Cambridge, Mass.: Perseus, 1999.

Frank, Adam. "Cracking the Quantum Safe." *New York Times*, October 14, 2012.

Gadamer, Hans Georg. *Truth and Method*. London: Continuum, 2004. First published in 1975 by Sheed and Ward.

Gamow, George. *The Great Physicists from Galileo to Einstein*. New York: Dover, 1961.

Gates, Henry Louis, Jr. *Figures in Black: Words, Signs, and the "Racial" Self*. New York: Oxford University Press, 1987.

———. *The Signifying Monkey: A Theory of African American Literary Criticism*. New York: Oxford University Press, 1988.

Giddings, Paula. *When and Where I Enter: The Impact of Black Women on Race and Sex in America*. New York: Bantam, 1985.

Gikandi, Simon. "Race and Cosmopolitanism." *American Literary History* 14, no. 3 (2002): 593–615.

Gilder, Louisa. *The Age of Entanglement: When Quantum Physics Was Reborn*. New York: Vintage, 2009.

Gilroy, Paul. *Against Race: Imagining Political Culture beyond Color*. Cambridge, Mass.: Belknap, 2002.

———. *The Black Atlantic: Modernity and Double Consciousness*. Cambridge, Mass.: Harvard University Press, 1993.

———. *Darker than Blue: On the Moral Economies of Black Atlantic Culture*. Cambridge, Mass.: Belknap, 2010.

Glymph, Thavolia. *Out of the House of Bondage: The Transformation of the Planta-tion Household*. Cambridge: Cambridge University Press, 2008.

Goodwin, Stefan. *Africa in Europe, Volume One: Antiquity into the Age of Global Exploration*. Plymouth, U.K.: Lexington, 2009.

Greene, Brian. *The Fabric of the Cosmos: Space, Time, and the Texture of Reality*. New York: Vintage, 2004.

Griffin, Farah J., and Cheryl J. Fish, eds. *A Stranger in the Village: Two Centuries of African-American Travel Writing*. Boston: Beacon, 1998.

Griggs, Sutton E. *The Hindered Hand: Or, The Reign of the Repressionist*. Google Ebooks, 2010. First published in 1905 by Orion.

Haggard, H. Rider. *King Solomon's Mines*. London: Penguin Classics, 2008. First published in 1885 by Cassell.

——. *She: A History of Adventure*. New York: Modern Library, 2002. First published in book form in 1887 by Longman, Green.

Halberstam, Judith. *In a Queer Time and Place: Transgender Bodies, Subcultural Lives*. New York: New York University Press, 2005.

Hall, Stuart. "Cultural Identity and Diaspora." In *Identity*, edited by J. Rutherford, 222–37. London: Lawrence and Wishart, 1993.

Hamilton, Ruth Simms, ed. *Routes of Passage: Rethinking the African Diaspora, Volume 1, Part 1*. East Lansing: Michigan State University Press, 2007.

Harper, Frances E. W. *Iola Leroy: Or, Shadows Uplifted*. Oxford: Oxford University Press, 1988.

Harris, Eddie L. *Native Stranger*. New York: Vintage, 1993.

Harris, Joseph E. *African American Reactions to War in Ethiopia, 1936–1941*. Baton Rouge: Louisiana State University Press, 1994.

Hartman, Saidiya. *Lose Your Mother: A Journey Along the Atlantic Slave Route*. New York: Farrar, Strauss and Giroux, 2007.

——. *Scenes of Subjection: Terror, Slavery, and Self-making in Nineteenth-Century America*. Oxford: Oxford University Press, 1997.

Henderson, Mae G. "Speaking in Tongues: Dialogics, Dialectics, and the Black Woman Writer's Literary Tradition." In *Changing Our Own Words: Essays on Criticism, Theory, and Writing by Black Women*, edited by Cheryl Wall, 16–37. New Brunswick, N.J.: Rutgers University Press, 1989.

Henderson, William Otto. *Studies in German Colonial History*. 2nd ed. New York: Routledge, 1962.

Henry, Annette. "There's Saltwater in Our Blood: The 'Middle Passage' Epistemol-ogy of Two Black Mothers Regarding the Spiritual Education of their Daughters." *International Journal of Qualitative Studies in Education* 19, no. 3 (2006): 329–45.

Hesse, Barnor. "Diasporicity: Black Britain's Post-Colonial Formations." In *Un/Settled Multiculturalisms: Diasporas, Entanglements, "Transruptions,"* edited by Barnor Hesse, 96–120. London: Zed, 2000.

Hicks, Jonathan P. "It's Rare to Find a Black American with 100 Percent African Ancestry." BET, March 28, 2012, http://www.bet.com/news/national/2012/03/28/it-s-rare-to-find-a-black-american-with-100-percent-african-ancestry-gates-says.html.

Hine, Darlene Clark. *Hine Sight: Black Women and the Re-Construction of American History.* Bloomington: Indiana University Press, 2007.

Hoffmann, Banesh. *The Strange Story of the Quantum: An Account for the General Reader of the Growth of the Ideas Leading to Our Current Atomic Knowledge.* 2nd ed. New York: Dover, 1959. First published in 1947 by Harper.

Holland, Sharon. *The Erotic Life of Racism.* Durham, N.C.: Duke University Press, 2012.

Hunter, Tera W. *To 'Joy My Freedom: Southern Black Women's Lives and Labors after the Civil War.* Cambridge, Mass.: Harvard University Press, 1998.

James, Jennifer. *A Freedom Bought with Blood: African American War Literature from the Civil War to World War II.* Chapel Hill: University of North Carolina Press, 2007.

Jayasurya, Shihan De Soto, and Richard Pankhurst, eds. *The African Diaspora in the Indian Ocean.* Trenton, N.J.: Africa World, 2003.

Jefferson, Thomas. *Notes on the State of Virginia.* New York: Palgrave Macmillan, 2002. First published in English in 1787 by John Stockdale.

Johnson, Charles. *Middle Passage: A Novel.* New York: Atheneum, 1990.

Johnson, E. Patrick. *Appropriating Blackness: Performance and the Politics of Authenticity.* Durham, N.C.: Duke University Press, 2003.

Johnson, Mat. *Pym: A Novel.* New York: Spiegel and Grau, 2010.

Jones, Colin. *Paris: The Biography of a City.* London: Penguin, 2005.

Jones, Sheilla. *The Quantum Ten: A Story of Passion, Tragedy, Ambition, and Science.* London: Oxford University Press, 2008.

Kaplan, Cora, and Bill Schwarz, eds. *James Baldwin: America and Beyond.* Ann Arbor: University of Michigan Press, 2011.

Kean, Sam. *The Disappearing Spoon: And Other True Tales of Madness, Love, and the History of the World from the Periodic Table of the Elements.* New York: Little, Brown, 2010.

Kelley, Robin D. G. *Race Rebels: Culture, Politics, and the Working Class.* New York: Free Press, 1994.

Keynes, John Maynard. "Newton, the Man." In *The Papers of John Maynard Keynes.* Cambridge: King's College Archive Center, Cambridge University Archives, 1942. http://phys.columbia.edu/~millis/3003Spring2014/Supplementary/John%20Maynard%20Keynes_%20%22Newton,%20the%20Man%22.pdf. (A lecture read posthumously by Keynes's brother in 1946 at the Proceedings of the Royal Society Newton Tercentenary Celebrations.)

Kim, Hyun Sook. "The Politics of Border Crossings: Black, Postcolonial, and Transnational Feminist Perspectives." In *Handbook of Feminist Research: Theory and Praxis*, 2nd cd., edited by S. Nagy Hesse-Biber, 107–22. Thousand Oaks, Calif.: Sage, 2012.

Large, David Clay. *Berlin*. New York: Basic, 2000.

Lawrance, Jeremy. "Black Africans in Renaissance Spanish Literature." In *Black Africans in Renaissance Europe*, edited by T. F. Earle and K. J. P. Lowe, 70–93. New York: Cambridge University Press, 2005.

Lebow, Richard Ned, Wulf Kansteiner, and Claudio Fogu, eds. *The Politics of Memory in Postwar Europe*. Durham, N.C.: Duke University Press, 2006.

Le Poidevin, Robin, and Murray MacBeath, eds. *The Philosophy of Time*. Oxford: Oxford University Press, 1993.

Levenson, Thomas. *Einstein in Berlin*. New York: Bantam Dell, 2004.

Levy, Andrea. *Small Island*. London: Headline Review, 2004.

Lindley, David. *Uncertainty: Einstein, Heisenberg, Bohr, and the Struggle for the Soul of Science*. New York: Doubleday, 2007.

Lorde, Audre. *Sister Outsider: Essays and Speeches*. Berkeley, Calif.: Crossing, 1984.

Love, Heather. *Feeling Backward: Loss and the Politics of Queer History*. Cambridge, Mass.: Harvard University Press, 2007.

Mann, Gregory. *Native Sons: West African Veterans and France in the Twentieth Century*. Durham, N.C.: Duke University Press, 2006.

Manning, Patrick. *The African Diaspora: A History through Culture*. New York: Columbia University Press, 2009.

Marchera, Dambudzo. *The Black Insider*. Harare, Zimbabwe: Baobab, 1990.

Massaquoi, Hans-Jürgen. *Destined to Witness: Growing Up Black in Nazi Germany*. New York: Perennial, 1999.

———. *Hänschen klein, ging allein . . . : Mein Weg in die Neue Welt*. Frankfurt am Main: Fischer Verlag, 2004.

Massey, Doreen. *For Space*. London: Sage, 2005.

———. "Politics and Space/Time." In *Space, Place, and Gender*, 249–72. Minneapolis: University of Minnesota Press, 1994.

McBride, Dwight. "'Can the Queen Speak?': Racial Essentialism, Sexuality, and the Problem of Authority." In *Black Men on Race, Gender, and Sexuality: A Critical Reader*, edited by Devon W. Carbado, 253–75. New York: New York University Press, 1999.

McGrayne, Sharon Bertsch. *The Theory That Would Not Die: How Bayes' Rule Cracked the Enigma Code, Hunted Down Russian Submarines, and Emerged Triumphant from Two Centuries of Controversy*. New Haven, Conn.: Yale University Press, 2011.

Medawar, Jean, and David Pyke. *Hitler's Gift: The True Story of the Scientists Expelled by the Nazi Regime*. New York: Arcade, 2000.

Melber, Henning. "How to Come to Terms with the Past: Re-Visiting the German Colonial Genocide in Namibia." *Africa Spectrum* 40, no. 1 (2005): 139–48.

Miller, Emily Budick. Review of *Color and Culture: Black Writers and the Making of the Modern Intellectual*, by Ross Posnock. *Modern Language Quarterly* 61, no. 4 (2000): 686–89.

Miller, James. "What Does It Mean to Be an American?: The Dialectics of Self-Discovery in James Baldwin's 'Paris Essays' (1950–1961)." *Journal of American Studies* 42, no. 1 (2008): 51–66.

Mintz, Sidney J., and Susan Reed. "'The Legacy of the Atlantic Program': A Conversation with Sidney Mintz." *Crosscurrents* 1 (1993): 43–52.

Monter, William E. *Frontiers of Heresy: The Spanish Inquisition from the Basque Lands to Sicily.* Cambridge: Cambridge University Press, 2003.

Morgenrath, Birgit, and Karl Rössel, eds. *"Unsere Opfer Zählen Nicht": Die Dritte Welt im Zweiten Weltkrieg.* Berlin: Recherche International, 2005.

Morrison, Toni. *Playing in the Dark: Whiteness and the Literary Imagination.* New York: Vintage, 1993.

Morton, H. V. *In Search of London.* Cambridge, Mass.: Da Capo, 2002. First published in 1951 by Methuen.

Moten, Fred. *In the Break: The Aesthetics of the Black Radical Tradition.* Minneapolis: University of Minnesota Press, 2003.

Murphy, Geraldine. "Subversive Anti-Stalinism: Race and Sexuality in the Early Essays of James Baldwin." *ELH* 63, no. 4 (1996): 1021–46.

Mwangi, Evan M. *Africa Writes Back to Self: Metafiction, Gender, Sexuality.* Albany: State University of New York Press, 2009.

Newton, Isaac, and John Machin. *The Mathematical Principles of Natural Philosophy.* London: Dawson's of Pall Mall, 1968. First published in 1729 by Benjamin Motte.

Okpewho, Isadore, and Nkiru Nzegwu, eds. *The New African Diaspora.* Bloomington: Indiana University Press, 2009.

Ouellette, Jennifer. *Black Bodies and Quantum Cats: Tales from the Annals of Physics.* London: Penguin, 2005.

Painter, Nell Irwin. *The History of White People.* New York: W. W. Norton, 2010.

Peters, Karl. *The Eldorado of the Ancients.* London: C. Pearson, 1902.

———. *New Light on Dark Africa.* Translated by H. W. Dulcken. London: Ward, Lock, 1891.

Peterson, Merrill D., ed. *The Portable Thomas Jefferson.* 3rd ed. New York: Penguin, 1977.

Pfaff, Françoise. *Conversations with Maryse Condé.* Lincoln: University of Nebraska Press, 1993.

Phillips, Mike, and Trevor Phillips. *Windrush: The Irresistible Rise of Multi-Racial Britain.* New York: HarperCollins, 1999.

Pinkard, Terry P. "Speculative *Naturphilosophie* and the Development of the Empirical Sciences: Hegel's Perspective." In *Continental Philosophy of Science*, edited by Gary Gutting, 19–34. Malden, Mass.: Blackwell, 2005.

Poe, Edgar Allan. *The Narrative of Arthur Gordon Pym of Nantucket*. London: Penguin Classics, 1999. First published in 1838 by Harper.

Polite, Carlene Hatcher. *Sister X and the Victims of Foul Play*. New York: Farrar, Strauss, 1975.

Polkinghorne, John. *Quantum Theory: A Very Short Introduction*. Oxford: Oxford University Press, 2002.

Popoola, Olumide, and Beldan Sezen. *Talking Home: Heimat aus unserer eigenen Feder/Frauen of Color in Deutschland*. Amsterdam: Blue Moon, 1999.

Posnock, Ross. *Color & Culture: Black Writers and the Making of the Modern Intellectual*. Cambridge, Mass.: Harvard University Press, 1998.

Powers, Thomas. *Heisenberg's War: The Secret History of the German Bomb*. New York: Da Capo, 2000.

Prince, Mary. *The History of Mary Prince*. London: Penguin Classics, 2001. First published in 1831 by F. Westley and A. H. Davis.

Pybus, Cassandra. *Black Founders: The Story of Australia's First Black Settlers*. Sydney: University of New South Wales Press, 2006.

———. "The World Is All of One Piece: The African Diaspora and Transportation to Australia." In *Routes of Passage: Rethinking the African Diaspora*, edited by Ruth Simms Hamilton, 181–90. East Lansing: Michigan State University Press, 2007.

Randall, Lisa. *Warped Passages: Unraveling the Mysteries of the Universe's Hidden Dimensions*. New York: HarperCollins, 2005.

Reid-Pharr, Robert. *Once You Go Black: Choice, Desire, and the Black American Intellectual*. New York: New York University Press, 2006.

Rimer, Sara, and Karen Arenson. "Top Colleges Take More Blacks, but Which Ones?" *New York Times*, June 24, 2004, A4, evening edition.

Rowell, Charles H., and Octavia E. Butler. "An Interview with Octavia E. Butler." *Callaloo* 20, no. 1 (1997): 47–66.

Sancho, Ignatius. *Letters of the Late Ignatius Sancho, an African*. New York: Cosimo, 2005. First published in 1782 by Books for Libraries.

Schleifer, Ronald. *Modernism and Time: The Logic of Abundance in Literature, Science, and Culture, 1880–1930*. Cambridge: Cambridge University Press, 2000.

Schwinger, Julian. *Einstein's Legacy: The Unity of Space and Time*. Mineola, N.Y.: Dover, 2002.

Seacole, Mary. *Wonderful Adventures of Mrs. Seacole in Many Lands*. Oxford: Oxford University Press, 1988. First published in 1857 by J. Blackwood.

Segrè, Gino. *Faust in Copenhagen: A Struggle for the Soul of Physics*. New York: Viking, 2007.

Sharpley-Whiting, T. Denean. *Negritude Women*. Minneapolis: University of Minnesota Press, 2002.

Shaw-Taylor, Yoku, and Steven A. Tuch, eds. *The Other African Americans: Contemporary African and Caribbean Immigrants in the United States*. Lanham, Md.: Rowman and Littlefield, 2007.

Shiroya, Okete J. E. *Kenya and World War II: African Soldiers in the European War*. Nairobi: Kenya Literature Bureau, 1985.

Sidbury, James. *Becoming African in America: Race and Nation in the Early Black Atlantic*. Oxford: Oxford University Press, 2007.

Simons, Marlise. "Brazil's Blacks Feel Bias 100 Years after Slavery." *New York Times*, May 15, 1988.

Smith, William Gardner. *Last of the Conquerors*. Chatham, N.J.: Chatham, 1973. First published in 1948 by the New American Library.

———. *Return to Black America: A Negro Reporter's Impressions after 16 Years of Self-Exile*. Englewood Cliffs, N.J.: Prentice-Hall, 1970.

———. *The Stone Face*. New York: Farrar, Strauss, 1963.

Smith, Zadie. *White Teeth*. New York: Penguin, 2000.

Smolin, Lee. *Time Reborn: From the Crisis in Physics to the Future of the Universe*. New York: Houghton Mifflin Harcourt, 2013.

———. *The Trouble with Physics: The Rise of String Theory, the Fall of a Science, and What Comes Next*. Boston: Houghton Mifflin, 2006.

Smoot, George, and Keay Davidson. *Wrinkles in Time*. New York: Avon, 1993.

Snobelen, Stephen. "Isaac Newton, Heretic: The Strategies of a Nicodemite." *British Journal of Historical Studies* 32, no. 4 (1999): 381–419.

Snorton, C. Riley. "Passing for White, Passing for Man: Johnson's Autobiography of an Ex-Colored Man as Transgender Narrative." In *Trans/Gender Migrations: Bodies, Borders, and the (Geo)Politics of Gender Crossing*, edited by Trystan Cotton, 107–18. New York: Routledge, 2011.

Spillers, Hortense J. "Mama's Baby, Papa's Maybe: An American Grammar Book." In *Culture and Countermemory: The "American" Connection*, special issue, *Diacritics* 17, no. 2 (1987): 65–81.

———. "'Watcha Gonna Do?'—Revisiting 'Mama's Baby, Papa's Maybe: An American Grammar Book.'" *Women's Studies Quarterly* 35, nos. 1/2 (2007): 299–309.

Starobin, Robert. *Industrial Slavery in the Old South*. New York: Oxford University Press, 1970.

Stephens, Michelle Ann. *Black Empire: The Masculine Global Imaginary of Caribbean Intellectuals in the United States, 1914–1962*. Durham, N.C.: Duke University Press, 2005.

Stolberg, Sheryl Gay. "Obama Has Ties to Slavery Not by His Father but His Mother, Research Suggests." *New York Times*, July 30, 2012.

Strogatz, Steven. *The Joy of X: A Guided Tour of Math, from One to Infinity*. New York: Houghton Mifflin Harcourt, 2012.

Thompson, Krista. "A Sidelong Glance: The Practice of African Diaspora Art History in the United States." *Art Journal* 70, no. 3 (2011): 6–31.

Touré. *Who's Afraid of Post-Blackness? What It Means to Be Black Now.* New York: Free Press, 2011.

Urdang, Stephanie. "Fighting Two Colonialisms: The Women's Struggle in Guinea-Bissau." *African Studies Review* 18, no. 3 (1975): 29–34.

Van Chet Btelanon, Lyric. *JUpen Interval.* Pittsburgh. University of Pittsburgh Press, 2009.

Van Jordan, A. *Quantum Lyrics.* New York: W. W. Norton, 2007.

Van Sertima, Ivan. *The African Presence in Early Europe.* Piscataway, N.J.: Transaction, 1986.

Von Eschen, Penny M. *Satchmo Blows Up the World: Jazz Ambassadors Play the Cold War.* Cambridge, Mass.: Harvard University Press, 2004.

Walker, Alice. *The Color Purple.* New York: Washington Square, 1983.

Walters, Ron. "Barack Obama and the Politics of Blackness." *Journal of Black Studies* 38, no. 7 (2007): 7–29.

Wells, Ida B., and Jacqueline Jones Royster. *Southern Horrors and Other Writings: The Anti-Lynching Campaign of Ida B. Wells.* Boston: Bedford/St. Martin's, 1996.

White, Debra Gray. *Too Heavy a Load: Black Women in Defense of Themselves, 1894–1994.* New York: W. W. Norton, 1999.

Williams, John A. *Clifford's Blues.* Minneapolis, Minn.: Coffee House, 1999.

Womack, Ytasha L. *Post Black: How a New Generation Is Redefining African American Identity.* Chicago: Chicago Review, 2010.

Woubshet, Dagmawi. "Tizita." *Callaloo* 30, no. 2 (2007): 509–10.

Wright, Michelle M. *Becoming Black: Creating Identity in the African Diaspora.* Durham, N.C.: Duke University Press, 2004.

Wright, Richard. *Black Boy.* New York: Harper Perennial Classics, 2008. First published in 1945 by Harper.

———. *Black Power.* New York: Harper, 1954.

Yancy, George. *Black Bodies, White Gazes: The Continuing Significance of Race.* Lanham, Md.: Rowman and Littlefield, 2008.

Young, Harvey. *Embodying the Black Experience: Stillness, Critical Memory, and the Black Body.* Ann Arbor: University of Michigan Press, 2010.

Young, Iris Marion. "The Logic of Masculinist Protection: Reflections on the Current Security State." *Signs: Journal of Women in Culture and Society* 29, no. 1 (2003): 1–25.

Young, Joseph, and Jana Evans Braziel, eds. *Race and the Foundations of Knowledge.* Urbana: University of Illinois Press, 2006.

Zamir, Shamoon. *Dark Voices: W. E. B. Du Bois and American Thought.* Chicago: University of Chicago Press, 1995.

Index

Abbott, Susan, 166
Africa Writes Back to Self (Mwangi),
  32, 159–60
Afrofuturism, 187n10
Against Race (Gilroy), 61
agency, Black, 5, 47, 59, 66–67, 70–72,
  79, 87–88, 104, 116–19, 154
Aidoo, Ama Ata, 113, 126–31, 135–36,
  139–40, 172
Alpers, Edward, 141
Althusser, Louis, 118
Andrade, Danilo de, 133
Andrade, Susan Z., 88, 89
Another Country (Baldwin), 138
Arianism, 170–71
Arius, 171
arrow of time, use of term, 28, 75–76
Atlantic Program (Johns Hopkins
  University), 141–42
Australia: forced migration to, 148–
  49; indigeneity and Blackness in,
  150–52

Bakhtin, Mikhail, 20–21
Baldwin, James, 30–31, 107, 132; on
  alienation, 122–23; on dehumanization of Blacks, 118–19; on
  homosexuality, 137–38; interpellation of Blackness, 113–14, 133,
  136; interpellation of women, 114;
  multidimensional blackness of, 109,
  111–12; quantum moment of, 109,

110–11; use of spacetime, 120–22; on
  Wright, 115. *See also specific works*
"Barack Obama and the Politics of
  Blackness" (Walters), 62–63
Barrow, Isaac, 39
Bayes's Theorem, 171–72
being. *See* knowing vs. being
Beloved (Morrison), 77
biraciality, 69–70, 101–2
bisexual Blacks. *See* LGBTTQ Blacks
Black Atlantic, The (Gilroy), 6, 27, 51,
  54, 56–61, 65
Black Atlantic studies, 141–43, 148–50,
  161
Black Bodies and Quantum Cats
  (Ouellette), 38–39
Black Founders (Pybus), 150–51
Black Nationalism, 63
Blackness: authentic, 64–65, 95–96;
  and black body, 1–2; constructs of,
  2, 4, 11–12, 14; definitions of, 1, 3, 5,
  6–9, 35; diversity of, 17, 25, 142–43,
  154; four grandparents rule, 67–70;
  globality of, 114; and identity, 3;
  and indigeneity, 150–51; interpellation of, 27–28, 111, 113, 119, 121, 124,
  147–48; Middle Passage, 10, 11–12,
  17–19, 66–68, 106, 123, 147, 150–51;
  multidimensional, 109, 111–13,
  118, 146, 154, 166; political, 64, 68;
  post-Blackness, use of term, 16, 113;
  poststructuralist theories, 5–6;

MICHELLE M. WRIGHT is an associate professor of Black European and African Diaspora literature and culture in the Department of African American Studies at Northwestern University in Evanston, Illinois. She has served as the Estella Loomis McCandless Junior Chair in Literary and Cultural Studies at Carnegie Mellon University, the Thomas E. Critchett Visiting Assistant Professor at Macalester College, and an associate professor of English at the University of Minnesota–Twin Cities. She is author of *Becoming Black: Creating Identity in the African Diaspora*, as well as many articles and book chapters, and is editor of several anthologies and journal special issues.

Printed and bound by CPI Group (UK) Ltd, Croydon, CR0 4YY

13/04/2025

14656504-0001